From Enemy to Friend

From Enemy to Friend

Jewish Wisdom and the Pursuit of Peace

Rabbi Amy Eilberg

ORBIS BOOKS

Maryknoll, New York 10545

ORBIS BOOKS
Maryknoll, New York 10545

Fathers and Brothers
MARYKNOLL

Founded in 1970, Orbis Books endeavors to publish works that enlighten the mind, nourish the spirit, and challenge the conscience. The publishing arm of the Maryknoll Fathers and Brothers, Orbis seeks to explore the global dimensions of the Christian faith and mission, to invite dialogue with diverse cultures and religious traditions, and to serve the cause of reconciliation and peace. The books published reflect the views of their authors and do not represent the official position of the Maryknoll Society. To learn more about Maryknoll and Orbis Books, please visit our websites at www.maryknollsociety.org and www.orbisbooks.com.

Library of Congress Cataloging-in-Publication Data

Eilberg, Amy.
   From enemy to friend : Jewish wisdom and the pursuit of peace / Rabbi Amy Eilberg.
      pages cm
   Includes bibliographical references and index.
   ISBN 978-1-62698-061-7 (pbk.)
      1. Peace—Religious aspects—Judaism.   2. Bible. Old Testament—Criticism, interpretation, etc.   3. Rabbinical literature—History and criticism.   I. Title.
   BM538.P3E35 2013
   296.3'827—dc23

                                                                    2013032365

To Louis,
the love of my life

Contents

Acknowledgments

This book is the fruit of a long journey, on which I was blessed to have many wise and loving guides and companions. I have reached this point in large measure owing to their help and support.

For inspiring me to begin my own journey as a pursuer of peace, I thank my rabbi and friend Sheldon Lewis. It is unlikely that my path would have led in the same direction without Shelly's gentle and loving presence in my life and in the world, and his bold passion for teaching about peace. Early on, Len and Libby Traubman served as important models and mentors for me. Leah Green, Carol Hwoschinsky, and their colleagues in The Compassionate Listening Project gave me treasured insights, practices, and models for the work of dialogue and peacebuilding.

I have been blessed with wonderful colleagues in the interfaith community in Minneapolis/St. Paul, Minnesota, my home during this important time of my life. Tom Duke, convener of SPIN (Saint Paul Interfaith Network), has been a treasured and precious colleague and friend in the work of interreligious dialogue. Along with him and the crew of devoted activists at SPIN, I learned much of what I know as an interfaith activist. During this period, Rabbi Barry Cytron graciously invited me to work at the Jay Phillips Center for Interfaith Learning at the University of St. Thomas, giving me a professional home for my peacebuilding work. His successor, Dr. John Merkle, has been a source of unstinting support and encouragement for my interfaith work and for my writing, and the person who persuaded me to submit my manuscript to Orbis Books. Dr. Curtiss DeYoung of Bethel University has been a valued colleague and friend.

I am immensely grateful to Dr. Debbie Weissman for inviting me into many remarkable experiences in international interreligious dialogue. Among them, I particularly cherished my time with the Thinking Together project of the World Council of Churches, where I had the honor of working with a group of world-class dialogue activists and scholars.

Dr. Robert Stains of the Public Conversations Project has been an important teacher and mentor for me in the theory and practice of conflict engagement, all the while, with characteristic humility and generosity, treating me more as colleague than student. My teachers and colleagues at the United Theological Seminary of the Twin Cities have been wonderful sources of learning and support. Jean Trumbauer encouraged me to write in my own authentic voice and timing, and Dr. Marilyn Salmon and Dr. Paul Capetz have been especially precious teachers.

Rabbi Melissa Weintraub and Rachel Eryn Kalish have been wonderful teachers and colleagues, as have Mitch Chanin and Dr. Eyal Rabinovitch, in the work of intra-Jewish dialogue. Recently, I have been delighted to work with and learn from Rabbi Dr. Daniel Roth of the Pardes Center for Judaism and Conflict Resolution at Pardes Institute in Jerusalem. Of course, I have learned a great deal from Dr. Marc Gopin, who essentially created the field of Judaism and Conflict Resolution. I have had the delight of working with Rabbi Steve Gutow and Ethan Felson of the Jewish Council for Public Affairs. I am grateful for their friendship and for welcoming me into national Jewish civility efforts.

I would not be the rabbi that I am without my teacher Sylvia Boorstein, who continues to be a primary spiritual teacher for me. I recognize that my colleagues in the Jewish healing movement, in the Jewish spiritual direction community, and at the Institute for Jewish Spirituality have profoundly shaped my spiritual identity, my aspirations, and my particular voice as a rabbi. I would be terribly lonely without them. Last but not least, all of the people whose names and stories appear in the book have been invaluable teachers for me.

Many friends have nourished me, cheered me on, and prayed for me throughout this journey. I am especially indebted to my long-time spiritual director, Janice Farrell, whom I consider to be the primary midwife of this book. So, too, my friend and weekly *hevruta* (sacred study partner)

Jacob Staub listened lovingly to the many twists and turns of this birthing process. My long-distance forever-friends Rabbi Cynthia Kravitz, Rabbi Nancy Flam, Rev. Sandee Yarlott, Ellen Bob, Dr. Ace Leveen, Diane Wexler, and Dr. Carol Winograd were treasured gifts in this writing project, as in my life. Rabbi Nancy Fuchs-Kreimer offered me friendship and many remarkable opportunities; Rabbi Sheila Weinberg shared invaluable insight on parts of the manuscript; and Drs. Riv-ellen Prell and Steven Foldes were generous with their expertise as well as with their love. In Minnesota, my sisters-in-law Jane Newman and Amy Lange and my friends Kimberley Treanor and Christine Lueck provided the circle of friendship essential to my life. Sam Freedman, of Columbia University and the *New York Times,* gave generously of his time and expertise. Last but certainly not least, I could not have found a better partner for bringing my book out into the world than Robert Ellsberg and the team at Orbis Books. I am very grateful.

The two years during which I wrote this book were the last year of my mother's life and the year following her death. It became clear that there were mysterious connections between the dying process—attending my mother during her last months of life—and the birthing process—bringing this book into the world. Even after my mother was no longer able to track the details of content, she would regularly ask, "How's the writing coming?" When I responded with excitement that I was making great progress, she beamed, reflecting, "You're really happy about this." I am very happy about it and grateful for the countless gifts my mother and father gave me. I am sad that neither of them lived to see the book completed and published, which would have made them both very proud.

My stepsons, Etan and Jonah Newman, are unique and unexpected blessings in my life. Their love, support, and affirmation for my work and my writing have been especially precious. My daughter, Penina, is an indescribable joy and blessing to me. She is a living model of the virtues I extol in this book. She has been an essential teacher for me, as well, as we learn together how two different people live in loving relationship together.

It is hard for me to imagine how I would have written this book without my husband, Louis Newman. He taught me to laugh at my own self-doubts, spent countless hours helping me think through conceptual issues, and brought his fine professorial eye to every word of this manuscript several times over. In this project, as in all things, he is my beloved partner and forever-husband. I am grateful beyond words for the blessing of sharing my life with him.

As ever, I am grateful to God for the gift of life and for all the abundance that is mine. On this occasion of the publication of my first book, I offer the traditional Jewish prayer of thanksgiving: Praised are You, O God, Sovereign of the universe, for giving me life at each moment, for sustaining and nourishing me every step of the way, and for enabling me to reach this blessed time.

Rabbi Amy Eilberg
Mendota Heights, Minnesota
June 2013 / Tammuz 5773

Notes on Hebrew Transliteration and Translation

In line with scholarly convention, in transliterating Hebrew words, I distinguish between "ḥet," the eighth letter of the Hebrew alphabet, and "chaf," the twelfth letter. Both are guttural versions of the English "h" sound, as in the "ch" sound in "Bach," not to be confused with "hey," the fifth letter of the alphabet, which is pronounced like the English "h" or is silent.

When translating biblical texts, I generally turn first to the standard Jewish Publication Society translations, such as *The Torah: The Five Books of Moses* (Philadelphia: Jewish Publication Society, 1962). I frequently adapt the translations based on my own understanding and interpretation of the verse, and to maintain gender neutrality.

My translations of Rabbinic works (e.g., Mishnah, Talmud, Midrash) are my own unless otherwise indicated.

Introduction

Who is the hero of heroes? . . . One who makes an enemy into a friend.

—*Avot d'Rabbi Natan, 23*

Return evil with good and your enemy will become a devoted friend.

—*Koran 41:34*

Early in my career, when I was working as a hospital chaplain, I was preparing to supervise a unit of CPE (Clinical Pastoral Education) training for a group of Christian chaplaincy interns. The training model includes some twenty hours per week of pastoral work in the hospital and nearly twenty hours per week of classes, along with individual and group supervision. The pastoral work with patients is intense, and the individual and group learning process is for most participants profound, even transformative. My co-supervisor and I, keenly aware of the power of the process, pored over the students' application essays to prepare ourselves to meet the participants and to decide which of us would offer individual supervision to which student.

My heart clenched when I saw the application from Dietrich (not his real name), a German Lutheran seminary student who had come to our center in California for his chaplaincy training. I sat for a long time with his essay in my hands, trying to imagine what it would be like for me, a rabbi, to supervise this student from Germany. I came to my co-supervisor and told her that, although I imagined it would be important for me to work with him in the group setting, I wanted her to be his individual supervisor. I didn't think I would be able to open my heart to him in the way that I must for the supervisory relationship to do its magic. My co-supervisor, a Protestant minister (and now, decades later, still a very close friend), looked me in the eye and said, without hesitation, "Amy, I think you have to supervise him."

I knew that I was frightened, and I knew that she was right. There was reason for my fear. My mother's immediate family had been attacked in pogroms prior to the war, and members of my extended family had been killed in the Holocaust. I knew better than to hold all Germans responsible for the crimes of the Nazis, but, as a family, we had avoided buying German products, not wanting to reward companies that had worked with the Nazi government. At that point in my life, I could imagine developing a loving relationship with a young person from Germany, but I knew that the sound of a German accent still instinctively made me stiffen, and I just didn't know if I'd be able to take this student fully into my heart.

At our first supervisory session we began the process of getting to know each other. Dietrich talked about his life and his training goals, and I told him about myself and my understanding of the supervisory process. We made a connection, leaning into a relationship we both sensed would be an important one. Suddenly, toward the end of the session, Dietrich spoke reverently about the unexpected opportunity to work with a rabbi as his chaplaincy supervisor. He spoke with deep personal pain and remorse about what his people had done to mine, and he began to cry. My heart opened, and I told him about the Jewish tradition of *tikkun olam*, the idea that human beings work together to repair brokenness in the world. He was moved by my words and replied, in heavily accented English, "So it seems we have some repair work to do, you and I." I have never forgotten his words.

Fifty years after the Holocaust, I had been forced to examine my visceral, negative reaction to all things German. I had good reason for that instinctive, heart-clenching response to the sound of the German language and the automatic thought that had always arisen in my mind when encountering someone from Germany: "I wonder what this person (or his or her parents) was doing during the Nazi Holocaust."

But sitting in the sacred space of the hospital's chaplaincy office, preparing to mentor this young seminarian to learn the art of offering spiritual care to the ill, I was released from the prison of my lifelong fearful instinct about Germans. This person was not my enemy. He was my student, preparing himself for a profound, introspective journey, seeking to cultivate his capacity for compassion for all those he would meet in the hospital. The very subject of spiritual care for the ill touches tender places in the heart, and I could imagine the many moving moments of learning we would share over the coming year. Even more, his deep and genuine remorse over the sins of his people toward mine inspired love rather than enmity.

I could almost feel God prying the walls of my heart open. In a single conversation, authentic human connection had allowed me to move past traumatic historical memory to engage in a relationship with one real, complex, and lovable human being.

This movement from the heart and mind closed in fear and wounding to a state of openness and curiosity about another human being is the work of moving from enemy to friend. The sometimes imperceptible shift from a stance of antagonism to acceptance and then to compassion is the work of making peace—be it in interpersonal conflict, in relationship to those different from us religiously, politically, or ethnically, and even in intergroup conflicts on the world stage. The goal of this book is to explore this inner work of peacebuilding,[1] explicating the beautiful rabbinic and Koranic teaching that the greatest heroism is to transform an enemy into a friend, to move from hatred to caring, from suspicion and fear, beyond tolerance, to embrace of the other.

The call to peace work had been growing in me for some time. I first became aware of its emergence in the aftermath of a terrible hate crime.

---

[1] I generally use the term "peacebuilding" in this work, as is becoming the norm in the field of conflict studies, to describe the work of ordinary people in addressing conflict in their lives and in the world. This is to be distinguished from "peacemaking," which is the work of diplomats in creating international agreements, and "peacekeeping," the work of military forces sent to prevent violence in conflict zones.

In August of 1999, a self-described white supremacist named Buford Furrow burst into the North Valley Jewish Community Center in Los Angeles and shot three children and a receptionist. His need to kill not yet sated, he left the center vowing to kill the first "nonwhite" person he encountered. The US postal service employee Joseph Ileto, a Filipino American, died in Furrow's violent spree.

I had lived through hate crimes before, but this one struck an especially tender chord in me. I learned that Furrow, living in Washington State, had researched several Jewish institutions along the West Coast, seeking one without substantial security that would impede his entry. This was a bone-chilling detail for me, because my daughter grew up at "our" Jewish Community Center, about five hundred miles north of Furrow's chosen target, just off Highway 101 that connected Los Angeles and San Francisco. Viewing the riveting photos of small children being guided out of the JCC, holding hands in a long line as they crossed the street, I felt that this had been an attack on my own children. What is more, at the time of the attack my daughter was at Camp Ramah in Ojai, California, a short distance from Los Angeles. This attack had struck very close.

In the aftermath of the attack, Jewish community centers, Jewish schools, and other institutions secured their entrances and hired security personnel. I grieved but also welcomed the appearance of guards, now needed to keep our children safe, at the places that had always felt like extensions of home for us. But most of all, I noticed a new reaction in me. Oddly, I felt neither great anger at the perpetrator nor fear of future attacks nor suspicion of others who might plan them. Rather, I felt the classic phrase, "If you are not part of the solution, you are part of the problem," resonating deep within me.

The reality of hatred had burst into my consciousness in a whole new way. As the Rabbis[2] used to say about a perplexing piece of sacred text, this incident said, "*Darsheini*" ("Seek to understand me"). I wanted to understand what engendered hate, and I wanted somehow to contribute to the solution.

---

[2] I capitalize the word "Rabbis" when describing the rabbis of the formative period of Rabbinic Judaism, from the first century B.C.E. through the seventh century C.E., but not when referring to contemporary rabbis.

A year later, in September 2000, the Second Intifada broke out. Like so many American Jews, Israel had been in my bones since my first visit as a teenager. I loved the streets, the stones, and the scents of Jerusalem with a powerful, irrational love. I had spent years in Jerusalem as an undergraduate and graduate student, and I had planned to "make *aliyah*" ("ascent"—the way Jews describe moving to Israel to make a life there). Watching violence erupt yet again in my beloved land, after years when peace had actually seemed within reach, was beyond heartbreaking.

But the heartbreak was compounded by a parallel conflict closer to home. I belonged to a synagogue called Kol Emeth (Voice of Truth). For years the place had been a home and a haven to me, the place where I had raised my daughter, grieved losses, and celebrated joys in my life. It was a community in the best sense of the word: a nonpretentious place where people came with a sincere desire to connect to one another, to Torah, and to God. People showed up for one another's sorrows and celebrations, and it felt like extended family.

But now, those on the left of the political spectrum—those with dovish views and deep concerns for justice issues—could not speak with those on the right—those holding more hawkish, security-conscious views. Lines of verbal battle were drawn, and ferocious arguments erupted on the congregation's listserv on a daily basis. There was no listening, only exchanges of aggressive tirades, apparently with little awareness of the humanity of the people on the other side. Some relationships ended; in other cases, only an agreement not to discuss the subject that most consumed us preserved the friendship.

The horror of renewed violence in Israel yet again was terribly painful but also familiar. But the new eruption of verbal violence in my home community was agonizing. What possible help could our furious debates be to our countrymen and women in Israel? We were making war on one another, an utterly futile rhetorical war as fierce in its own way as the war for whose end we fervently prayed. Why were we turning on each other at this time of deep pain for all of us? How could we make it stop?

Then came September 11, 2001, and I was suddenly surrounded by a world of people struggling, like me, to fathom violence, hatred, and division in our world. I invited members of the congregation to services of healing, filled with prayers for peace. I studied with my rabbi, Sheldon Lewis, who had begun to comb the classical sources of Jewish law and lore for teachings on peacemaking that might bring a measure of comfort and hope.[3] And I made my own first foray into the world of conflict resolution, hoping to learn about systems of facilitation that held promise in bringing peace to conflict-ridden relationships between people and among nations. I attended my first workshop in Compassionate Listening,™[4] a mode of listening that has the power to humanize enemies and transform relationships.

Seeds had been planted in me, and my call to peace work was growing imperceptibly within. So perhaps I should not have been surprised when I found myself summoned to turn the central focus of my work toward the pursuit of peace.

While visiting my stepson who was spending a year in Israel, my husband and I had the opportunity to visit a place I had long admired: the School for Peace at Neve Shalom/Wahat al-Salaam/ Oasis of Peace, halfway between Tel Aviv and Jerusalem. Neve Shalom/ Wahat al-Salaam would be a remarkable place anywhere, but most especially in the midst of one of the most intractable conflict zones in the world. It is a village created[5] as a living exercise in coexistence for Israeli Jews and Arabs. The community, having had its share of challenges over the years, is now thriving, home to over one hundred families who live together, raise their children together, and work together for peace and understanding between Jews and Palestinians around the region.

The town houses the world-renowned School for Peace, which serves as a laboratory, educational center, and think tank for peacebuilders from around the region and around the world. The school's signature program is a three-day residential encounter program for high school juniors from Jewish and Palestinian[6] schools within Israel. This may

---

[3] The fruit of his research is now published in *Torah of Reconciliation* (Jerusalem: Gefen Press, 2012).

[4] The Compassionate Listening Project, http://www.compassionatelistening.org.

[5] By Father Bruno Hussar, a Jewish-born Roman Catholic priest, in 1970.

[6] In Jewish and Israeli circles, it is common to describe Arabs, both Muslim and Christian, who live within the State of Israel, as Israeli Arabs, and those in the

sound unremarkable until one realizes that the school systems in Israel are almost completely separate, so that the group of approximately one hundred sixteen-year-olds, half of them Jewish Israelis and half Israeli Palestinians, who attend each workshop have virtually never before met "the other" in a positive context.

During their three days together, the young people at the School for Peace do far more than discover the commonalities in their language and culture or even uncover one another's common humanity. In the program, the participants actively engage the dynamics of the conflict that defines all of their lives. Highly trained facilitators apply a sophisticated educational methodology that pays rigorous attention to and redirects power dynamics within the group that mirror those outside the sheltered environment of the school. Thus Hebrew is not privileged over Arabic; every activity is run with the full and equal collaboration of Jewish and Palestinian educators; and the facilitators are quick to point out ways in which the Jewish kids begin to claim more airtime or assume a position of superiority in the mixed groups. This is no "hummus and pita" or "kumbaya" stereotype of dialogue based on avoidance of real issues. This is intergroup education at its finest.

My husband and I watched from behind a one-way mirror as the young people settled into their groups together, learned one another's names, and negotiated about the name they would give to their groups. In any other circumstance, this would have been a simple set of icebreakers at

---

West Bank and Gaza as Palestinians. But as frequently happens in the development of group identity of people struggling against discrimination, those "Israeli Arabs" are now in a state of flux as to how to describe themselves. Heightened demands for their rights as citizens within Israeli democracy, their own emerging national identity, and their connectedness to Palestinian nationality in the Occupied Territories have led many to describe themselves not as "Israeli Arabs" but as "Palestinian Arabs" or "Palestinian Israelis" or "Palestinian citizens of Israel." This linguistic fluidity is challenging, to be sure, and has political implications. But an analogy is to be drawn with the process by which white Americans came to honor the name and self-understanding of African Americans. I believe that calling people by the name they choose for themselves is a mark of respect. Therefore, I will honor these people's dignity by calling them what they are beginning to call themselves: "Palestinian Israelis" or "Palestinian citizens of Israel." I will generally use that language here.

the beginning of a youth group conference. But there was nothing simple or ordinary about this encounter.

Far too soon, the person who had brought us said that it was time for us to go. For my part, I was riveted to the floor, gripped by a powerful instinct to roll up my sleeves. Every time I told the story of what had happened to me that day, I found myself reaching for my sleeves. Although the God I believe in neither literally sends messages to individuals nor communicates like a human being, I felt a visceral sense of having been called by God to roll up my sleeves and find some way to help.

I returned to my home in Minnesota, as if stumbling off a mountaintop revelation experience, determined to find some way to serve the cause of peace. I spent two years reading everything I could get my hands on about the Israeli-Palestinian conflict. Desperately curious about theories of conflict in general and the characteristics of conflict interaction, I read widely—in conflict studies, communication theory, postmodern philosophy, and cognitive neuroscience, as well as works of Jewish theology. I attended several peace camps and put myself through multiple training programs in conflict-resolution techniques, including advanced training in Compassionate Listening and several forms of mediation. The fire to help burned brightly within me, but I had still not found the place where I could serve in a meaningful way.

One day, a phone call from a colleague led to a job offer, supporting me in creating programs of person-to-person interreligious dialogue among synagogues, churches, and Muslim communities in the Twin Cities. I had found a way to my heart's desire: to do meaningful work as a peacebuilder.

This book is the fruit of my reflections on seven years of pursuing the cause of peace in my life and work, drawing on my perspective as a rabbi and spiritual teacher. I do this using the methods of what many Christian theologians call "theological reflection," considering a blend of different sources of truth: my own experience of interpersonal, intracommunal, and intergroup conflict, wisdom found in ancient Jewish sacred texts, and perspectives from the academic study of peace and conflict and communications theory. In each case, I explore the inner work of peacebuilding: what happens to the human heart and mind under threat and in the midst of conflict, and what it takes to pry open the heart and mind to meet the other and to see him or her, as the Torah[7] teaches, as ourselves. I offer here a conceptual framework, grounded in Jewish theology and practice, for the personal work of conflict transformation as a spiritual practice, in both interpersonal and intergroup contexts.

My call to serve the cause of peace has led me to explore the dynamics of interpersonal conflict, a primary source of pain for countless individuals in their lives, in both personal and professional relationships. In my own Jewish community, in North America, and around the world, civil dialogue on contentious issues such as the Israeli–Palestinian conflict has become extremely antagonistic, endangering the fabric of community. Throughout the world, violence remains an all-too-present reality in intergroup and international relations.

In all of these contexts, parties to conflict tend to feel that their dispute is uniquely intractable and immune to efforts at resolution. Yet surprisingly, contemporary conflict and communications theorists teach that many of the same dynamics animate all conflict—be it interpersonal, intracommunal, intergroup, or even international. In essence, conflict thrives when minds are closed by histories of wounding, and resolution becomes possible when hearts and minds open to the humanity of the other side. Thus the inner work required of those seeking to pursue peace and reconciliation is essentially the same, regardless of the nature or scope of the conflict.

In this book, I explore this spiritual truth and offer practices fashioned to address it. Although many others have written on interfaith relations and international conflict, and some recent works examine the Jewish peace tradition from a scholarly perspective, this book is distinctive in that it presents traditional Jewish concepts of peace and conflict as a spiritual practice that can guide the lives of faithful people seeking to contribute to a more peaceful world.

As indicated, I teach the everyday practice of pursuing peace by integrating insights from three sources of knowledge: (1) my own experience

---

[7] I use the word "Torah" in three ways, in accordance with standard Jewish usage. Most narrowly, "Torah" (literally, "teaching,") refers to the first five books of the Hebrew Bible, or the scroll on which this text is written in the synagogue. "Torah" is often used more broadly to describe the entire Rabbinic tradition, and more broadly still, to describe the whole corpus of Jewish sacred literature, up to the present.

in conflict engagement, (2) classical Jewish texts on peacemaking, and (3) peace and conflict theory. The blending of these three elements provides a richer understanding of the dynamics of peacebuilding than any of them could do independently.

The personal experiences in the book will provide you with accessible and compelling models of how hostility and estrangement can be transformed. These stories of engagement across lines of difference demonstrate how relationships can move from estrangement, entrenched bigotry, and fear to positive, engaged encounter. These stories will enable you to see that the work of peacebuilding, contrary to popular opinion, is not restricted to diplomats and politicians, on the one hand, or unusually pious or gifted individuals, on the other. "It is not in heaven" (Deut. 30:12)—not a far-distant goal, but a real possibility for all of us in our lives.

The study of classical texts brings ancient sacred wisdom to bear on our understandings of conflict. These traditional texts convey with resounding clarity that the work of conflict engagement is an imperative for every one of us. In presenting and interpreting the texts, I move the discussion of conflict beyond the level of psychological or political analysis to the realm of sacred truths that inspire faithful response. These sources have put words to my burning desire to work for peace, both in my personal life and in the world, and they have urged me on in dark times, when peace seemed an impossible goal. They are the captions and the lyrics of the passion for peace that burns in my heart.

The textual passages also challenge the widespread assumption that religious texts and leaders too often contribute to intergroup hostility and hatred. The strands within our religious traditions that require us to transform conflict, to journey from discord to harmony and from enemy to friend, are less familiar, as the news media so regularly amplify the voices of religious violence and extremism. I believe that peace-loving religious teachings are essential for our contemporary world and rarely receive the public attention they richly deserve. I delight in giving them voice in my writing and teaching.

The sections on conflict and communications theory in the book provide theoretical scaffolding for the ways in which I read the texts and interpret the acts of peacebuilding I have witnessed and in which I have participated. These theoretical insights also confirm that there is a body of literature and practice to inform and guide the practice of conflict transformation, even for the most intractable of conflicts.

Toward these ends, the book begins with a chapter focusing on the experience of conflict in interpersonal relations, the crucible in which everything we know (and think we know) about conflict was formed. The three chapters that follow explore conflict engagement in different spheres: between faith communities (in chapter 2), across ideological lines within the North American Jewish community on the subject of Israel (in chapter 3), and in the context of grassroots Israeli-Palestinian peacebuilding (in chapter 4). In the final chapter, I synthesize the tradition's teachings on the pursuit of peace as spiritual practice, focusing on the cultivation of qualities of soul that are essential to the art of pursuing peace in interpersonal, interfaith, or intergroup relations. Every chapter of the book integrates accounts of personal encounters and interpretations of sacred texts. Some chapters include theoretical insights as well, drawn from peace and conflict and communications theory and from cognitive neuroscience.

Everywhere I go, I encounter people in pain about the interpersonal conflicts in their lives. They are frequently at a loss about how to mend the torn tapestry of family and community. In American society, we live in the midst of a deteriorating spiral of polarized rhetoric and ideological combat. With depressing frequency, people respond disparagingly to any mention of the word "peace," so disillusioned are they about the possibility of building a more peaceful world. As a Jew and an American citizen concerned about the future of our society, I know how desperately needed this message is in our society and our world.

I strongly suspect that, in these few pages, I have already alienated many readers, for whom the word "peace" evokes complicated and negative feelings. Because I have used this word, you may have already jumped to conclusions about my political outlook and concluded that this book will be one more infuriating analysis of the politics of the Middle East.

For a long time I refused to accept the reality that I encountered in so many places, that the words "peace" and "reconciliation" have become charged—laminated with assumptions about the political orientation of those who use these terms and infused with years of pain and disappointment about attempted peace processes between Israelis and Palestinians. I have come to understand that the word "peace" has, for many people, come to evoke all the pain of the past twenty years, or sixty years, or one hundred years, of the Israeli-Palestinian conflict.

Still, I cannot stop using this word. Jewish tradition is in love with the subject of peace. As has often been pointed out, every section of every Jewish prayer service ends with prayer for peace, often with multiple prayers for peace. The Rabbis said, among other things, that God's very name is peace, that peace is the concluding wish of all of our prayers, and that peace is the container that allows us to experience all the blessings in our lives.[8] My friend Rabbi Sheldon Lewis writes that the Rabbis regularly erupt into cascades of praise of peace whenever the topic arises.[9]

Surely we cannot abandon the word *shalom* to the purview of political analysts, pundits, and activists. The pursuit of peace lies at the very heart of our tradition, so the word "peace" cannot be the property of one segment of the community—left, right, or center. We must acknowledge and grieve the pain and hopelessness we feel at the very sound of the word, reflecting on how battered we feel by so many years of conflict, trauma, fear, and death, and how exhausted we are by the roller coaster of optimism and dashed hopes. In this book I seek to reclaim the concept of peace as a centerpiece of Jewish theology, prayer, and practice. I present the pursuit of peace as an essential imperative of our tradition and describe a path to serving the cause of peace in our lives, in all of our relationships.

Each of the major world religions is an old, vast, and complex tradition, including multiple viewpoints on most topics. A short answer to the question, "What is the Jewish view of _____?" is almost always inadequate, if not downright deceptive. Rigorous study of Jewish sources nearly always reveals multiple, if not contradictory, strands within the tradition about any important issue.

---

[8] Babylonian Talmud, *Perek Hashalom* (Chapter of Peace). The Talmud is the sixty-three-volume corpus of Rabbinic law, lore, and commentary. The term generally refers to the Babylonian Talmud (henceforth BT), edited in the early sixth century, as opposed to the Jerusalem—or Palestinian—Talmud (henceforth JT), edited in the early fifth century.

[9] Lewis, *Torah of Reconciliation*.

The corpus of Jewish sacred texts includes a vast repository of beautiful teachings about the nature of peace and the process of peacebuilding. I will introduce a small sampling of these texts in this book.[10] It is surely the case that there are also Jewish sacred texts that advocate, or at least condone, hatred and/or violence under certain circumstances.

Some scholars and Jewish leaders assert that the most honest and educationally sound course is for all those who take this literature seriously to engage deeply in study and discussion both of texts that promote the value of peace and those that do not. Professor Robert Eisen has written a remarkable volume based on this theory, reviewing four different stages of Jewish history, and in each, pointing out both examples of pro-peace texts and texts that gravitate toward ethnocentrism, enmity, and violence.[11] Rabbi Melissa Weintraub has likewise made the case that all of us must become "exegetical warriors," actively exploring and debating sacred texts on both sides of the peace and violence debate.[12] I honor this point of view, and heartily agree that one must never pretend that Jewish tradition is univocal on this, or any other, topic. This would be to whitewash and ultimately betray the richness and complexity of the tradition.

However, I am more persuaded by Marc Gopin's argument[13] that, at this troubled moment in history, we must affirmatively engage in a "hermeneutic of peace-making," intentionally mining the pro-peace and pro-social dimensions of the tradition, so needed in our community and in our world. Arguably, the Rabbis did the same thing, as in their famous adaptation of the climactic verse of the golden calf narrative.

---

[10] More scholarly expositions of these and many other Jewish peace texts appear in Robert Eisen, *The Peace and Violence of Judaism, from the Bible to Modern Zionism* (Oxford: Oxford University Press, 2011); Lewis, *Torah of Reconciliation*; and in Marc Gopin, *Between Eden and Armageddon: The Future of World Religions, Violence, and Peacemaking* (Oxford: Oxford University Press, 2000), and *Holy War, Holy Peace: How Religion Can Bring Peace to the Middle East* (Oxford: Oxford University Press, 2002).

[11] Eisen, *Peace and Violence in Judaism*.

[12] Melissa Weintraub, "Waging Peace in the Context of Violent Conflict," public lecture at University of St. Thomas, St. Paul, Minnesota, November 2, 2011.

[13] Gopin, *Between Eden and Armageddon*, 12.

> *Adonai, Adonai*, a God compassionate and gracious, slow to anger,
> abounding in kindness and faithfulness, extending kindness to the
> thousandth generation, forgiving iniquity, transgression, and sin;
> yet God does not remit all punishment, but visits the iniquity of
> fathers upon children and children's children, upon the third and
> fourth generations.[14]

The entire verse includes both compassionate and vengeful dimensions
of God. But when the Rabbis use the verse in liturgical texts (as an oft-
repeated mantra, for example, in the *Yom Kippur*—Day of Atonement—
service), they cut the verse in half, omitting the punishment of sinners, thus
reversing the message of the original verse. Although much more could
be said about this example, it is clear that the Rabbis were intentionally
elevating and reinforcing God's qualities of mercy and compassion over
descriptions of God as punishing and vengeful.[15]

In the violent times in which we live, I see it as a value, even a religious imperative, to engage in such selective hermeneutics. I believe that
all religious traditions must be rigorously honest about these matters,
exploring their own traditions deeply and acknowledging ways in which
their own tradition has brought more division and less love into the world.
We must certainly refrain from the temptation to compare our own
peace texts with another tradition's violent texts. Such comparisons are
dishonest and defensive, violating one of the great principles of interfaith
dialogue, by comparing the best of our own tradition with the worst of
another.[16] If all religions acknowledged that all of our traditions include
texts that may support our fellow religionists in exclusivist, even hateful
and violent, attitudes and actions, there would be far less religiously sanc-
tioned violence in the world.

We must own and engage with the fullness of our tradition—the troubling texts as well as the favorites. But it is the texts that inspire caring,

---

[14] Exodus 34:6; translation adapted from *The Torah: The Five Books of Moses*
(Philadelphia: Jewish Publication Society), 1962. A very similar verse appears at
the climax of the narrative of the spies, Numbers 14:18.

[15] My analysis here is influenced by Lewis, *Torah of Reconciliation*, 166–68.

[16] Will Joyner, "Krister Stendahl, 1921–2008," April 16, 2008, obituary at
Harvard Divinity School website, http://www.hds.harvard.edu.

compassion, respect, and reconciliation that need to be heard widely and convincingly to counter the myriad voices of violence and hatred in our world. The best response to those who claim that religion is responsible for violence in today's world is to identify and disseminate powerful religious words that move people to act with compassion, kindness, and love, to treat others with dignity, and to live with humility and genuine curiosity for all beings. The world needs to hear and absorb these commanding and evocative religious texts, inspiring us all to live up to the high ideals that all religions revere.

> Hizkiah said: Great is peace, for with regard to all the commandments in the Torah it is said, If [you should be in a given circumstance], "if you should see" . . . "if you come upon" . . . "if it happens" . . . "if you build" . . . if the commandment is available to you, you are obliged to do it. But with peace, what is written? "Seek peace and pursue it. Seek it in your place and pursue it in another place."[17]

The Rabbis observed that most of the legislation in the Torah is case law. If we find a lost object, we are to return it to its owner. If we own property, we must take precautions to ensure the safety of those who enter it. If we see our enemy's animal struggling under its load, we are to help him. When Shabbat (Sabbath) or a holy day comes, we are to observe it.

Notably, two commandments are explicitly articulated not as responses to a particular situation, but as imperatives to be followed—indeed, pursued—at all times. We are not only to act in accordance with these imperatives passively when the occasion arises. We are to actively seek out opportunities to engage in them. The two cases are the pursuit of justice, of which it is said, "Justice, justice shall you pursue" (Deut. 16:20) and the pursuit of peace, of which it is said, "Seek peace and pursue it" (Ps. 34:15).

Although this formulation of the *mitzvah* (commandment) appears in the book of Psalms and not in the Torah itself, the Rabbis apply their practice of assuming that every apparently superfluous word in the text is there for a reason. In this case, they implicitly ask why the verse employs two verbs ("seek" and "pursue") when one would have

---

[17] BT *Perek Hashalom* and Jerusalem Talmud (henceforth JT) *Peah* 1:1.

sufficed. Their answer: "Seek it in your place and pursue it in another place." The two verbs convey different elements of the command: seek peace when conflict comes to your doorstep, but do not stop there. You must energetically pursue opportunities to practice peace, near and far, for it is the work of God.

The Ḥafetz Ḥayim[18] continues the tradition's musing on the verse, teaching:

> Seek it (peace) for your loved one and pursue it with your enemy. Seek it in your place and pursue it in other places. Seek it with your body and pursue it with your material resources. Seek it for your own benefit and pursue it for the benefit of others. Seek it today and pursue it tomorrow. With reference to "seek it tomorrow," it teaches that one should not despair, thinking that one cannot make peace, but rather one should pursue peace today and also tomorrow and on the day afterwards, until one reaches it.[19]

This rabbi of the nineteenth and the early twentieth centuries expands on the earlier interpretation, elaborating on the verse's message to reach beyond one's home and comfort zone in the pursuit of peace. What is called for, he insists, is not passive or occasional practice, but a constant, relentless seeking after opportunities to respond to the command.

We are not to wait for conflict to come to us before offering a peaceful presence; we must actively seek out ways to help. We are to practice peace with those nearest to us and with those we would prefer to avoid. We are to make the pursuit of peace central to our relationships, both with those we love and with those we might consider to be enemies. We are exhorted to build peace both at home and when in foreign territory. We are to seek peace every day of our lives.

But then comes the Ḥafetz Ḥayim's most striking and original addition to Rabbinic reflections on the pursuit of peace: "With reference to 'seek it tomorrow,' it teaches that one should not despair, thinking that

---

[18] Pen name of Rabbi Yisrael Meir Ha-Kohen Poupko, 1838–1933, Vilna See *Encyclopedia Judaica* (Jerusalem: Keter, 1972), 9:1067.

[19] Rabbi Yisrael Meir Kagan (1838–1933, Poland), Ḥafetz Ḥayim, *Shmirat Halashon, Sha'ar Haz'chirah,* chap. 17.

one cannot make peace." I wonder what historical circumstances impelled him to urge his followers not to lose hope about the prospect of peace.

Many years later, I identify with his impulse to counsel hopefulness and perseverance in the pursuit of peace, for I encounter so many people who are discouraged and disdainful about the prospect of conflict transformation in their lives and in the world. This sense of hopelessness, fear, and anger has been bred in us by many decades, or even centuries or millennia, of trying, without success, to live in peace with our neighbors.

Although we might think of the demon of despair as a uniquely contemporary obstacle to the practice of peacebuilding, the rabbi exhorts his people not to allow hopelessness, discouragement, or compassion fatigue to keep them from responding to the command to seek and pursue peace. Rather, he says, we must live out this sacred directive one day at a time, and then the next day, and then the next. He whispers words of encouragement: if we all begin to live this way, then yes, peace will come.

I pray that, in some small way, the reflections in this book will encourage you to take the mitzvah/commandment of peacebuilding more fully into your life. This is not easy work. Many obstacles stand in our way. First, we must banish the notion that "peacemaking" is only the purview of politicians and diplomats or that the peace we seek is some utopian, unattainable, and even dangerous goal. If this were the case, the tradition would not present the pursuit of peace as a command to every one of us, throughout our lives. Rather, the tradition exhorts us to work persistently for reconciliation because it knows that conflict is an everyday reality for us. What is more, the larger peace that the world longs for depends on all of us, not just an elite few; as in the beautiful phrase attributed to Gandhi, we must be "the change we wish to see in the world."

We will face obstacles both external and internal in our own personal work for peace. Externally, we may meet the nonresponsiveness of our "enemy" to our efforts, the experience of unfairness embedded in experiences of conflict, and the sheer unlikelihood that long-entrenched disputes will somehow find quick resolution. Many more of the obstacles are internal—our own hurt, anger, and sense of betrayal, our attachment to our own version of the truth, and the sheer discomfort of stretching beyond our comfort zone for the sake of maintaining or restoring relationships. These are all natural, even necessary, elements of our experience of conflict.

But we also carry within us our traditions' wise teachings, inspiring us to see the pursuit of peace as a command for all of our lives and prescribing practices that help us live, as best we can, with compassion, gentleness, generosity, and even a measure of holiness. Although feeling wounded, angry, and stuck are understandable human responses to conflict, religious traditions call us to aim higher, allowing our lives to be guided by a set of values that can override our baser emotions, even emulating divine qualities of compassion, loving-kindness, and forgiveness.

I hope that the experiences, portraits, sources, and theory contained in this book will inspire you with confidence that you can in some way contribute to the cause of peace in your own life and in the world. May we all claim the role of peacebuilder in our own lives, adding to the reservoirs of peaceful energies in the world and filling the universe with fervent prayers for peace. When more of us do so, our world will become a more peaceful place.

1

On Peace and Conflict

May the One who makes peace on high make peace for us, for all Israel, and for all the inhabitants of the earth.

—*Jewish Daily Prayer Book (my translation)*

Bar Kappara said: Great is peace. If heavenly beings, among whom there is no jealousy, hatred, rivalry, strife, conflict, nor the evil eye, need peace, as it is written "the One Who makes peace on high" (Job 25:2), how much more so do earthly beings, among whom all these things exist [need peace]!

—*Leviticus Rabbah 9:9*

The description of God as "Maker of peace on high" is ubiquitous in Jewish liturgy. Multiple times during every prayer service, every day of the year, Jews around the world fervently pray for the Maker of peace in the celestial realms to make peace for us on earth. Relatively few people who love this prayer realize that the image first appears, of all places, in the Book of Job. What is more, what does this image mean? We know that we need all the help we can get in moving toward peace among the human family. But who on high is locked in conflict, in need of God's help to bring them peace?

The author of this midrash[1] implicitly asks why heavenly beings need God's help to make peace. Do angels have jealousy, competition, strife, and argument among them? Ancient mythologies aside, the answer is decidedly not. Celestial beings, the author imagines, are spared the vicissitudes and challenges of human life that give rise to conflict. The author therefore understands the image of God making peace on high as a reminder of how profoundly we earthly creatures need God's help in making peace. If celestial beings, among whom there is no low self-esteem, envy, jockeying for power, scarcity, or discord, nonetheless need God's help as a peacemaker, how much more do we humans need the ultimate source of peace in the universe to come to our aid.

All of this raises the basic question: What do we mean by peace? I asked this question of a group of people studying Jewish texts on the pursuit of peace. They all agreed that absence of conflict and violence is the minimal definition of peace. But, in offering their own definitions, they all went beautifully far beyond this narrow understanding. The students responded, aware that the root meaning of the word "*shalom*" in Hebrew and hence in the Jewish imagination is "wholeness." So they elaborated that peace means wholeness, harmony, and balance among individuals, among groups, and among nations. They suggested that peace includes a sense of well-being, contentment, completeness, and tranquility—within individuals, among people, and among communities. Peace also implied for them qualities of trust, patience, openheartedness, respect, integrity, and gratitude. Some imagined peace as a quality of joy, lightness, and connection to others and to all things. One suggested that peace is the absence of fear. Another offered that peace is not a goal or destination so much as a daily practice, recalling A. J. Muste's statement, popularized by Thich Nhat Hanh, "There is no way to peace. Peace is the way."[2]

What comes to mind when you pray for peace? Close your eyes for a moment and consider: What does peace mean to you? What do you envision when you pray for peace?

---

[1] Literary, legal, or folkloristic commentary on a biblical text or free-standing homiletical composition.

[2] See the website of the A. J. Muste Memorial Institute, http://www.ajmuste. org. The saying was popularized by Thich Nhat Hanh, *Peace Is Every Step: The Path of Mindfulness in Everyday Life* (New York: Bantam Books, 1991).

Not surprisingly, ancient Jewish texts also offer different understandings of peace. Consider, for example, these two descriptions by Rabbi Don Yitzhak Abrabanel.[3]

> In all places in which "peace" is mentioned in the Bible, some commentators think that its meaning is always agreement between conflicting parties. . . . as if the matter of peace is only when there has been quarrel and struggle. . . .
>
> They [such commentators] did not know the great value of *shalom*, and they did not see its precious, splendid greatness. . . . *"Shalom"* is also used without fighting or conflict, [with regard to] the common good and agreement and love among people that is necessary for the unity of a nation. It is the tie that binds and connects everything.
>
> In general, *shalom* refers to the health, wholeness, good and beauty of a matter. Therefore, G-d is called *Shalom*, since God connects the whole world, sustaining everything according to its particular nature, for when everything is in its proper order, there will be peace and righteousness.[4]

Thus, both ancient commentators and contemporary people recognize the range of meanings of the concept of peace. We sometimes speak of peace in its minimal sense, as in the absence of violence or the absence of conflict between people. Surely, an end to violence and discord would make for a very different world from the one in which we live. But I am convinced that the prayers for peace offered by people all over the world every day express more far-reaching yearnings—for wholeness, balance, acceptance, and ease.

Meanings of Conflict

Early in a mediation training course I attended some years ago, participants were asked to draw a visual image of conflict. It was a remarkable question, and we all gathered art materials and sat down to work. The drawing that emerged from my art-challenged hand was one of dangerously

---

[3]   Don Yitzhak Abarbanel (1437–1508), philosopher and biblical exegete, Spain.

[4]   Abarbanel, *Nahalat Avot* 1:12, cited in Rabbi Daniel Roth, "Rodef Shalom: Pursuing Peace in Judaism" teaching materials, Pardes Center for Judaism and Conflict Resolution, www. pcjcr.pardes.org.

sharp-edged objects rubbing against one another. One could almost hear ominous sounds of growling and grinding in the background. In my own subconscious, conflict is strongly associated with pain and hurt.

We were then invited to walk around the room in silence and look at the variety of images created by our fellow students. I have done this with many groups over the years, and usually most of the people in the room, like me, produce pictures of violence, injury, and loss. There are often likenesses of people—often children—injured or alone and crying. There are images of ruptures, chasms, and explosions—in every case, a palpable sense of sorrow and destruction.

In each group, in my experience, a few participants create representations of creative clashes, say, between water and rock, resulting in a beautifully sculpted wonder of nature. These drawings depict collisions, even damage to the two sides, but from the site of the injury something new and beautiful arises. The people who fashion these images seem to know, deep in the unconscious from which such artistic creations emerge, that without conflict little growth and transformation can occur. For the rest of us, conflict means painful and frightening experiences, to be avoided whenever possible.

What are we to make of these radically different understandings of conflict? What do we mean when we speak of conflict?

> Why does the Torah not say the words, "And God saw that it was good," [in its account of] the second day of creation? Rabbi Hanina explained: Because on the second day separation [i.e., division or estrangement] was brought into being, as indicated in "Let [the firmament] separate water from water" [Gen. 1:6]. In this regard, Rabbi Tavyomi noted: If there is no mention, "that it was good," about an act of separation that is conducive to the world's improvement and well-being, all the less so should these words occur in describing acts of separation that lead to the world's disarray.[5]

As is well known, the account of the creation of the world in the first chapter of Genesis contains evaluative statements. At the end of most of the days described in the narrative, the text records that "God saw

---

[5] *Genesis Rabbah* 4:6. *Genesis Rabbah* is a midrash on Genesis, edited in the early fifth century.

[what God had created] that it was good." After the sixth day, following the creation of the human person, the text speaks more positively: "God saw everything that God had made and, behold, it was very good" (Gen. 1:31). Only in one case, after the second day, when the "firmament" was created to divide between celestial and terrestrial waters, does the day end without praise for God's own work.

Rabbinic commentators, ever attuned to the finest nuances in the biblical text, suggest that God could not have seen the work of this day as good, because this was the day when separation or estrangement, the roots of conflict, came into the world. Even though this act of division was generative, even essential for the creation of the world, it was seen as a sad day when disunity became a reality in the universe. Rabbi Tavyomi indicates that he is aware that in this case the rupture lay at the core of a great creative act. Yet he imagined that God is displeased even by separation that is beneficial or generative. Surely, then, conflict among human beings—obviously a cause of suffering in the world—is seen as negative, as a threat to the well-being of relationships and communities.

By contrast, consider this very different view:

> Understand that a disagreement is a kind of creation of the world. For the essence of the creation of the world was that it required an empty space, since without it, everything would be the infinite presence of God and there wouldn't be any place for the creation of the world. So God pulled the light back to the sides and the empty space was created and in it God created everything—days and measures—using speech. . . . This is similar to disagreement. If the Sages were united, there would be no place for the creation of the world, which only happens through the disagreements between them. They move away from each other, each one pulling back towards a different side. Thus a kind of empty space is created between them, which is like pulling back the light to the sides. This is where creation can happen through speech. Everything that they say should only be for the sake of creating the world, which is done by them in the empty space between them, for the Sages create everything with their words.[6]

---

[6] Rebbe Nachman of Bratzlav (1772–1810, Poland), *Likutei Moharan*, 64:4, with thanks to Rabbi Lisa Goldstein for sharing this text with me.

In this remarkable text, Rebbe Nachman of Bratslav presents a radically positive view of intellectual debate among the Sages. Drawing on Kabbalistic[7] creation mythology, Nachman asserts that before the creation of the world, nothing existed but the Divine Presence. In order for there to be space for the universe to occupy, God needed to self-contract. Nachman imagines that in order to create this generative space, God separated the all-encompassing divine light to leave room for the universe-to-be. Ingeniously, he adds that God's act of creation took place by way of divine speech, when God declared, "Let there be . . ."

Acts of division and of speech, then, are a prerequisite to existence itself. So too, Nachman asserts, religious truths are articulated through speech. In order for new discoveries to be revealed, the Sages must divide themselves into different views on an issue. Only from the verbal space created by this differentiation of perspectives can new understandings emerge. Thus, although members of the academy may be grieved by vigorous disputes among colleagues, they should remember that such argument is essential to the pursuit of divine truth.

On the basis of this source alone, one might conclude that Nachman's analysis pertained only to a very particular kind of conflict—intellectual debate within the walls of the *beit midrash* (house of study) or religious academy. Such debates are disagreements among a circumscribed group of people who are bound by a shared body of beliefs, practices, and life circumstances. But consider this second Nachman text.

Through arguments in which (people) disagree with a person, they do him good, for through this he can grow and flourish. When a seed is planted in the ground, if all of the land were bound together, it would not be possible for a seed to grow and flourish and become a tree. Knowing that the land will be separated a bit, there will be room for the tree to grow.[8]

---

[7] "Kabbalah" (literally, "receiving"), refers to the whole body of Jewish esoteric teachings and Jewish mysticism, especially from the twelfth century onward.

[8] Rebbe Nachman of Bratzlav, *Gesher Tsar Me'od* (Very Narrow Bridge), cited in Roth, "Rodef Shalom."

Here, Nachman is clearly talking about interpersonal conflicts wherever they may arise, not necessarily among sages or community leaders. Still, Nachman uses a similar metaphor, drawing on an analogy with the created universe, in which division is necessary for growth. Just as a seed can only become a tree if the earth parts a bit to allow for it to be planted, so too, people only grow from the generative conflicts that develop in relationships. In our day we might extend the biological metaphor, adding that without the process of cell division, life as we know it could not exist. Again, existence depends on serial separations and ruptures.

These images of rifts and schisms as integral to life and growth challenge the intuitive assumption that disunity and disruption are necessarily dangerous. Strikingly, this view, expressed by Rebbe Nachman, parallels an idea commonly found in contemporary conflict resolution theory. Consider, for example, the following statements.

> Many persons believe that conflict, properly institutionalized, is an effective vehicle for discovering truth, for attaining justice, and for the long-run benefit of a society as a whole.[9]

> It may come as a surprise, particularly since we often dwell on the costs of conflict, that conflict also has benefits. Yet, clearly there are significant benefits to conflict or it would not be the prominent characteristic of human relationships that it is. Conflict is often driven by a sense of grievance, be it scarcity, inequality, cultural or moral differences, or the distribution of power. Thereby, engaging in the conflict provides one means of addressing these concerns—either affirming a position of advantage or overcoming perceived shortcomings.[10]

> Conflict is natural; neither positive nor negative. It just IS. Conflict is just an interface pattern of energies. Nature uses conflict as its

---

[9] Louis Kriesberg, *The Sociology of Social Conflicts* (Englewood Cliffs, NJ: Prentice-Hall, 1973), 3.

[10] Eric Brahm, "Benefits of Intractable Conflict," in *Beyond Intractability*, ed. Guy Burgess and Heidi Burgess. Conflict Information Consortium, University of Colorado, Boulder. Posted: September 2004, http://www.beyoninstractability. org, with thanks to Rabbi Daniel Roth for identifying this source.

primary motivator for change, creating beautiful beaches, canyons, mountains and pearls. It's not whether you have conflict in your life. It's what you do with that conflict that makes a difference.... Conflict can be seen as a gift of energy in which neither side loses and a new dance is created.[11]

Thus we have seen in Jewish sources, as in personal experience, two very different ways of relating to conflict. In one view, conflict is seen as necessarily divisive and dangerous, even tragic. In another, conflict is seen as a dynamic and vital process essential to biological, interpersonal, and social growth.

What is true about this for you? Close your eyes for a moment and see what image arises in your mind's eye when you silently say "conflict." How would you draw this image?

This chapter presents different ideas about the nature of conflict in contemporary peace and conflict studies. The goal is to investigate what goes wrong when discord becomes harmful to relationship and community, examine what distinguishes generative conflict from destructive conflict, and explore a mindful approach to engagement with conflict and difference.

The Roots of Conflict

Take a moment and ask yourself another question: Where and when have you encountered conflict today? If you are like most people, you will immediately notice the different levels of seriousness and different contexts in which conflict appears in our lives. We know conflict internally (I knew I had lots of work to do today, but I really wanted to sleep a little longer), interpersonally (I was irritated with my husband for lingering over the newspaper just when I was waiting to see it), ideologically, politically, and internationally (as became evident as soon as I began to read the newspaper).

A preliminary glance at dictionary entries likewise reveals the multiple layers of meaning associated with the term "conflict." *The Oxford Dictionary* defines conflict as "a serious disagreement or argument, typically a

---

[11] Thomas Crum, *The Magic of Conflict: Turning a Life of Work into a Work of Art* (New York: Touchstone, 1987), 49.

protracted one; a prolonged armed struggle; a state of mind in which a person experiences a clash of opposing feelings or needs; or a serious incompatibility between two or more opinions, principles, or interests."[12] This set of definitions highlights issues of significance (a trivial disagreement versus a profoundly important matter), level of seriousness (from mild tension to international violence), duration, and scope (within one person or among people, among groups holding different viewpoints, or in international contexts).

Similarly, the mediator Sam Leonard suggests that conflicts can be described and categorized by considering three criteria: intensity (ranging from discomfort to need for resolution, all the way to breakdown in communication, depersonalization, and annihilation); level of "healthiness" and quality of communication; and substance (conflict over resources, intrapsychic struggles, relationships, systems and structures, or values).[13]

Scholars of conflict resolution differ on the nature of conflict and what, if any, kind of resolution is needed. Various theorists and practitioners believe that discord arises fundamentally from real or perceived scarcity of resources, from frustrated human needs (as in needs for security, control, dignity, self-determination, affirmation, and love), and/or from a clash of nonnegotiable existential needs, values, or identity issues. Robert A. Baruch Bush and Joseph P. Folger summarize these differences of perspective elegantly by stating that people are understood to come to mediation when conflict (a) threatens their power over others (according to the power theory of conflict), (b) threatens their rights (as in the rights theory of conflict), or (c) threatens their assurance of their needs being met (as in the needs/interests theory of conflict).[14]

Intriguingly, Bush and Folger's "transformative theory of conflict" asserts that

> what people find most significant about conflict is not that it frustrates their satisfaction of some right, interest, or pursuit, . . . but

---

[12] *Oxford Dictionaries Online,* http://oxforddictionaries.com.

[13] Sam Leonard, *Mediation: The Book: A Step-by-Step Guide for Dispute Resolvers* (Evanston, IL: Evanston Publishing, 1994), 37–46.

[14] Robert A. Baruch Bush and Joseph P. Folger, *The Promise of Mediation: The Transformative Approach to Conflict* (San Francisco: Jossey-Bass, 2005), 43–44.

that it leads and even forces them to behave toward themselves and others in ways that they find uncomfortable and even repellent. . . . It alienates them from their sense of their own strength and their sense of connection to others, thereby disrupting and undermining the interaction between them as human beings.[15]

For Bush and Folger, conflict is at its core an "interactional crisis,"[16] a sense of personal powerlessness and alienation from others with whom they are in relationship.

To illustrate these broad descriptions of conflict, consider the case of Jacob and Esau. What lies at the root of their conflict? The story certainly contains issues of scarcity of resources, embedded in biblical assumptions about the birthright and its accompanying blessing. Esau's plaintive cry, "Have you only one blessing, father?" (Gen. 27:38) speaks powerfully to his belief that the giving of the firstborn's blessing to his brother means that his own basic needs will not be met. Or is the blessing primarily a symbol of power, dignity, and parental affirmation? By contrast, some commentators understand the brothers' conflict as a matter of core values and identity, given the text's implication that the brothers emerged from the womb with different personalities and inclinations. Still others see the narrative as a story about the use and misuse of power, since the narrative comes to be used as textual confirmation of the spiritual superiority of Jacob's descendants over Esau's.

Whichever theory is most compelling for you, note that conflict scholars create their analytic schema with reference to all kinds of conflict, from interpersonal to intergroup to international. This may at first be counterintuitive. Surely what happens between spouses or friends in dyadic conflict is different from what occurs between different ethnic or racial groups. Obviously, international conflict has dimensions that are quite different from the interpersonal realm.

Of course, scope matters. Yet when we step back from our view of particular conflicts to a consideration of the phenomenon of human conflict, scholars agree that common patterns of thought and behavior arise in all

---

[15] Ibid., 45.

[16] Ibid., 46.

sorts of conflict, for regardless of scale, human beings are involved. This insight may be counterintuitive at this point. But I invite you to consider trying on the striking suggestion that distinctive patterns and behaviors arise in all kinds of human conflict, regardless of scope or subject.

Interpersonal Conflict in our Lives

For individuals seeking to understand conflict in the world and in our lives, it is most fruitful to begin by looking at what we know about conflict from our own experience. But first a note of caution. It is in the nature of painful conflict that when we call such a situation to mind, we are likely to focus on what the other person did to harm us. On deeper reflection, it becomes clear that the path of wise and sacred engagement with conflict always demands looking first at ourselves. My colleague Rabbi Alan Lew said it best when he wrote, "Conflict begins in our own heart and then we project it onto others and this kind of projection proliferates until the world is full of violence and conflict."[17]

We each come into adult life with a plethora of experiences, images, assumptions, and attitudes about the role of conflict in relationship. Take a moment and ask yourself: What were your formative experiences of conflict as a child? Who was in conflict and how did this affect you? Did the sound of raised voices bring dread to your heart, evoking fears of judgment, humiliation, loss, or abandonment? Or does argument conjure memories of vibrant, life-giving, and connecting exchanges of ideas over the family dinner table, strengthening loving relationship and a sense of shared commitments? Each of us carries an inner photo album of such memories and emotions. Consciously or not, these core images powerfully affect how we conduct ourselves in conflict situations throughout our lives.

So, too, we each have characteristic patterns that we tend to employ in a wide range of conflict situations in our lives. For some, the eruption of disagreement triggers an instinct to prepare for battle, to mount convincing arguments in hopes of wrestling a rhetorical opponent to victory. Such people may lie awake at night reviewing enraging snippets

---

[17] Alan Lew, *Be Still and Get Going: A Jewish Meditation Practice for Real Life* (New York: Little, Brown, 2005), 94.

of dialogue or rehearsing indignant accusations of injustice. For others, a predominant response is to run away in the face of discord, denying issues in order to avoid at all costs the pain of explicit conflict. For still others, argument causes us to shut down, disengage, and space out—to allow the conflict to wash over us in order not to be overwhelmed by it. Not coincidentally, as we shall see, these general categories of conflict response parallel the well-documented inner mechanisms of "fight, flight, or freeze," in the presence of physical threat.

Most people who have satisfying relationships in their adult lives have, to a greater or lesser degree, learned about their own inner-conflict landscape. Based on early experience, on neurology, and God knows what else, we each have certain issues that are our characteristic hot-button emotional issues. For some people, even the slightest insult to self-esteem causes such intense pain that anger and conflict are sure to follow. For others the primary vulnerability is a fear of abandonment or of annihilation, and for others, the issues are power and control. In young relationships, partners tend to stumble unawares into their own and the other's "trigger" issues, "pushing buttons" in a way that creates pain and discord. With increasing maturity, we learn to bring more self-awareness to our relationships. Knowing the places inside us that are most susceptible to uncontrollable spasms of pain, we are more likely to avoid engaging in unwise speech and action that only cascades into more suffering for both parties.

> When we go from situation to situation and we realize that the same kind of conflicts have followed us from place to place, we begin to get a glimmering that the problem might be within us and not just in the circumstances. . . . The source of this conflict is within and not without.[18]

> So it is that I find myself fighting with people all the time over scraps of love and attention, that I become vulnerable to their provocations, that they can always touch me in that inner place of lack and draw me into conflict with them. It has very little to do with them. It mostly has to do with me, with the torn and hurting

---

[18] Ibid., 103.

places my heart is trying to cover over, the deep wells my disappointment is trying to stop up.[19]

Don't say, "Since I have been humiliated, let my neighbor be humiliated also." Know: it is the image of God you would be humiliating
in your neighbor.[20]

It may be said that experiences of humiliation lie at the heart of all interpersonal conflict. If so, then in very few words, this deceptively simple text
goes to the heart of why healing interpersonal discord can be so difficult,
and it also hints at the path to transformation.

Consider, for example, this grimly vivid description of a marriage in crisis.

Some time ago, I had the opportunity to do therapeutic work with
a professional couple who were involved in bitter conflicts over
issues they considered non-negotiable. The destructiveness of their
way of dealing with their conflicts was reflected in their tendency
to escalate a dispute about almost any specific issue (for example,
a household chore, the child's bedtime) into a power struggle in
which each spouse felt that his or her self-esteem or core identity
was at stake. The destructive process resulted in (as well as from)
justified mutual suspicion; correctly perceived mutual hostility; a
win-lose orientation to their conflicts; a tendency to act so as to
lead the other to respond in a way that would confirm one's worst
suspicion; inability to understand and empathize with the other's
needs and vulnerabilities; and reluctance—based on stubborn pride,
nursed grudges, and fear of humiliation—to initiate or respond
to a positive, generous action so as to break out of the escalating
vicious cycle in which they were entrapped.[21]

Most people who have ever experienced an intimate relationship in crisis
will find this description painfully familiar. In its author's penetrating

---

[19] Ibid., 107.

[20] Ben Azzai in *Genesis Rabbah* 24:7.

[21] Morton Deutsch and Peter T. Coleman, eds., *The Handbook of Conflict Resolution* (San Francisco: Jossey-Bass, 2000), 1.

description, it contains all the hallmarks of intractable interpersonal discord: conflict over issues of great emotional import, communication patterns suffused with power struggle, suspicion, hostility, and mortal threats to self-esteem on both sides, and the rest. Put in the terms of our ancient text, each partner feels chronically humiliated by the other. Under attack, each repeatedly does what human beings do under threat: they attack back, consciously or unconsciously seeking to inflict the same kind of hurt on the other that was done to them. As for seeing the image of God in the other, or even in oneself, who has time for such luxuries when one feels that one's very essence is under attack?

In the heat of conflict, it is extremely difficult to pay attention to what is happening inside us. Right now, sitting quietly with this book in your hands, close your eyes for a moment or two and think about a person who has wronged you or from whom you are estranged. As you hold that person's image in your mind, what do you notice in your body, in your breath, and in the pace, tone, and content of your thoughts? Do you notice your heart beginning to race, your fists clenching, and thoughts racing through your brain, reviewing familiar dialogues and self-righteous arguments over and over again? Did you ever wonder about this set of visceral responses to conflict? What is the body doing here?

Now try shifting your attention from your response to conflict with an individual, and consider how you react to a political or religious leader with whom you strongly disagree. If you commit to a moment of honest self-reflection while holding such a figure in your mind, you may gain a wealth of knowledge about how you regard "the other." It is very common for us to leap unconsciously to righteous indignation, exaggerated certainty about our beliefs, superiority toward those who hold other beliefs, and/or deep fear and vulnerability about the very existence of such convictions in our nation and in our world.

Try disengaging for a moment in the midst of a political argument at your dinner table or while watching your favorite cable TV news program. Be silent for a moment and tell yourself the truth: Do you feel an adrenaline rush, as if preparing to jump into battle, and a powerful certainty that any view other than your own is absurd or dangerous and must be rhetorically demolished? Notice the fascinating similarity between this set of responses to a political "other" and feelings we have in the midst of interpersonal discord in our lives. The really interesting question is this: What lies beneath this rush to verbal warfare, or its apparent opposite, a retreat into fearful avoidance of disagreement—whether in personal relationship or in connection with a political or religious opponent?

The Neurobiology of Conflict

For years I was desperately curious to understand these visceral responses to conflict and difference that I experienced in myself and observed in others. What is this strange reaction, I thought, that makes the body clench, the fists tighten, the breath constrict, and thoughts race into high gear? I knew it had the quality of a hardwired pattern. I knew that it was present in myself and in others in the midst of the most ferocious arguments— interpersonal, religious, or political—and that it generally operated outside of the combatants' conscious awareness. How was I to understand this strange human instinct that had the power to turn ordinary disagreement into destructive, dehumanizing battles, which endangered relationships and at times even encouraged violence?

Then I began to read popular works of neuroscience. I am certainly not an expert on this subject, but I have learned that in recent decades, brain scientists have come to understand a great deal about the structure of the brain and its evolutionary history. Researchers have demonstrated the central role of the amygdala, an almond-shaped pair of structures deep in the brain, in the activation of sensations of fear and the physical responses that make up the "fight or flight" response in the presence of threat. Scientists believe that the limbic system, of which the amygdala is a part, belongs to an ancient layer of the human brain's evolutionary development.[22]

---

[22] Rick Hanson with Richard Mendius, *Buddha's Brain: The Practical Neuroscience of Happiness, Love, and Wisdom* (Oakland, Calif.: New Harbinger Publications, 2009), 34–35. Other sources on this material include Richard J. Davidson with Sharon Begley, *The Emotional Life of Your Brain: How Its Unique Patterns Affect the Way You Think, Feel, and Live—And How You Can Change Them* (New York: Hudson Street Press, 2012); Daniel Goleman, *Emotional Intelligence: Why It Can Matter More than IQ* (New York: Bantam, 1995); John Gottman, *The Science of Trust: Emotional Attunement for Couples* (New York: Norton, 2011); and Daniel J.

Imagine prehistoric human communities living in small, self-sustained enclaves. Living in caves or other protective natural structures, they cared for their basic needs and for their young. When an unknown person appeared over the horizon, the amygdala leaped into high gear. The other was surely not coming on a friendly visit, but with hostile intent. The ancient brain, responsible for self-preservation, evolved to assume that an "other" was an approaching threat, endangering community members, food supply, and homestead. Were it not for this stage of brain development, humans would have been wiped off the evolutionary map.

At some point, the more sophisticated layers of the brain developed, areas that facilitate rational thinking, critical analysis, and weighing of alternatives. Only at this stage did it become possible for the frontal cortex to execute a reflective, rather than an instinctive and emotional evaluation of perceived danger. Sometimes, as Rick Hanson describes,[23] the long narrow object slithering along the forest path is just what the amygdala instantly recognizes it to be—a mortal danger. Only the frontal cortex can take another second to review its memory stores to compare this object to others it has encountered. The frontal cortex can then conclude that the object is a harmless stick and override the powerful limbic reactions already coursing through the body. Nonetheless, we may notice that we are left with the vestiges of the adrenaline rush (heart racing, limbs poised to sprint) that flooded our system instantaneously when the amygdala's powerful alarm system was activated.

I think of Abraham and Sarah, known in the Bible and in Rabbinic tradition as masters of hospitality. It is said that Abraham so delighted in the practice of hospitality that he actively sought out wayfarers in order to offer them lavish food and drink.[24] Similarly, as is well known, the command repeated more frequently than any other in the Torah—thirty-six times, in fact—is the command to love, reach out to, and do justice to the stranger.

The fact that the commandment is repeated so many times testifies to its religious significance but also to the visceral difficulty we human

---

Siegel, *The Mindful Brain: Reflection and Attunement in the Cultivation of Well-Being* (New York: Norton, 2007).

[23] Hanson, *Buddha's Brain,* 34.

[24] *Avot d'Rabbi Natan* 7:1. *Fathers according to Rabbi Nathan,* a volume of commentary on *Mishnah Avot*, printed as a minor tractate of the Talmud.

beings have in upholding it. In developing the value of hospitality and care for the stranger, religion both reflects and nurtures the development of the frontal cortex, the part of the mind that can evaluate and sometimes supersede physical sensations of danger when, on reflection, there is really no need for fear. These religious values positively empower the frontal cortex to pause and reflect on the veracity of a potential threat, to question limbic panic more often, and to supersede the automatic instinct to fear the other in the absence of real danger.

We still need these deep, primal structures in the brain. We need the amygdala to alert us rapidly to imminent dangers such as the smell of fire or gas, an oncoming car in our lane on the freeway, or a threatening shadow climbing through the bedroom window in the middle of the night. In the infinite wisdom of the Divine, our body is still able to spring rapidly into action, helping us fight, flee, or get help to save ourselves and our loved ones from danger.

But many have observed that the limbic system is an anachronism in contemporary life. The amygdala responds to work stress, traffic, perfectionist instincts, and irritable colleagues as if to mortal danger in the forest. Consequently, the "fight or flight" response gets stuck in the "on" position and stress hormones flood our bodies continuously, as we fruitlessly try to tell our body and mind to relax and approach a nonlethal situation more thoughtfully.

The meditation teacher Arnie Kozak writes that the good news is that our body-mind has exquisitely effective systems, evolved over millennia to recognize dangers and keep us safe, and the bad news is that these mechanisms evolved perhaps a hundred thousand years too early to be appropriate for most of the threats we face on a daily basis.[25] The brain and its hormonal partners are honed through evolution to be particularly vigilant to mortal danger, because the price of inattention can be so dire. The limbic system's modus operandi, as Kozak describes it, is "Shoot first, ask questions later."[26] Thus the peculiar quality of the mind (not just yours but everyone's) to react more strongly to negative stimuli (e.g., criticism or conflict) than to positive ones (e.g., affirmation or harmony) makes

---

[25] Arnie Kozak, *Wild Chickens and Petty Tyrants: 108 Metaphors for Mindfulness* (Boston: Wisdom Publications, 2009), 74.

[26] Ibid., 92.

perfect sense against the background of the evolutionary development of the brain. Species bred to be too mellow did not survive.

Those instincts so essential in a world filled with mortal danger are ill-suited to today's everyday fears, such as fear of disapproval, failure, or disagreement. Yet most of us, if we pay close attention, will notice fight-or-flight responses surging within us when we have the first inkling that discord is developing in an important relationship or when we find ourselves in the presence of a representative of a religion or ideology we find foreign or offensive.

The real surprise here is that the limbic brain—right now in the twenty-first century—cannot distinguish between "I disagree with you," "I'm afraid you're going to hurt me," "I hate what you are saying," and "You endanger my way of life (or my dignity), so I must kill you." The amygdala, developed to be quick and effective rather than nuanced and reflective, jumps instantly into action in the presence of perceived threat, be it personal insult, simple diversity (i.e., a person of a different race, religion, or political persuasion), or mortal threat.

This is a compelling explanation for the strange dimension of conflict interaction I have described. In the presence of perceived threats to our well-being (e.g., emotional safety, self-esteem, or empowerment) or in the presence of difference (religious, ethnic, or political) the brain's ancient systems often catapult ordinary conversation into aggressive confrontation. Awareness of difference often resonates as a threat to our need for love, dignity, or power; it can evoke deep fear and vulnerability, which in turn can rapidly erupt into adrenaline-driven aggressive patterns of thought and speech. The leap into hypervigilant battle mode makes no sense but for the understanding that the limbic brain reacts to personal challenge or communal diversity as to a threat, creating physical responses to difficult conversations and to divergent values as if one's life depended on it. It is the ancient brain's survival mechanism that is responsible for those mystifying moments when hurtful words erupt from our mouths before we are able to pause and choose how to respond as the more reflective people that we are.

Yes, there is bad news and there is good news. The bad news is that the problem is as deeply rooted as the oldest structures of our brains. Some may stop here and proclaim that it is hopeless. We can't teach our brains new tricks, and so humanity is doomed to play out these ancient dynamics, both in individual and collective relationships, predisposing us to violence and hate until eternity.

But the same neuroscience that illuminates the problem can bring us to the solution. The brain is more than the hyperactive amygdala. The brain's reflective frontal cortex can override the limbic response, which is why we can sometimes apologize after exploding at our kids or even take a deep breath or a time out in the midst of a combustible conversation and then return and reengage wisely and lovingly, before regrettable words are spoken.

It is essential to know that there is a deep, ancient reason why it is difficult to respond thoughtfully and compassionately when we feel attacked. But it is even more vital to know that the uniquely human parts of the brain give us choices about how to respond to the limbic hormonal surges when they arise. We are not at the mercy of our fears of attack when they turn out to be distorted. We can practice consciously engaging our higher self when we feel frightened—whether by a family member challenging our self-esteem or by a person holding a political or religious worldview very different from our own.

This, I think, was precisely the intent of the author of the ancient midrash above. When Ben Azzai cautioned against humiliating a person who has humiliated us, he could not have known what we know about the evolutionary development of the brain. Yet he knew the solution to the problem. "Don't say, 'Since I have been humiliated, let my neighbor be humiliated also.' Know: it is the image of God you would be humiliating in your neighbor."[27] When we experience the primal pain of assault on our dignity, the urge to retaliate is strong in us. But we can choose to reach for a place of wisdom that is also embedded deep within us before we respond. The primal instinct, Ben Azzai knew, could easily lead us to counterattack. But spiritual awareness could inspire in us a righteous response, even in the midst of a challenging interaction.

We are not doomed to respond impulsively when we feel threatened. We simply need to practice skills that strengthen our capacity to shift our attention from the dynamics of threat and counterattack to the level of

---

[27] Ben Azzai in *Genesis Rabbah* 24:7.

soulful response. As the conflict specialist Dave Joseph puts it, "For me, the central challenge of human existence is to figure out how we can ... [avoid] visiting on others the hurts, misunderstandings and pain that each of us has experienced, in our own unique ways."[28]

Destructive and Constructive Conflict

Conflict, then, is not necessarily a source of irritation or danger in our lives. Handled mindfully, discord in relationships and uncomfortable encounters with difference can become a laboratory for learning, soul-purification, and growth. With the needed skills in place, dispute and difference—like the division that gives rise to life itself—may actually bring blessing and new understanding in its wake. In the words of one scholar of conflict resolution,

> Conflict, says Guy Burgess, "is the engine of social learning." Without conflict, attitudes, behavior, and relationships stay the same, regardless of whether they are fair. Conflict reveals problems and encourages those problems to be dealt with. Whether they are dealt with constructively or destructively depends on how the conflict is handled.[29]

What, then, makes the difference between disagreement that is a source of anguish, estrangement, and violence, on the one hand, and disagreement that is creative, enlivening, and even holy, on the other? As one pioneering conflict scholar puts it, "What leads to lively controversy rather than deadly quarrel?"[30]

In the conflict resolution field, there is considerable reflection on the difference between "constructive" and "destructive" dispute. The notion of "constructive conflict" refers to a kind of conflict interaction that

---

[28] Dave Joseph email, "Regarding the Tragedy in Newtown," sent by Public Conversations Project on December 21, 2012, in the aftermath of the Newtown, Conn., shooting.

[29] Brahm, "Benefits of Intractable Conflict."

[30] Morton Deutsch and Peter T. Coleman, eds., *The Handbook of Conflict Resolution: Theory and Practice* (San Francisco: Jossey-Bass, 2000), 9.

actually strengthens relationship and contributes to the development of knowledge and understanding.

> Constructive controversy occurs when one person's ideas, information, conclusions, theories, and opinions are incompatible with those of another, and the two seek to reach an agreement. Constructive controversies involve what Aristotle called *deliberate discourse* (discussion of the advantages and disadvantages of proposed actions) aimed at synthesizing novel solutions (*creative problem solving*).[31]

> The major difference between constructive controversy and competitive debate is that in the former people discuss their differences with the objective of clarifying them and attempting to find a solution that integrates the best thoughts that emerge during the discussion, no matter who articulates them. There is no winner and no loser; both win if during the controversy each part comes to deeper insights and enriched views of the matter that is initially in controversy. Constructive controversy is a process for constructively coping with the inevitable differences that people bring to cooperative interaction because it uses differences in understanding, perspective, knowledge, and world view as valued resources.[32]

Thomas Jefferson is said to have observed that "difference of opinion leads to inquiry, and inquiry to truth."[33] Scholar-practitioners David Johnson, Roger Johnson, and Dean Tjosvold articulate the potential value of opposing views in psychological, cognitive, and moral development, in the development of knowledge, in problem solving, and in combating social injustice. They assert these benefits in theory and then test them in practice, distinguishing between "constructive controversy" and "debate," revealing the following intriguing patterns.

---

[31] David W. Johnson, Roger T. Johnson, and Dean Tjosvold, "Constructive Controversy: The Value of Intellectual Opposition," in *Handbook of Conflict Resolution,* 65.

[32] Deutsch and Coleman, *Handbook of Conflict Resolution,* 28.

[33] Johnson, Johnson, and Tjosvold, "Constructive Controversy," 65.

In both constructive controversy and debate, proponents of different points of view categorize and organize information to form opinions, present and advocate for their conclusions, and experience being challenged by proponents of different views. However, constructive controversy evokes "epistemic curiosity motivating active search for new information and perspectives" versus "closed-minded rejection of opposing information and perspectives" in debate formats. That is, when the disagreement is explored in a collaborative context, the exploration of ideas produces curiosity, which, in turn, results in more nuanced and better-reasoned ideas by all participants. By contrast, in competitive, debate-style formats, speakers and observers tend to emerge having absorbed nothing about perspectives other than their own. Rather, their "closed-minded adherence" to their own points of view has often been strengthened.[34]

Controversy for the Sake of Heaven

Remarkably, the Mishnah[35] contains a very similar concept.[36]

> A controversy for the sake of Heaven will have lasting value, but a controversy not for the sake of Heaven will not endure. What is an example of a controversy for the sake of Heaven? The debates of Hillel and Shammai. What is an example of a controversy not for the sake of Heaven? The rebellion of Korach and his associates.[37]

This renowned text is the locus of classical Jewish reflection on the phenomenon of debate and discord in the ancient Rabbinic academy and beyond. Its central teaching is the distinction between "contro-

---

[34]   Ibid., 67.

[35]   The Mishnah is the sixty-three-volume foundational work of Jewish law, compiled around 200 C.E. by Rabbi Judah the Prince, reflecting the first stage of Rabbinic law, including sources from several centuries of reflection in Rabbinic academies in Palestine.

[36]   With thanks to Rabbi Daniel Roth for alerting me to the connection between this ancient text and the contemporary literature on constructive controversy.

[37]   *Mishnah Avot* 5:17.

versy for the sake of Heaven" and "controversy that is not for the sake of heaven."

The word *maḥloket*, translated as "controversy," "debate," or "dispute," frequently refers to classical scholarly debates about matters of Jewish law and interpretation. The word is also used to connote differing schools of thought on religious and philosophical matters and the general phenomenon of discord in human relationship. The word literally means "division" or "separation," suggesting how destructive conflict can divide and damage relationships and communities. Intriguingly, the word contains the Hebrew root for "part," highlighting an essential teaching about the nature of conflict. When engaged in heated argument, we tend to grow rigidly certain of the rightness of our position and the wrongness of any other view. In fact, no human being can have access to more than part of the truth. It is only when we mistake our partial view for the whole, invalidating and deriding the part that is visible to others, that disagreement grows toxic and destructive.

The Mishnah's distinction, it seems to me, refers simultaneously to three dimensions of dispute: (1) subject matter, (2) tone and style of communication, and (3) the parties' intentions in the conduct of the debate. On the level of content, a controversy for the sake of heaven is a strong, reasoned disagreement about a matter of sacred import, or at least a matter related to the common good. (An argument about who will take out the trash is unlikely to meet this criterion.) On the level of process, an argument is sacred or righteous to the degree that parties comport themselves with seriousness, dignity, and respect, honoring the matter at hand and all persons engaged in the dispute. (Derisive language and ad hominem attacks would not qualify.)

Most deeply, righteous debate arises from the intention of the parties to explore important issues, to learn from others about weighty truths, even to discern the will of the Divine. Why are we having this debate? A sacred argument is a conversation grounded neither in ego needs, power struggles, nor desire to shame or defeat the other. Honorable debate emerges from a sincere desire to explore issues of great import, including reasonable expectations about the outcome, beyond self-centered desire for victory. The following checklist summarizes the matter nicely:

It is the subtext that most often determines a controversy's outcome. Do we seek to vanquish? Punish? Mend? Do we differ over goals or over strategies toward the same goal? Do we seek reconciliation or rupture?[38]

The Mishnah illustrates the distinction between "sacred" and "not sacred" conflict vividly with reference to two examples. As is often observed, the Talmud regularly records the content of debates on virtually every imaginable matter, including opinions later determined to be minority views. In some cases, particular pairs of rabbis are known as consistent rhetorical opponents. Among the first of these pairs is Hillel and Shammai, two great rabbis of the first century before the Common Era, who disagreed about a wide range of religious and scholarly matters, but who sustained their communal ties with each other even when differences might have divided them.[39] In particular, Hillel and his students were known to comport themselves with humility and respect toward their rhetorical opponents, giving honor to the other side's views even while advocating their own.[40] This is "controversy for the sake of heaven." Imagine stopping in the middle of a heated political discussion to calmly and respectfully articulate the other side's view and you will immediately notice how difficult this can be.

The counterexample is the biblical figure of Koraḥ (Num. 16:1–35), who challenged Moses' divinely given authority over the Israelite community in the wilderness. According to the biblical account, God's displeasure at Koraḥ's revolt resulted in Koraḥ and his two hundred and fifty supporters being swallowed up by the earth. The Rabbis therefore understand Koraḥ's complaint to be an ego-driven control battle, motivated by narcissistic needs rather than by genuine concern for communal well-being and faithfulness to God. Although the subject of Koraḥ's challenge—the proper authority structure during the people's journey through the wilderness—was surely a matter of great import, his intention was self-centered, impervious to the needs of the community and the will of God. This is a controversy decidedly *not* for the sake of heaven.

---

[38] Sh'ma 28/543 (December 12, 1997): 1.

[39] BT *Yevamot* 14b.

[40] I explore these figures in greater depth in chapter 3.

Thus, "controversy for the sake of heaven" becomes the classic Jewish definition of what is now known as "constructive controversy." When disputes are carried out not only functionally but righteously, exploration of various points of view becomes the hallowed path to a sacred system of law and interpretation, of continuing to discern God's will for subsequent generations of Jews. In the words of Gerald Steinberg, a contemporary Israeli conflict scholar,

> The process of "*machloket*" [disputation and conflict] is a central mechanism for discerning the meaning of texts and their implications, as well as for renewal and adaptation in response to a changing environment. Through the continuous process of explication and *machloket*, the law (halacha) and meaning of revealed texts are in constant revision—the canon of interpretation is never closed. In these debates, which continue in the Responsa, in the *yeshivot* (schools of Jewish learning), and among commentators, rabbis discussed specific instances of community strife covering a very wide range of issues. As a result, *machloket*, in the form of constructive conflict, is viewed as a part of community life.[41]

In its secular iteration, "constructive" or "generative" conflict refers to a set of circumstances and structures—including format, facilitation design, collaborative intent, and readiness of participants—that predisposes rhetorical opponents to conduct their disagreements in fruitful ways. Johnson, Johnson, and Tyosvold articulate the following list of "collaborative and conflict management skills" that make for "skilled disagreement."[42]

- I am critical of ideas, not people. I challenge and refute the ideas of the other participants, while confirming their competence and value as individuals. I do not indicate that I personally reject them.

---

[41] Gerald M. Steinberg, "Jewish Sources on Conflict Management Realism and Human Nature," in *Conflict and Conflict Management in Jewish Sources*, ed. M. Roness (Ramat Gan: Bar Ilan University, Program on Conflict Management and Negotiation, 2008), 13.

[42] Deutsch and Coleman, *Handbook of Conflict Resolution,* 70–71.

- I separate my personal worth from criticism of my ideas.
- I remember that we are all in this together, sink or swim. I focus on coming to the best decision possible, not on winning.
- I encourage everyone to participate and to master all the relevant information.
- I listen to everyone's ideas, even if I don't agree.
- I restate what someone has said if it is not clear.
- I differentiate before I try to integrate. I first bring out *all* ideas and facts supporting both sides and clarify how the positions differ. Then I try to identify points of agreement and put them together in a way that makes sense.
- I try to understand both sides of the issue. I try to see the issue from the opposing perspective in order to understand the opposing position.
- I change my mind when the evidence clearly indicates that I should do so.
- I emphasize rationality in seeking the best possible answer, given the available data.
- I follow the *golden rule of conflict*: act toward opponents as you would have them act toward you.[43]

This is a remarkable list of commitments that, if agreed upon, would radically transform conflict conversations between warring family members or work associates, among political leaders engaged in polarized public discourse, or among diplomats negotiating international agreements. They are commonsensical and, once articulated, obvious—truly basic expressions of emotional intelligence and maturity in the midst of conflict or difference. Yet they are rarely followed, because in the midst of passionate disagreement, the reactive limbic brain rather than the reflective frontal cortex is so often in charge.

Strikingly, at the end of this list, the scholars turn philosophical, adapting the Golden Rule to conflict situations. "Act toward rhetorical opponents as you would have them act toward you" tersely summarizes the whole matter. It seems to me that the authors invoke these words not only for

---

[43] Ibid.

their descriptive value but for their religious and moral power. So, too, when we aspire to conduct our conversations in the spirit of "controversy for the sake of heaven," we seek not only functionality and minimal harm. We appeal to a higher standard, reaching toward a righteous, even holy, way to navigate conflict and negotiate difference.

In this spirit, we turn to the work of the twentieth-century philosopher Martin Buber, whose writings figure prominently in contemporary literature on communications and dialogue. Buber's penetrating approach to dialogic communication can help illuminate how conflict engagement can be not only constructive but sacred—deeply respectful of all parties to passionate conversation and the role of such conversation in our world.

Buber on Dialogue

One of the wonderful surprises in my research in contemporary communication theory was reencountering the work of Martin Buber. I had studied Buber in college, rarely feeling that I had understood him very well. Here he was again, referred to by many as the patriarch of theories of dialogue, prefiguring postmodern scholarship on dialogic communication.

"All actual life is encounter."[44] "In the beginning is the relation."[45] "'Real' life begins with two."[46] With these and many other majestic words, Buber expresses his fundamental theology of human nature and human relationship.

Contrary to many modern psychological theories of human development, which imagine that human beings first create an autonomous self and only later learn to be in relationship, Buber boldly asserts the reverse. Relationship creates us; at birth, we emerge into the bosom of loving relationship. We know our primary others—the sensations of the womb and sound of our mother's heartbeat, the feel of our parents' touch, the comfort of our caregivers' arms, and the soothing sound of their voices—

---

[44] Martin Buber, *I and Thou*, ed. and trans. Walter Kaufmann (New York: Charles Scribner's Sons, 1970), 62.

[45] Ibid., 69.

[46] Ronald C. Arnett, *Communication and Community: Implications of Martin Buber's Dialogue* (Carbondale: Southern Illinois University Press, 1986), foreword by Maurice Friedman, xiv.

long before we know ourselves to be separate human beings. We become human beings in relationship to them—shaped by their language, their ways of relating, and their strengths and weaknesses.

For Buber, what is most important about our lives is not what is contained within us, but what happens between us and other people, in what he calls the sphere of "the between." It is in the "interhuman" dimension of life where we become ourselves, where truth and meaning are created, where I and Thou meet, and where we may glimpse the divine.

> The Hasidic movement . . . teaches that the true meaning of love of one's neighbor is not that it is a command from God which we are to fulfill, but that through it and in it we meet God.
>
> This is shown by the interpretation of this command. It is not just written, "Love thy Neighbor as thyself," as though the sentence ended there, but it goes on. "Love thy neighbor as thyself, I am the Lord" (Lev 19:18). The grammatical construction of the original text shows quite clearly that the meaning is: You shall deal lovingly with your "neighbor," that is, with everyone you meet along life's road, and you shall deal with him as with one equal to yourself.
>
> The second part, however, adds, "I am the Lord"—and here the Hasidic interpretation comes in: "You think I am far away from you, but in your love for your neighbor you will find Me: not in his love for you but in yours for him. He who loves brings God and the world together.[47]

Human communication, in Buber's view, is far more than a way to exchange information, explore ideas, or even share feelings. It is an expression of the fundamental command to love the other. In performing this *mitzvah* (commandment), we engage in an essential spiritual practice, perhaps the quintessential way we find the sacred in our lives. When we communicate in thoughtless, selfish, or belligerent ways, we sully the image of God in the other.

Therefore, Buber rails against several forms of "false dialogue," in which "the participants do not really have each other in mind, or they have

---

[47] Martin Buber, *On Judaism*, ed. Nahum N. Glatzer (New York: Schocken Books, 1967), 212.

each other in mind only as general and abstracted opponents and not as particular beings. There is no real turning to the other, no real desire to establish mutuality."[48] Such conversations may claim to be dialogic, but they have little of the essence of sacred human encounter.

> There is *genuine dialogue*—no matter whether spoken or silent— where each of the participants really has in mind the other or others in their present and particular being and turns to them with the intention of establishing a living mutual relation between himself and them. There is *technical dialogue*, which is prompted solely by the need of objective understanding. And there is *monologue disguised as dialogue,* in which two or more men, meeting in space, speak each with himself in strangely tortuous and circuitous ways and yet imagine they have escaped the torment of being thrown back on their own resources.[49]

Just as Buber fully recognized that we spend more of our lives in "I-It" relationships than in the "I-Thou" stance, Buber knew the pervasiveness of "technical dialogue," in which we engage one another for a purpose, without regarding the other as a full human being. Buber seems to have some sympathy for our inability to treat everyone in our lives with the full reverence and attention that is ideally called for. The real problem is when we confuse genuine dialogue with its opposite, thinking we are relating to another when in fact we are speaking and listening only to ourselves.

Buber offered devastating descriptions of debate, which figures so prominently in our own public life: a recitation of serial attacks, without real listening, interaction, or dynamic learning, "a *debate* in which the thoughts are not expressed in the way in which they existed in the mind but in the speaking are so pointed that they may strike home in the sharpest way, and moreover without the men that are spoken to being

---

[48] Maurice Friedman, *Martin Buber: The Life of Dialogue* (Chicago: University of Chicago Press, 1976), 123.

[49] Martin Buber, *Between Man and Man* (New York: Macmillan, 1972), 19 (emphasis mine). I have quoted Buber's own language, even when it violates contemporary norms of gender neutrality.

regarded in any way present as persons."[50] This is debate as combat, an aggressive exchange of prepackaged monologues, pseudocommunication that is completely unaffected by the presence of one's conversation partner, another human being.

Buber also disparages what we innocently call "conversation," highlighting how different it is from intentional, sacred dialogue: "a *conversation* characterized by the need neither to communicate something, not to learn something, not to influence someone, not to come into connexion with someone, but solely by the desire to have one's own self-reliance confirmed by marking the impression that is made."[51]

Buber is even more critical of the rhetorical manipulations of much persuasive speech (even in advocacy for good causes). In the words of the Buber scholar Maurice Friedman,

> The distinction between propaganda and education does not lie in whether one is a communist or a pacifist but in whether one approaches another wishing to impose one's truth on him or whether one cares enough for him to enter into dialogue with him, see the situation from his point of view, and communicate what truth one has to communicate to him within that dialogue. Sometimes that dialogue can only mean standing one's ground in opposition to him, witnessing for what one believes in the face of his hostile rejection of it. Yet it can never mean being unconcerned for how he sees it or careless of the validity of his standing where he does. We must confirm him even as we oppose him, not in his error but in his right to oppose us, in his existence as a human being whom we value even in opposing.[52]

When the goal is to persuade people to sign up for a political action or protest an injustice, there is little room for the qualities of dialogue

---

[50] Ibid.

[51] Ibid., 19–20.

[52] Maurice S. Friedman, *Touchstones of Reality: Existential Trust and the Community of Peace* (New York: E. P. Dutton, 1974), 284, quoted in Kenneth N. Cissna and Rob Anderson, *Moments of Meeting: Buber, Rogers, and the Potential for Public Dialogue* (Albany: State University of New York Press, 2002), 252.

described above. When influence is the goal, we have less interest in what might motivate an individual to see things differently than we do. We select the evidence that best proves our point and choose the words that communicate our own perspective in the sharpest way possible. The person on the other side is a means to an end, a potential new team member or reliable vote for our side. In such a stance, that person's full human beauty and complexity is beside the point. The problem, as the communications scholar John Stewart affirmed, is that "persons, because of their intrinsic value, should never be treated as the means to achieve some end, but should always be treated as an end in themselves. . . . You cannot value all human behavior positively, but you can value each human positively. That's another way we distinguish between things and people."[53] Stewart is referring, of course, to Kant's categorical imperative, according to which "rational beings stand under the *law* that each of them should treat himself and all others *never merely as a means* but always *at the same time as an end in himself.*"[54] This, in turn, hearkens back to the principle of love of neighbor as oneself. When we view a rhetorical opponent as an object to be engaged or demolished for the sake of a cause, we violate this most basic of moral principles.

Buber's Genuine Dialogue

Human encounter at this level, as Buber understood it, requires a number of special attitudes and essential qualities of being.

1. Awareness of the other's humanity. Dialogue requires us, first of all, to enter into relationship with another human being. This may sound obvious, even tautological, but how often do we sit with another, even face-to-face, much less with technology intervening, and speak and listen

---

[53] John Stewart, "Interpersonal Communication—A Meeting between Persons," in *Bridges Not Walls: A Book about Interpersonal Communication*, ed. John Stewart (Reading, MA: Addison-Wesley, 1982), 18, quoted in Ronald C. Arnett, *Communication and Community: Implications of Martin Buber's Dialogue* (Carbondale: Southern Illinois University Press, 1986), 106.

[54] Immanuel Kant, *Groundwork for the Metaphysics of Morals*, trans. Arnulf Zweig, ed. Thomas E. Hill Jr. and Arnulf Zweig (Oxford: Oxford University Press, 2002), 234.

only to ourselves? It is so much simpler to talk only to myself. But if we want to enter into relationship, we must do so with another human being, even if the other may challenge, frighten, and disappoint us.

By definition, the other person in any relationship is separate and different from ourselves—complex, multidimensional, and ever-changing, with human doubts and vulnerabilities as well as convictions and certainties. We are commanded to love the other—not only those with whom we agree—as a whole person. Like ourselves, the other is far more than his or her political, religious, or ideological opinions. The other is a whole, divinely inspired being, just as we are.

I am reminded of an exercise I first experienced in a mediation training course. The teachers asked us to pair up, then tell our partner about something disturbing that had happened to us in the past week. We were told we would have one minute to speak. Just before we were asked to begin our sixty-second story, we heard the concluding instruction: both members of the dyad were to speak for one minute at one and the same time.

Some people in the room laughed. In later years, when I have used this exercise in my own teaching, I find that there are generally some participants in the group who refuse to follow the instruction. They are offended by the idea of speaking while pretending to listen. They are the heroes of the experience. But most participants (as I did when I first encountered the exercise) follow instructions and try to speak and listen at the same time. Later, in debriefing the experience, some people claim to have been able to hear as they spoke. But most admit the truth: it is impossible to attend deeply to another while we are speaking.

I love this exercise, and not only because it gets people actively engaged in a workshop and fills the room with laughter. I love it because I know how often people—including myself, of course—pretend to listen to another while actually listening only to an internal monologue, reviewing past experiences and preparing an impactful response. It is good to call attention to this pattern and laugh about how often we feign attention to another but are actually talking and listening only to ourselves.

2. Acceptance of the other as different from ourselves. How often do we rage and fume that the other is not like us? Like Professor Higgins ironically musing, "Why can't a woman be more like a man?" we all too frequently respond with judgment or outrage to the fact that the other—whether in interpersonal conflict, ideological or intergroup conflict—is different from us. We so regularly forget that being in relationship with another person necessarily means encountering a being who is different from us. The alternative is to be, like Narcissus, engaged only with ourselves. If only we could see ourselves clearly when we are foolishly staring at our own reflection while pretending to engage in relationship.

In sacred human encounter, we must not only notice (so often with anger, incredulity, or derision) that the other is different from us; we must actively accept that the other is who he or she is. This emphatically does not mean that we agree with the other's opinions. It does, however, mean that the other has the same right—and obligation—as we do to be the person that he or she is. Further, we recognize that actively exploring the differences between us can bring great gifts and opportunities for learning and connection. Here, again, Buber's words are instructive.

> The chief presupposition for the rise of genuine dialogue is that each should regard his partner as the very one he is. I become aware of him, aware that he is different, essentially different from myself, in the definite, unique way which is peculiar to him, and I accept whom I thus see, so that in full earnestness I can direct what I say to him as the person that he is. . . . I accept this person, the personal bearer of a conviction, in his definite being out of which his conviction has grown—even though I must try to show, bit by bit, the wrongness of this very conviction. I affirm the person I struggle with: I struggle with him as his partner, I confirm him as creature and as creation, I confirm him who is opposed to me as him who is over against me. . . . If I thus give to the other who confronts me his legitimate standing as a man with whom I am ready to enter into dialogue, then I may trust him and suppose him to be also ready to deal with me as his partner.[55]

Notice that this is a far cry from "tolerance," which may mean, "I hate your guts, but I'll put up with you if I must."[56] Rather, dialogue requires

---

[55] Martin Buber, *The Knowledge of Man: A Philosophy*, ed. Maurice Friedman (New York: Harper Torchbooks, 1965), 79–80.

[56] I am grateful to my friends Rabbi Gerry Serotta and Imam Yahya Hendi, of Clergy Beyond Borders, for this stark framing.

an affirmative desire to enter into an exploration of differences, while rigorously affirming the full personhood of our conversation partner. As Buber put it,

> Every true . . . existential relationship between two persons . . . begins with acceptance, . . . being able to . . . make it felt to the other person, . . . that I accept him just as he is . . . and accepting the whole potentiality of the other . . . I can . . . recognize in him, know in him, more or less, the person he has been created to become.[57]

3. Intentional "turning toward" the other. A third prerequisite for Buber's stance of "genuine dialogue" is what he poetically calls "turning toward" the other, of reaching into "the unpredictable and mysterious other . . . and 'imagining the real' of the other life as it is lived,"[58] "a bold swinging . . . into the life of the other."[59] We all know this experience of "turning toward" the other, of intentionally reaching for connection and understanding with another human being, animated by genuine curiosity and desire to learn.

To choose a simple example, when I travel abroad, I relate to cab rides as opportunities for learning. If I share some common language with the cab driver, I lean into conversation with him (and even more so on the rare occasion when the driver is a woman). Like a journalist on assignment, I turn my full attention to the opportunity to learn something new about another's experience. This is a chance for me to conduct a "person on the street" interview, an invitation to learn about the reality of a human being who lives a very different life from my own. My natural curiosity flows. Even when the driver expresses views I find implausible or discordant with my own, I want to make the most of the rare opportunity to learn about another's world.

By contrast, I know when the gates of curiosity in my mind and heart have shut down, and I simply do not want to engage. Often on an airplane, I am intent on the work I want to get done on the flight or the rest that

---

[57] Quoted in Cissna and Anderson, *Moments of Meeting*, 149.

[58] Ibid., 200.

[59] Ibid., 54.

I am counting on. In such a state of mind, if the person sitting next to me is "too friendly," I nonverbally communicate that I'm not available for conversation. If the person does not get my hint, I convey, in as kindly a tone as I can muster, that I have work that I need to do or am desperate for a nap. I dread the moment when the person, irresistibly curious, asks about the *kippah* (traditional Jewish head-covering) that I wear. She has surely guessed that I am a rabbi and wants to ask me all her questions about Judaism or about Israel. In such a state of mind I may reject the potential gift of the encounter and groan at the time and energy the conversation will require of me.

I remember once flying back from Israel, an exhausting eleven-hour journey under the best of circumstances. I was seated next to a woman who was, by her dress, obviously ultra-Orthodox. I had planned to read a book about Sufism written in Hebrew by a Muslim peacebuilder friend in Israel, but I dreaded the series of questions that would surely ensue if she saw what I was reading. I said to myself repeatedly, "This is a dialogue opportunity! This is your chance to learn something about the world of the ultra-Orthodox!" Because of the length of the flight, I dreaded being stuck for hours in exhausting, contentious conversation. I put my book away and did my best to get some rest.

Eventually my neighbor's extroversion won out and she asked me the dreaded question, "What do you do?" I could not refuse to answer her direct question, so I responded that I was a rabbi. She asked a series of questions, feigning nonjudgmental interest, but eventually came to the punch line. As if concerned for my soul and God's plan for my life (rather than just being caught in her own absolutist ideology), she said, "Oh, I can see that you are a wise and compassionate woman, and that God has much good work for you to do. What a shame that you are wasting your life working with Conservative Jews!" In such moments I honestly do not feel curious. I do not want to engage with a person that I believe will bring only negative judgment to our encounter.

It is no great sin to turn away from airplane conversations, espe-cially for the sake of self-care. I tell these stories only to illustrate the experience of Buber's "turning toward," the quality of wholeheartedly reaching for learning and connection in human encounter. We all know from our own lives the difference between turning toward and turning away from another, when engagement feels easy and when it feels nearly impossible.

4. Presence and authenticity. Fourth, for Buber, real dialogue requires that both conversation partners are fully present, willing to bring all of themselves, including doubts as well as convictions, vulnerabilities as well as certainties. This is not habitual repetition of long-held opinions, but the meeting of two hearts and two whole human beings. The contemporary philosopher Alphonso Lingis describes it in this way:

> To enter into conversation with another is to lay down one's arms and one's defenses; to throw open the gates of one's own positions to expose oneself to the other, the outsider; and to lay oneself open to surprises. . . . It is to risk what one found or produced in common . . . to expose oneself to the alien.[60]

The British philosopher Charles Hampden-Turner describes the risk differently.

> The risk I undertake is permitting my structure to crumble, with the knowledge that a new element supplied by him [my conversation partner] may prevent the logical restructuring of my beloved ideas. I risk being ridiculed by him at a moment when my competence is not firmly in my grasp. By investing my undefended worth, I am risking the verdict that I am worthless. I tell him something which shows that I value his judgment but leave him free to disconfirm and devalue my judgment and so alter the definition of our relationship. I do this because I am seeking confirmation from him and the expansion of my ideas—yet I cannot gain these without temporarily "surrendering" and risking permanent loss.[61]

Dialogue requires opening our belief systems to challenge, thus opening ourselves to ridicule, shame, and disorientation. At the same time, it also

---

[60] Alphonso Lingis, *The Community of Those Who Have Nothing in Common* (Bloomington: Indiana University Press, 1994), 86.

[61] Charles Hampden-Turner, *Radical Man: The Process of Psycho-social Development* (Garden City, NY: Anchor Books, 1971), 48.

requires that we come to the dialogue fully dedicated to our own beliefs, willing to hold our own ground in conversation, balancing our conviction with concern for the other. On the one hand, without a willingness to articulate our own views, we are not fully present to the dialogue. On the other hand, without willingness to be changed in the dialogue, we are not allowing the other to be fully present to us.

5. Openness to being changed. Buber believed that when we enter into conversation utterly convinced of the rightness of our view, without any possibility of learning anything from the other, we are not engaging with another, only talking to ourselves. Although I may or may not adopt the other person's view, to enter into real dialogue is to know that I may emerge changed from the encounter.

> Partners in genuine dialogue also say no: they oppose, explore, argue, and willingly influence others. But all this occurs under the responsible condition of remaining open to influence. "Even as a young man, I [Buber] felt I have not the right to want to change another if I am not open to be changed by him as far as it is legitimate."[62]

Contemporary scholars of communications, influenced by postmodernism, understand that meaning is not located in the self but only in the sphere of human interaction, Buber's sphere of "the between." By this logic, meaning is created anew each time we listen attentively to another's view and seek to be heard, adjusting our own communication in order to be heard by the other. If truth is to be found between, not within, persons, then reciting predetermined thought constructions to one another, without any possibility that our conversation partner can contribute anything to our thinking, cannot reveal truth.

This awareness that meaning is co-created in human relationship can radically shift our understanding of our ideological debates. If the truth is ours to co-create, the right question becomes not, "How can I win this argument?" but "How can you and I create something constructive in our communication with one another?"

With this kind of consciousness, we might pause at entangled moments of conversation, step back from our certainties, and ask instead, "How did

---

[62] Cissna and Anderson, *Moments of Meeting*, 6.

this piece of conversation emerge? Is it useful? Is there another way to put all of this together so that it will work for all of us?" Dialogue can become less of a duel and more of a collaboration to find truths and solutions that are life-enhancing for all partners to the conversation.

6. *Non-negotiable concern for dignity of both self and other, even in the midst of conflict.* Contrary to the popular image of Buber's dialogic stance as soft and fuzzy, Buber's dialogic experience requires holding two paradoxical attitudes in tension, courageously walking what he calls a "narrow ridge."[63] This dialogue practice is a challenging and precarious balancing act that includes willingness to argue vigorously for our understandings of truth, on the one hand, and passionate affirmation of the full personhood of our "opponent," on the other.

Buber's dialogue is no parody of active listening, in which one mechanically mirrors back another's view. Nor is it to be confused with conflict avoidance or passive, false politeness. Rather, for Buber, real dialogue is an ardent seeking after truth and meaning. It is a fierce and complex practice of balancing genuine concern for self and other, of speaking passionately of our own reality without compromising the well-being and dignity of our "opponent." This level of engagement is not for the faint of heart, the lazy or the arrogant. It is the way we engage with another being who is, like us, beloved of God.

With Buber's understandings of dialogue in mind, I now offer introductory elements of a spiritual approach to conflict engagement. I delve more deeply into the ingredients of this practice in chapter 5, but this introduction identifies core themes that emerge in the coming chapters. The central practices and perspectives introduced here point the way toward a spiritual orientation to conflict, allowing us to stay in touch with our best selves even in the heat of interpersonal, intracommunal or intergroup discord.

Sacred Conflict Engagement

"I place God before me always" [Ps. 16:8]. "Before me"—"*lenegdi*"—from the word "*negdi'ut*"—"opposition." And I have heard that

---

[63] Arnett, *Communication and Community*, 30.

the person should return to herself, for she has gone far from the Blessed One. It seems to me that, according to what I have received from my teachers and friends, one should behave compassionately with every person. Even when one sees something ugly in another person, one should give heart to the fact that there, too, dwells the name of the Blessed One, for there is no place empty of God. Therefore it is for one's own good, for there is in you, too, a trace of it, and you should give heart, to do *teshuvah* (repentance).[64]

This piece of Ḥasidic[65] commentary takes as its jumping off point the verse from the Psalms, "I place God before me always," a verse that often appears in artistic form on the eastern wall of a home or synagogue. Ḥasidic commentators tend to take this verse almost literally, imagining the letters of God's name as a lens through which to perceive the world. Imagine viewing the moments of your day through God-colored glasses!

The author of this text focuses on the word "*lenegdi*" in the verse, generally translated as "before me," but literally meaning, "opposite me" or "against me." Thus, the rebbe looks to the verse for instruction on how to relate to our opponent, the one who is "against us." One senses that the rebbe knows all too well the natural human tendency to attack the one who is "against us"—in words, thoughts, identity, or worldview. Based on this verse, he teaches that we are to do precisely the opposite. Rather than turn against our opponent, we are to gently "return to ourselves," turning our attention back inside with compassion, knowing that we are suffering in this interaction, churning with animosity, hurt, and suspicion.

Here he articulates a breathtaking spiritual instruction: "one should behave compassionately with every person." Having soothed our own aching heart, we are to look again at the person who has harmed us, gaze directly at the trait in the other person that has given rise to

---

[64] Rabbi Jacob Joseph Katz of Polonnoye (eighteenth-century Poland), *Toldot Ya'akov Yosef, Ḥayye Sarah*, translated by Rabbi Jonathan Slater, teaching materials for Institute for Jewish Spirituality.

[65] Ḥasidism refers to an ultra-Orthodox revival movement beginning among Eastern European Jewry in the second half of the eighteenth century onward. The Hasidic rabbis, or "rebbes," left a body of literature, including homiletical, exegetical, and philosophical works.

the hurt, and remember that here, too, the Divine resides. The rebbe draws on Kabbalistic[66] principles, asserting that there is no place in the universe devoid of God. If there is, by definition, no place where the divine presence is absent, then the Holy must be present even in the "ugly" place inside our opponent that allowed him to wound us. In yet another remarkable leap of theological logic, the rebbe says that since the Eternal is present in that "ugly" place in our adversary, and we, too, are made of the Divine, that same trait must live in us as well.

More simply, we might say that since we and the other are both human beings, made of the same raw material; the flaw that exists in the other is present in us as well. In the light of this awareness, our aversive reaction to the other becomes a welcome invitation to attend to this imperfection within ourselves, to purify ourselves from it through a process of *teshuvah* (repentance). We are actually to see the other person's failing as "for our own good," for it provides us an opportunity to grow closer to our aspiration for our own lives.

This text beautifully illuminates the central role of self-awareness in the work of sacred conflict engagement. As long as we stay focused on the maddening flaws of the one who has harmed us, we will pour energy into the dynamics of assault and counterassault—whether in verbal retorts in troubled personal relationships or in our angry reactions to challenging beliefs or perspectives. The text prescribes a three-step process to use our energy in a more productive way:

1. bringing attention back to ourselves
2. compassionately tending to our own pain, and then
3. observing the other empathically, with the expectation that the interaction is an opportunity for growth and learning.

One could construct an entire theory of conflict transformation based on these steps. If you consider these practices in relationship to a personal conflict in your own life, you will readily see just how complex they are. (1) Bring attention back to my self? Why should I? He/she is the one who has committed terrible wrongs against me! (2) A response of compassion,

---

[66] From the Jewish mystical tradition.

particularly toward our own pain, is the precise opposite of the limbic panic reaction. Who has time for compassion when it feels like values we hold dear are endangered? (3) This positive, humane and caring reaction to the other is obviously the key to conflict transformation. But even for the most empathic people, in the midst of a disturbing altercation we are generally far too tense to ascend into these evolved states of being.

In the following three brief sections, I discuss three practices that are essential for moving through the process the rebbe described: opening the heart, seeing the other, and the process of listening. In chapter 5 I elaborate on the cultivation of our capacities to engage in these practices.

Opening the Heart

Hillel taught, "Be of the disciples of Aaron, loving peace and pursuing peace, loving your fellow creatures and bringing them close to the Torah."[67]

What is "loving peace"? One should love peace among all people, as Aaron loved peace among all people, as it is said, "Great is peace, for Aaron the Priest was only praised for peace, for he was a lover of peace and a pursuer of peace. He opened conversation with peace and responded with peace, as it is said, "He walked with Me in peace and virtue" [Mal. 2:6]. Afterwards it is written, "He brought many back from transgression" [Mal. 2:6]. This teaches that when he saw two people hating one another, he would approach one of them and say to him, "Why do you hate so and so? He came to me at my home, prostrated himself before me, and said to me, 'I have sinned against so and so. Please go and placate him.' Then he would depart and approach the other person and say to him as he had said to the first. He would bring peace, love, and friendship between one and another. And he brought many back from transgression."[68]

Rabbinic tradition, beginning with Hillel's teaching here, identifies

---

[67] *Mishnah Avot* 1:12.
[68] *Avot d'Rabbi Natan* 12:3.

Aaron as a model peacebuilder, "a lover of peace and a pursuer of peace." I have long been fascinated by the way in which the Rabbis draw from the biblical text to construct this portrait of Aaron as peacebuilder and contrast his style of leadership with that of Moses.[69] But this second text has long troubled me. Are we really to emulate Aaron's model of lying to the two parties, pretending to each side that the other is remorseful and desirous of reconciliation when this is not the case? I couldn't imagine how this kind of deception could be helpful as the basis for mediation of conflict.

Over the years, the text has begun to reveal itself to me. Some time ago I participated in a workshop led by Rabbi Melissa Weintraub, the founding director emerita of Encounter,[70] in which she asked us to think of an occasion in our lives when we were engaged in distressing conflict with a person who mattered to us, a conflict that was later resolved. I immediately thought of a moment when there had been intense conflict between my husband and me that, thankfully, had long ago been completely resolved. She asked us to recall how we had felt in the midst of the conflict, to notice what thoughts and feelings were moving in us. Then we were asked to similarly investigate our inner experience when the conflict had found resolution.

This exercise powerfully illustrated the way in which, in the midst of painful conflict, regardless of the specific content, we tighten. I can literally feel tightening in my throat, chest, and hands, and a narrowing of my mind into thoughts of anger, hurt, judgment, and self-righteousness. I may experience a cascade of indignant thoughts, rehearsing my grievances against the other and my own utter blamelessness. When the conflict is resolved, I sense an opening, a release from my fist-clenching anger and obsessively antagonistic thoughts, and the relief of being reconnected with someone I love. The Public Conversations Project, to whose work I will return in chapter 3, summarizes this phenomenon with the mantra "Conflict narrows; inquiry expands."[71]

---

[69] See, for example, *Tosefta Sanhedrin* 1:2. *Tosefta* means, literally, "addition"; it is a collection of tannaitic materials (prior to 200 C.E.), parallel to the Mishnah in content and organization, edited in the late fourth century C.E.

[70] Encounter is a nonprofit organization "dedicated to strengthening the capacity of the Jewish people to be constructive agents of change in transforming the Israeli–Palestinian conflict." See www. encounterprograms.org.

[71] Concept taught by Bob Stains at Public Conversations Project "Power of Dialogue" Workshop, February 2, 2011, Minneapolis.

With awareness of this quality of conflict interaction, by now familiar as part of the limbic "fight or flight" response, the text about Aaron's "shuttle diplomacy" makes sense. The text is saying that Aaron had a gift for opening the hearts of people, even in the midst of painful conflict. First, Aaron had the wisdom to sit with each person separately so that each could feel deeply heard in his or her pain for as long as was needed. Only then would Aaron reach for the person's heart by evoking an image of the other person as caring and connected, not only as the source of the current hurt. Describing the other as remorseful (which he knew the other surely would be once the period of anger had passed), Aaron reminded each person of his or her feelings for the other. Thus he helped each one shift out of an attitude of constriction, bitterness, and blame, restoring their ability to see their opponent as the person they once cared about. When the two came together, they did so with a renewed desire for connection, seeing the other not just as the person who had hurt them, but as a whole and once again beloved person.

Stop for a moment and ask yourself the question I described. Think of an experience of significant conflict with someone you care about that was later resolved. How did you feel and what kinds of thoughts moved through your mind when you were locked in conflict? Then, after harmony was restored, how did you think and feel about the other person and about yourself? I suspect that your reaction will resemble my own, that in the midst of conflict you felt tense, constricted, embattled, angry, and perhaps frightened—hardly your best self. After the conflict was over, you no doubt felt more at ease, more capable of compassion and of loving relationship.

This description is reminiscent of a wonderful concept in Kabbalistic and Hasidic literature, the distinction between *moḥin d'katnut* ("small mind") and *moḥin d'gad'lut* ("big mind"). "Small mind" is ordinary consciousness, in which, most of the time, we go about our business, pursuing our personal needs and agendas, only occasionally reaching out to another in empathic connection or seeking a larger perspective on our lives. "Big mind" is elevated consciousness—those graced moments of mental clarity, renewed perspective, prayer, or reflection, when we get beyond the habit of attending only to our own needs and views. In small mind, all I know is what I think, what I need, and where I need to be. In big mind, I want more: I am blessed with a sense of connection to the much wider circle of life of which I am a part.

In the midst of conflict, we instinctively cringe, resisting the pain of attack and preparing counterattack. We have energy only for the battle, for self-protection, for awareness of the hurt inflicted on us by the other, and plans for defensive action. We are tight and constricted—narrow versions of ourselves. When a sense of safety, possibility, and connection is renewed, we can breathe again, and we may open to awareness that others, too, have needs and wounds. We can again see the other as a beloved human being with whom we desire ongoing connection.

This phenomenon of the closing and opening of consciousness, so central to the human experience, provides a key to conflict transformation. When we have a sense of safety and a glimpse of caring and connection, we can return to our larger view of ourselves and the other as images of the divine, fellow members of the human family. That is to say, when the heart relaxes from fear and constriction, we are naturally more open to knowing, hearing, and accepting one another. Bringing healing to a destructive conflict requires creating the circumstances—in ourselves and in others—that elicit the opening of the heart.

Seeing the Other

You shall not take vengeance or bear a grudge against your coun-trymen. Love your neighbor as yourself: I am God. (Lev. 19:18)

Why the juxtaposition of "I am God" to the beginning of the verse? . . . The intention is to explain the beginning of the verse: "You shall not take vengeance . . ." Should you say in any form, "How can I work on myself so that there will be no ill feeling against the other and I can even love him?" the verse comes to respond, "I am God." I am God who has loved him. . . . Likewise you can love him. In truth it is a simple matter. For when one sees in one's fellow only the aspect of the material in which he or she is clothed, the other seems as nothing in one's eyes. And, in particular, if in any matter the other is against you, you dismiss the other in your thoughts. It is not the same with the Blessed Holy One, who knows the essence of the holy root of a human soul.[72]

---

[72] Kagan, Ḥafetz Ḥayim, *Shmirat Halashon, Sha'ar Hat'vunah,* chap. 6.

The best-known phrase in the Torah, "Love your neighbor as yourself," is rarely read in its original context. As a free-standing expression, a mere three words in Hebrew, it reads like a banner headline, an overarching principle governing all kinds of human behavior and ethical life. It is eminently familiar, but often feels too lofty and abstract to relate directly to ordinary life. In its original context, however, it is associated with some of the most painful experiences in everyday human relations.

It is a mistake to think of the "vengeance" in our verse only as violence committed by terrorists in distant parts of the world. Rabbinic commentators[73] understand the commandment, "Do not take vengeance or bear a grudge," in connection with the most ubiquitous of interpersonal interactions. Vengefulness is the eminently understandable instinct to get back at someone who has hurt us. The weapon may, God forbid, take someone's life. More commonly, our words, thoughts, or affections are the weapons we use against the other.

Think of a recent time when someone hurt you, when a family member spoke cutting words in the midst of an angry exchange, or a friend failed you. When we are rigorously honest with ourselves, we notice that our feelings of pain are frequently mixed with an instinct to cause pain to the other, if only by replying with equally hostile words or actions. We may deliver an angry tirade out of conscious desire to retaliate. Or it may be instinct that impels us to yell back when someone has shouted at us, to counter one accusation with another. This is clearly a verbal expression of the limbic brain's impulse to attack when threatened. Hence the common subjective experience that the hurtful words have flown out of our mouths, beyond our conscious control.

So, too, to bear a grudge is to hold on to vengeful thoughts, even when we refrain from acting on the instinct to cause the other pain. The Torah and subsequent Rabbinic commentaries see carrying a grudge, or holding on to negative feelings about the other person, as closely related to vengeance. Some readers may protest that Judaism only legislates action, not thoughts and feelings. It is true that, generally speaking, Jewish texts are more focused on behavior than on emotions, but there are exceptions to this rule, and two of them—grudge-bearing and love of neighbor—appear in this key verse.

---

[73] BT *Yoma* 23a and Rashi (Rabbi Shlomo Yitzhaki, preeminent biblical commentator, eleventh-century France) on Leviticus 19:18.

When vengeance and resentment are placed in their everyday inter-personal context, it becomes clear why this mitzvah is juxtaposed with the grand category of love of neighbor. The Torah is commanding us to counter our natural tendency to retaliate in words, deeds, or thoughts when we have been hurt, because such attitudes and behaviors threaten the fabric of relationship and of community. The Torah knows that these inclinations will arise in us and even understands how difficult it can be to resist them. But when we fail to overcome our instinct for reprisal, we violate the most fundamental mitzvah of love of neighbor and fail to be the people we were created to be.

The Ḥafetz Ḥayim interprets the commandment in an even more demanding way, asserting that when we are hurt we are required to ask a remarkable question: "How can I work on myself so that I will have no ill feeling against the other and even come to love him?" Not only does the Ḥafetz Ḥayim want us to refrain from speaking harsh words to a person who has insulted us. He wants us to respond to the affront by going inside and asking what inner work we need to do in order to flush out any negative feeling against the other, even to love him. He sets a high bar indeed.

Lest you think this is an impossible task, he offers a path to help us get there, in the guise of an exegetical question. He asks, "What is the phrase, 'I am God,' doing at the end of this verse?" His answer: "I am God who has loved him . . . likewise you can love him." If you see only this person's outer trappings, you will see human failings and limitations. If the person has upset you, you may want to shut him or her out of your heart. But if you try to see the person who has offended you as God, his or her Creator, sees him or her, you will easily see beyond human imperfections. If you get a glimpse of this person as a child of the divine, then you will love him or her too.

Does this sound impossible? Try one of these formulations if they work better for you. Bring your adversary into your mind's eye and think, "This person, just like me, was created in the image of God. Image of God. Image of God." Or imagine her as a five-year-old child, naturally lovable and vulnerable to failure and to being hurt herself. Imagine her as a baby in her mother's arms. Can you see her differently now? Difficult as it may be, it is possible to do this even in a situation in which a person who matters deeply to you has grievously failed you. Our religious traditions teach that only if we open our awareness to include such expanded, sacred perspective will we be able to see the other—and ourselves—as the persons we truly are. From such broadened and deepened view of self and other, the transformation of hurtful conflicts becomes possible.

Sacred Listening

Shema Yisrael Adonai Eloheinu Adonai Echad.
Hear O Israel: Adonai our God, Adonai is one.[74]

Over the years, I have taught many training sessions and scholar-in-residence weekends in synagogues on the subject of listening. I start with a question that gets a laugh from the audience every time. "How many of you think that Jews are good listeners?" The question is funny because of the sociological fact that many Jews have a culturally syntonic style of speech that includes high volume and velocity of speech and mutual interruption.[75]

In all seriousness, Jews *should* be extraordinarily good listeners, for at the center of our daily liturgy is this prayer, the *Shema*, a prayer about listening. Traditional Jews recite the Shema at least three times every day (in morning and evening services and before slipping off to sleep). The Shema is the prayer that Jews hope to say just before death, as Jews have throughout the ages. I daresay that of all Jewish prayers, this is the one best known by the greatest number of Jews, including many long alienated from active Jewish life.

When I ask groups of Jews what the Shema means, some talk about the fundamental unity of all things, and many more simply reply, "It's the watchword of our faith." My colleague Barbara Breitman teaches that this central prayer is at its core an affirmation of the importance of listening: "The central statement of the Jewish faith, the *Shema* . . . declares that hearing is the quintessentially sacred act for Jews."[76] Surely, without listening,

[74] Deut. 6:4, and in all Jewish prayer books, morning and evening services.
[75] More on this pattern in chapter 3.
[76] Barbara Breitman, "Holy Listening: Cultivating a Hearing Heart," in *Jewish Spiritual Direction: An Innovative Guide from Traditional and Contemporary Sources,* by

one cannot observe the central commandment of love of neighbor, the core principle of so many religions and ethical systems.

The practice of listening figures prominently in the Hebrew Bible, postbiblical text, and Jewish liturgy. For example, the Book of Deuteronomy constantly exhorts the Israelites to listen, connoting attentiveness and obedience to God. In Jewish prayer, traditional Jews describe God three times every day as the "Hearer of prayer." So, too, during the High Holy Days, Jews repeatedly call on God to "hear our voices," a plaintive and passionate cry for presence and responsiveness. If God is the ultimate Listener, then we honor the image of the Divine within us most fully when we listen to others, to ourselves, and to the Holy in our lives.

Shortly after the Shema ("Hear O Israel") in the traditional Jewish prayer book, twice each day, Jews recite a biblical passage that begins, "It shall come to pass, if you listen diligently to My commandments that I command you this day, to love Adonai your God, and to serve God with all your heart and with all your soul" (Deut. 11:13–21). The passage continues by promising that if the Israelites are attentive and obedient to God's commandments, the rain will come in due season, the land will be fruitful, and the community's life will be blessed. At first glance, this text strains credulity.

But, as is so often true, the realm of personal experience makes sense of things that are puzzling on the level of theory. I often ask people to remember a time when they were deeply listened to, and then describe what it was like to be attended to in that way. Across a wide range of experiences, people use such words as "healed," "loved," "whole," and "at peace." Many people recall occasions when, at a very dark time of life, being deeply listened to brought enormous comfort, even a sense of transformation.

Then I ask people to think of a recent time when they listened to someone absently and to note what ensued after that kind of inattentive presence. The differences are stark. Many think of occasions when a tantrum followed a moment of ignoring a child's need for attention. Others remember times when distracted or self-centered listening with

Howard A. Addison and Barbara Eve Breitman (Woodstock, VT: Jewish Lights, 2006), 73.

an intimate partner evoked a storm of negative emotion. In the realm of personal experience, it is palpably true that life is profoundly different when we are listened to fully, lovingly, and wholeheartedly. The puzzling passage predicted dire consequences for poor "listening." Relationally speaking, this is a description of life as it is.

I have come to love a classic story about listening at the beginning of a beautiful book called *Holy Listening.*[77] The author, Margaret Guenther, an Episcopal priest and now a beloved teacher in the spiritual direction community, writes of her days working as a hospital chaplain, when she encountered a woman she called "Mrs. G." "A formidable woman," she tells,

> who looked like the Red Queen in Alice, she was seriously ill and—with her ceaseless demands—a source of annoyance to the nursing staff. One day after I had fetched her glasses and found her teeth, adjusted the television and repaired the Venetian blind, put fresh water in her pitcher and plumped her pillow, I assumed that Mrs. G. had run out of urgent needs. But she beckoned me close and said, "One more thing. Get me out of here!" When I protested that, much as I would like her to be well, granting this particular request was out of my power, Mrs. G looked at me with disappointment and some disgust. "You mean you just walk around and listen to people?" I felt very small and very fake when I answered, "I'm afraid that's it, Mrs. G." A slow smile crept over the Red Queen's face. "Well, I guess that's work too."[78]

The story beautifully illustrates the continually surprising power of listening to contribute to healing, growth, and well-being.

Before coming to the work of conflict transformation, I had served for many years as a chaplain, sitting at the bedside of the ill and the dying and their loved ones. I had specialized training for this work, but in truth, it was all about listening. For many years I had worked as a spiritual director, bringing reverent, prayerful listening to an individual or group seeking to discern how the Holy was present in their lives. Whether I was training

---

[77] Margaret Guenther, *Holy Listening: The Art of Spiritual Direction* (London: Darton, Longman and Todd, 1992).

[78] Ibid., 1–2.

chaplains, lay volunteers for the art of hospital or hospice ministry, or spiritual directors, for many years my teaching had been all about the power of listening to transform lives.

The kind of listening I aspired to teach and practice was not just an activity but a way of being in the world. Listening—whether to one's own inner voice, to loved ones, or to the needs of a troubled world—requires humility, respect for others and genuine curiosity. As has often been said, offering one's full attention is the greatest, most generous gift of caring and compassion one person can give to another.

Having thought deeply about these issues for my whole adult life, I am still regularly astounded by the profound difference this kind of listening makes in my own life. So I probably should not have been surprised that, although I surely had a great deal to learn from conflict theorists and practitioners, what is healing in other difficult times of life is profoundly impactful in the presence of conflict as well. There is simply no skill more basic to the conflict transformation process than deep listening.

Listening in the Presence of Conflict

Early in my peacebuilding journey, I encountered Leah Green and The Compassionate Listening Project.™[79] One of Leah's penetrating training exercises encapsulated for me the process of listening in the presence of conflict with empathy, compassion, self-awareness, and openness to learning. The exercise was predicated on the fundamental idea that in every piece of human communication, the spoken content is only the tip of the iceberg, only the superficial layer of a multidimensional process. That is, what makes conflict interaction so difficult is not the content of disagreement or even difference, but the unspoken layers of emotion, personal values, and identity that underlie the words.

The Compassionate Listening Project calls these layers "facts," "feelings," and "values."[80] The first level is the verbal content—what, when, who, where, and why. But this verbal level is animated by the feelings beneath the words. The speaker's (or writer's) emotions determine the tone, volume,

---

[79] The Compassionate Listening Project, http://www.compassionatelistening.org.

[80] Andrea Cohen, with Leah Green and Susan Partnow, *Practicing the Art of Compassionate Listening* (Philadelphia: Quaker Books, 2011), 22.

and intensity of communication. I have heard communication scholars say that the verbal content is a small fraction of what a listener (or reader) receives from spoken (or written) communication. The emotional content determines how listeners will respond, how much they will remember, and how they will store the memory of what they have heard.

Still deeper than the level of emotions is the layer of core values or essence, or what I might call "soul." As powerful as they are, feelings come and go. We all regularly experience angry words that later melt into contrition and search for understanding. But some important pieces of communication are animated by a person's core essence—his deepest values and commitments, her identity, and what makes them who they are.

I later learned that many other conflict resolution experts have similar schemas. For example, Harvard Negotiation Project faculty and best-selling authors Douglas Stone, Bruce Patton, and Sheila Heen separate conversation into layers of "facts," "feelings," and "identity."[81] Similarly, author and practitioner Marshall Rosenberg[82] trains individuals all over the world, including in conflict zones, to communicate by attending to four distinct layers of interaction. He trains speakers first to offer nonjudgmental observations (e.g., "I noticed a pair of your socks on the floor of the bathroom"), then feelings about what was observed ("I felt angry, because I felt that I was obligated to pick up your socks and put them in the laundry, and I feel that I have to clean up after you more than I am comfortable doing"), then needs ("I need to feel that you are my partner in taking care of basic household care"), and then requests ("I need for you to more consistently put your own socks in the laundry basket promptly after you take them off"). If you can get beyond the obvious absurdity of my example, you will notice a very similar concept about the layers present in all human communication.

In an impactful Compassionate Listening exercise, participants are placed in groups of four. In the first round, one person begins by telling a story of something irritating that happened that week or a conflict in which she's been engaged. The person to her immediate right is assigned

---

[81] Douglas Stone, Bruce Patton, and Sheila Heen, *Difficult Conversations: How to Discuss What Matters Most* (New York: Penguin Books, 2000).

[82] Marshall B. Rosenberg, *Nonviolent Communication: A Language of Life* (Encinitas, CA: PuddleDancer Press, 2003).

to listen specifically to the level of "facts," the next person around the circle to "feelings," and the last person to the level of "values" or "identity." The speaker has five minutes to tell her story. Then the "facts" listener has three minutes to reflect back to her, "This is what I heard you say on the level of facts," retelling what she heard as accurately as she can, after which she checks in with the original speaker to see if any of her account needs to be corrected. Then the "feelings" listener has three minutes to mirror back, "This is what I heard you saying on the level of feelings," and likewise the "values" listener. Then the circle is rotated, and a different person has a turn being the storyteller, and so on, until all four members of the circle have experienced each role.

I have seen and used this experience in training situations many times. There are occasionally a few people in a large training group who protest the unnatural separation of the strata of communication, which are blended in normal speech. But that, of course, is precisely the point of the training activity. The exercise requires participants to artificially attend to the three layers separately, in order to bring heightened attention to the various component parts of what would ordinarily be a single piece of human communication.

I never fail to be amazed by how many participants—even in groups of rabbis, spiritual directors, therapists, and other "expert" listeners—respond to the exercise with awestruck exclamations of how precious and rare an experience it was to have been listened to so attentively. Gradually other reactions come out: people observe how humanizing and clarifying it was to bring special focus to the emotional and values dimensions of speech, even when the "facts" of the story inspired judgment or condemnation. Participants regularly say that they have learned a powerful lesson in how to get beneath the verbal content that we so often mistake for the essence of communication, when really the spoken content is but a small fraction of how human beings interact with one another.

The trick, of course, is to take this lesson back into our lives. How often can we remember this insight about the multilayered nature of communication when a loved one, housemate, or co-worker comes at us with critical speech? In all of these situations, when we are able to listen to the deep feelings and animating convictions that underlie the challenging words, we can avoid useless and hurtful rounds of accusations, defensive responses, and misunderstandings. So, too, when we can muster the courage and empathy required to hear beneath the offensive ideological content of a relative or neighbor's political speech, we can learn something important about another human being and about the world.

Perhaps the most important learning of all from this exercise would be to learn to listen to ourselves in that same honest and compassionate way. If in a wise pause before voicing an angry comment we could remember to listen to the pain and the deep sense of threat fueling our instinctive reaction, we would take far better care of ourselves and do far less damage in our own relationships with others.

Soul Traits

In this last section, I have begun to describe sacred perspectives and practices that can play a central role in the transformation of conflict. More such practices will be explored throughout this book.

But shifting relationships from enmity to restored connection depends on far more than tools and techniques. Every conflict specialist I know agrees that peacebuilding is far more than a matter of technique. There is no tool that works in every situation, as the work of conflict transformation is delicate and complex human work. Seeking peace in our relationships and in our world is a way of being.

Teachers of the *Mussar* (literally, "instruction" or "morality") movement[83] articulate a set of *middot* ("soul traits"), which together provide a path to rigorous moral and spiritual development. This ancient system of cognitive-behavioral spiritual practice has undergone a revival in our generation. Jewish leaders and individuals have returned to the deep teachings of Mussar as an aid in creating a life of balance, connection, and awareness. In chapter 5, I offer an extended treatment of middot that support the work of conflict engagement and embrace of difference. These are qualities that, when cultivated over the course of a lifetime, prepare a person to respond productively to conflicts in one's own life, and to respond to the tradition's call to serve the cause of peace in the world.

---

[83] The Hebrew word *mussar* means both "correction" and "instruction," and "*Mussar* literature" hence refers to a genre of pietistic literature that began in the tenth century and continues to develop into the present.

Seeking peace depends on awareness of self and other, compassion, and empathy. Peacebuilders must practice humility, respect for all persons, willingness to learn what is needed in a particular situation and to change course when needed for the greater good, and an ability to step back when others' work is most helpful. Peacebuilders must be patient, for the process can be agonizingly slow, and generous with their time and energy. The quest for peace includes the flexibility to let go of old baggage and move toward forgiveness; it includes gentle ways of speech and presence that can inspire a sense of safety, soothe hurt, and support hopefulness.

All of these qualities, articulated in ancient sacred texts as the basis of responsible and righteous living, directly address the troubled dynamics of entrenched conflict. Whether in arguments among family members or political rivals, compassion and empathy, humility, respect, curiosity, and generosity are the traits that can loosen the tendencies of heart and mind to constrict, self-protect, attack, and blame. These are the attributes that can liberate us from distorted views, by which the one who hurt us or threatens us (whether personally or ideologically) becomes dehumanized and even demonized in our eyes. This way of being, when practiced consistently, is what prepares us to unclench our fists, minds, and hearts when we feel wounded. These traits of the reflective mind and spirit can counter the reptilian brain's instinctive surges of fear, rage, and hate, helping us quiet primal impulses and live instead as the sacred beings that we aspire to be.

Whether in personal discord, intracommunal conflicts, or international struggles, these fundamental spiritual virtues lie at the center of peacebuilding practice.

2

Peace among Religions

They will beat their swords into plowshares and their spears into pruning hooks. Nation will not take up sword against nation; they shall never again know war. They will sit beneath their grapevine or fig tree with no one to disturb them, for *Adonai Ts'va'ot* has spoken. All the peoples will walk, each in the names of their gods, and we will walk in the name of *Adonai* our God forever and ever.

— *Micah 4:3–5*

Like any Jewish youth group member, I had probably sung the song, "*Lo yisa goy el goy ḥerev*" ("Nation will not take up sword against nation . . . "), hundreds of times by the time I had graduated from youth group and college. This text was an old friend by the time it unexpectedly revealed itself to me anew in the context of my interreligious work.

Healing Fear in the Pursuit of Peace

Preparing for an interreligious program on religious pluralism some years ago, the third verse of the passage leaped off the page at me. "All the peoples will walk each in the names of their gods, and we will walk in the name of Adonai our God forever and ever." One could read this as an exclusivist text, as if it meant to say, "All of them (foolish, sinful people) will worship their own (pagan) gods, but *we* will walk in the name of the true God forever."[1] But I think the text suggests something very different: parallel streams of worshippers each offering their own devotions, praying in their own particular language and cadence, all going about their lives in relationship to the God of their understanding.

In this joyous cacophony of religious voices, the Israelites (and their heirs, the Jewish people), for their part, will raise their voices to Adonai, their name for God. No judgment, no comparison, no denigration of another's religious path. Just the human family with all of its God-given diversity, living along separate paths, together.

With this insight, I understood for the first time why this portrait of religious pluralism is placed just two verses after the beloved vision, "Nation will not take up sword against nation; they shall never again know war." Some twenty-seven hundred years after this text was written, theologian Hans Küng wrote, "There can be no peace among the nations without peace among the religions. There can be no peace among the religions without dialogue between the religions."[2] In order to help create a more peaceful world, religions and religionists must not only tolerate but celebrate difference as a fundamental gift of God's creation.

The text implores us to believe that the end of war is a possibility—not only in the world to come but in this world that we inhabit together. But it will not happen as long as we begrudge the "other"—the one religiously, ethnically, racially, or ideologically different from us—his or her place in the landscape of God's creation. Conversely, as we cultivate the ability to recognize and appreciate the beauty of another's words and ways, we contribute to a world in which the human family lives together in peace.

Later still, I came to understand why the intermediate verse of the passage—"All will sit beneath their grapevines or fig trees with no one

---

[1] Rashi, for example, based on *Targum Jonathan*, interprets Micah 4:5 in this way: "They will walk . . . to destruction, because they committed idolatry." *Targum Jonathan* is the ancient Aramaic translation of the prophetic books of the Bible, edited in the seventh century.

[2] Talk delivered by Hans Küng at Santa Clara University's Markkula Center for Applied Ethics on March 31, 2005, http://www.scu.edu.

to disturb them"—is placed here, in the midst of a vision of a world of peace and mutual respect. Micah places a description of the healing of fear between the vision of peace and the practice of positive interreligious engagement. What obstructs the achievement of a world at peace and a global practice of interfaith respect? It is the reality of fear. The prophet exhorts us to work for a world without violence by reaching out to the religious other. And he tells us that what is most likely to interfere with this practice is fear among people.

The prophet Micah seems to have anticipated by three millennia what we now know about how fear can impede our capacity to serve as instruments of peace in the world. The ancient part of our brain, primed to protect us from harm, cannot allow us to be curious or openhearted toward the other, to open ourselves to learning, or to explore relationship. Only when fear is soothed and the thinking mind is engaged can we stop and reflect, question our prejudices, and consider whether stepping into relationship with the other might be enriching rather than perilous. Only then can we move closer to a vision of peace.

In this chapter, I reflect on experiences drawn from my seven years of work in interreligious dialogue, viewing this work as a laboratory for transcending fear of the other in order to build positive relationships in the presence of difference. I include portraits of local, grassroots interfaith dialogue work, national dialogue projects, and international leadership dialogues. In each of these contexts, I focus on the inner process of moving from fear and suspicion to embrace of the religious other. I also consider ancient Jewish reflections on religious pluralism, on relations between religious groups, and on the process of learning to recognize the value and beauty in traditions other than one's own.

Surely some interreligious dialogues include memories of past traumas, when members or leaders of one religion have inflicted suffering on another, sometimes on a massive scale (e.g., in Jewish-Christian relations). Such history makes the encounter complex and difficult. However, many interfaith encounters evoke fear chiefly because members of the other religion are seen as different from ourselves. I begin my exploration of intergroup encounter with interreligious dialogue precisely in order to investigate this primal fear of difference and how it can be transformed into the joy of being enriched by acquaintance with "the other." This ability to transcend the instinct that associates difference with danger is one layer of the work of moving from fear to reflection and, perhaps, to acceptance, of allowing the "enemy" to become a friend.

Reaching Out to the Religious "Other"

Since my call to peace work in 2004 had come in the context of Israeli-Palestinian reconciliation efforts, I thought that I was being asked to find a way to work for peace in the Middle East. How was I to respond to this call from my home in St. Paul, Minnesota?

I entered into an extended period of discernment, including reading, networking with scholars and practitioners, and attending several training programs. I learned about many scores of grassroots groups working on the conflict in various ways, both in the Middle East and here in the United States. I learned an enormous amount by connecting with many such groups and their leaders, but I had not yet found the way to use my own unique set of gifts and experiences to serve the cause of peace.

The answer came from an unexpected direction. Rabbi Barry Cytron invited me to lunch to talk about the work of the interfaith learning center that he directed. By the end of lunch, it seemed that I had found my place to serve. Before long I was employed by the center, creating congregationally based programs of interfaith trialogue, bringing Jews, Christians, and Muslims together for interreligious education and relationship building. Along with a wonderful multifaith circle of colleagues throughout the community, I created structures that would invite Jews, Christians, and Muslims (and at times, Buddhists, Hindus, Baha'is, Native Americans, and committed atheists) to cross religious divides in order to know one another more deeply, to explore one another's faith and humanity, and to learn to hear truths different from their own.

My first step was to meet with a range of local Muslim leaders, for I knew I faced a steep learning curve in learning about Islam and about the local Muslim community. For many months, I came home in an exuberant mood after one or another of my networking lunches with a Muslim leader. I had sat in a café with an imam or Muslim community leader. We had shared parts of one another's personal and professional stories and affirmed our shared belief in the importance of building interreligious understanding. We had tasted the mutual delight of learning about the many similarities between Judaism and Islam.

I was always elated to discover yet another commonality between Hebrew and Arabic. I never tire of this experience, always sensing that the connection between our languages confirms the truth that we are family to one another. I loved comparing my observance of *kashrut* (the Jewish dietary laws) with the Islamic practice of *hallal* food, noticing what questions I asked the server about the ingredients in a particular menu item and which questions my new Muslim friend asked in order to be faithful to Islamic dietary laws.

I was amazed to discover cultural similarities as well. What I thought of as "Jewish time," the Jewish cultural habit of arriving late for every engagement, my new friends called "Muslim time." Every joke I had ever heard or told about the centrality of food in Jewish culture had its analog in Muslim communities. Once a new Muslim colleague, in a sheepish tone, suggested that he and I study Jewish and Islamic sacred texts together, as a way of exploring how we might bring our two communities together. As if revealing an embarrassing oddity about his culture, he said, "Muslims are really into text study." I burst out laughing, delighted by the parallel. "Muslims are into text study? Jews are *really* into text study!" I knew that Jews to whom I told this story would share my delight.

I bubbled with joy about my newfound discoveries. I felt keenly that every hour I spent building these relationships was sacred work, a palpable fulfillment of my call to pursue peace. One hour at a time, sitting in cafés in Minneapolis and St. Paul, a rabbi and a Muslim leader, I knew that we were making peace together. I hoped that others in the café would notice us, remarking with surprise, "Oh, look at the imam and the rabbi having lunch and laughing together!" Rabbi and imam enjoying food together, leaning into deep and delight-filled conversation, we were a tableau of a more peaceful world.

As relationships grew, deeper dimensions of dialogue emerged, and some conversations grew more challenging. One of my most faithful partners has been a Muslim leader originally from Pakistan. During the first year of our work together, I heard him say over and over again that this work was not about geopolitics. What happens "over there" is a million miles away, he would say; our task is to learn about our neighbors, about their families, their communities, and their faith lives, not to talk about political struggles beyond our control or influence. We both knew where "over there" was, and we were well aware of the significance of a Muslim leader and rabbi working together, seeking to draw our people into more peaceful relationship with one another.

One day, over a year after we began to work together, we sat at a planning committee meeting, creating a program on justice in Judaism, Christianity, and Islam. When our planning was nearly complete, in a temperate and matter-of-fact tone, my Muslim colleague asked the rabbi at the table who would be presenting the Jewish view of justice, "Have you thought about how you will respond if someone asks, given the Jewish passion for justice, how you understand Israel's treatment of the Palestinians?"

The Jews at the table grew tense and frightened; our Muslim friend was confused, for he thought he had asked a simple question. After the group meeting ended, he asked me sincerely, "Why did my question create so much tension in the room?"

A few days later he and I went out to dinner to explore his question. We chatted for a bit, then dove into the momentous conversation we needed to have. Like many rabbis, I am normally a person of many words. I have a lot to say about most things, especially those religious and political issues about which I feel most passionately. So it must have been by the grace of God that, when the moment came for me to respond to his question, "Why was the Israeli-Palestinian question so sensitive for the Jewish members of the committee?" I responded briefly and from the heart.

I can't honestly say that I intentionally did anything. I did not review my favorite principles of dialogue or take a moment for prayer; I did not even choose to take a long conscious breath, as I often teach others to do. Somehow, beyond my conscious control, I dropped into my heart and spoke what was for me the simple truth. I said that the Jewish people, my people, have suffered greatly throughout history, and that while we—and our brothers and sisters in Israel—may look strong and powerful, inside we are very frightened.

Remarkably, I knew that those few words were more impactful than a flood of other explanations I could have offered, and I stopped talking. My friend began to talk about how Muslims in Pakistan see the world, and I was aware that I was being blessed with a glimpse of reality I might never have encountered but for my relationship with this man. In that graced, quiet space of heartfelt communication, it became clear that our relationship had changed. We were having a boundary-crossing encounter that was new for both of us, and it was deeply moving. In subsequent conversations, it became clear that we had reached a different stage in our relationship.

We did not bring peace to the Middle East that evening. We did not fall into one another's arms, professing lifelong friendship despite the ways in which culture and religion divided us. But two leaders from different religions, different cultures, and different continents had shared our perspectives on a highly contentious issue that normally evokes heated passion and embattled debate. Instead, we had heard perspectives that would otherwise have been inaccessible to either of us from within our own communities. Our worlds expanded to include the perspective of the other.

This is the fundamental work of peacebuilding, when human relationship allows us to move beyond generalized thinking about "the other." In the safety of genuine face-to-face encounter, we begin to see the other as a trustworthy and admirable human being, even in the presence of real religious and/or ideological differences. The fearful amygdala quiets down; we become calm enough that the frontal cortex reasserts itself; and we are ourselves again. Just as we are naturally curious about unfamiliar sights, sounds, and beliefs when traveling in distant lands, we become curious about how someone with a very different background from our own can construct a worldview so different from what seems obvious to us. If one party insists that the other must change his or her view, fight or flight instincts can become engaged again. But if both conduct themselves in a spirit of respectful inquiry, both are enriched by the opportunity to learn something more about God's world.

Confusing Our Part with the Whole

Let us imagine . . . a little worm, living in the blood. . . . This little worm would live in the blood, in the same way as we live in a part of the universe, and would consider each part of blood, not as a part, but as a whole. . . . I believe that, if a triangle could speak, it would say, in like manner, that God is eminently triangular, while a circle would say that the divine nature is eminently circular. Thus each would ascribe to God its own attributes, would assume itself to be like God, and look on everything else as ill-shaped.[3]

This text makes me laugh, and I assume that is precisely the reaction its author, a bold fifteenth-century theologian far ahead of his time, intended. The notion of a microscopic organism, an infinitesimally small part of the grandeur of creation, confusing itself with the whole of the universe is laughable. For such an organism (endowed with the capacity for philosophical thought, no less) to think that its tiny corner of the cosmos is all there is is palpably absurd. Yet of course we do this on a daily basis, thinking that what we see and believe is the only possible truth.

The absurdity is multiplied when we consider Spinoza's triangle (also capable of philosophical contemplation) inventing God, as it were, in its own image. To the triangle, it is inconceivable that God could be anything but triangular, and to the octagon, octagonal. But these images are comical only on their surface, for, on reflection, we recognize that such absurd thinking has done enormous harm in the world.

Some white Christians believe that Jesus, born in Palestine, is white and blond, and that God is surely a white man. This assumption has contributed to prejudice against people of color on a massive scale for millennia. Likewise, male religious leaders have assumed that God is obviously male, hence affirming the exclusion and oppression of women throughout history. It is not only Spinoza's hypothetical triangle or circle that projects its own image heavenward and calls it God, willing to judge and persecute those who do not match that very limited and self-serving image. We are the worm, the triangle, and the circle committing these destructive absurdities.

Spinoza is asking us to interrogate our own ethnocentrism, the all-too-entrenched idea that what seems true to us is the absolute truth for all people. My reality is born of my own historical, religious, social, and familial context, yet I am astonished when others do not see the world in precisely the same way I do. I am moved to outrage that Republicans are not Democrats, that Muslims are not Jews, and that the poor and the very rich do not think just like me. It is silly, yet we do it all the time.

From this ridiculous presumption grows the sense that the "other," the one who is not like me, is wrong, insane, or evil. The other—the

---

[3] Baruch de Spinoza, *Spinoza: Correspondence*, http://www.sacred-text.com.

one whose story I have not yet heard and understood[4]—is a threat to be defended against or annihilated.

What if, instead, the triangle were a curious creature, genuinely interested in exploring this peculiar octagonal being or the circular one with no sides at all? What if difference inspired not judgment, fear, and aggression but excitement and the desire to learn? What if we grew beyond the instinct that makes us associate difference with danger and we cultivated instead a childlike expectation that new experience is likely to be fun, that difference will bring new growth and expansion of our own beings? What a different world it would be.

Learning from the Religious Other

Through an extraordinary stroke of good fortune, I was invited to participate in a think tank called "Thinking Together," exploring cutting-edge issues in interreligious dialogue under the sponsorship of the World Council of Churches. For three consecutive summers, I traveled to Geneva, Switzerland, to meet with this exceptional group of people: a senior Jewish educator from Jerusalem, a progressive imam and Islamic scholar from South Africa, a Buddhist professor of conflict resolution from Thailand, a professor of Hinduism from India and Trinidad, a senior leader of the Presbyterian Church in the United States, an internationally known Christian scholar and leader of the interfaith dialogue movement, and a hilariously witty Buddhist monk and scholar from Sri Lanka who wore bright orange robes, among others. Since September 11, 2001, the group had studied, talked, and written on issues related to religion and violence and views of "the other" in various religious traditions. The group had recently turned its attention to the issue of religious conversion.

I learned that many Christian leaders around the world are deeply concerned about what they consider to be unethical missionizing, as in seeking to convert vulnerable populations in the course of distributing humanitarian aid following natural disasters. Still, as the only Jew at this

---

[4] Gene Knudsen Hoffman, "An Enemy Is One Whose Story We Have Not Heard," first published in *Fellowship, Journal of The Fellowship of Reconciliation*, May/June 1997, website of New Conversations Initiative, http://www.newconversations.net.

particular meeting and a newcomer to the group, I grew uneasy as I listened to my new colleagues discuss what might distinguish ethical from unethical conversion. My heart began to beat rapidly, and angry thoughts arose in me from a very deep and old place. "Do these people know," I thought heatedly, "what it is to be on the receiving end of coerced conversion?" Have these people, gracious and sophisticated as they are, done their own work to truly understand the wrongs that have been done to the Jewish people in the name of what they were now euphemistically calling "faith sharing"?

At a break in the day's discussions, I shared my concerns with my new friend Thomas Thangaraj. A renowned Christian theologian from India, Thomas had a loving, authentic presence and had already reached out to help me feel welcome in the group. Trusting him, I told him about my discomfort in rather blunt terms. I said, "For me, as a Jew, conversion lies on one end of a continuum that has included persecution, expulsion, and genocide." He responded just as starkly. "For me," he said, wanting me to understand his life experience as I wanted him to understand mine, "conversion means liberation."

I learned that Thomas was born a Dalit in India, and, like many people of his caste, had converted to Christianity to escape the oppression that otherwise would have been his fate in his native land. From a completely different cultural context than my own, Thomas indeed understood, at least as deeply as I did as a Jew, what it is to live as a persecuted minority. In fact, he had devoted a great deal of his academic career working to understand and atone for Christian sins against the Jewish people.

Sitting at the table with my colleagues, my fight-or-flight reflexes had been activated by the discussion of conversion. The very word conjured images of Jews throughout the ages, my own ancestors, suffering prejudice, persecution, expulsion, and murder because of Christian insistence on religious hegemony. Their words touched a place of fearful collective memory in me. Under threat, though it was only rhetorical threat, I became embattled, imagining myself locked in adversarial debate with the others at the table.

But in conversation with one wonderful human being who, as it turns out, knew even more about religious persecution than I did, my well-rehearsed Jewish sensibilities cracked open. I was safe with these people. They were not related to the millennia of enemies of the Jews. We were on the same side, albeit from different vantage points. As such, there was much for me to learn from them about how the world looked from the perspective of different religions, different parts of the world, and different ways of constructing reality.

It was a moment I knew I would never forget. Thomas and I had reached across boundaries of religion and nationality to share the heart of our respective people's pain. In so doing, I learned about a part of the world that was utterly new to me and recognized how a particular issue (in this case, conversion), very charged and laden with pain in my own cultural and historical context, had completely different meanings for him and his people. It was a deep moment of learning about how what seems from one perspective to be the only possible truth on an issue looks very different from a different personal or national perspective. The Jewish people's perspective surely reflects the reality of our experience through history. But I grasped that what is absolute truth from my own people's perspective has very different meanings for others. My world had been expanded.

Later in the week, Wesley Ariarajah, a Christian scholar of religion originally from Sri Lanka and a celebrated pioneer in international inter-religious dialogue efforts, spoke with frustration of Christian colleagues who were so committed to the practice of evangelism that they violated far more important tenets of their shared faith. In a moment of rigorously honest critique of his own tradition, he said that missionary work had become "an obsession" (his word). "I want to say to these guys, 'What difference would it make if we made another million people Christians, and we were still killing each other all over the world? What difference would that make?'"

His words rang with revelatory power, as if I'd heard the voice of God. This religious leader was leveling a powerful critique at one of the central imperatives of his own religion. Given the state of the world today, he was willing to ask, "What difference would it make?" of a core practice of Christianity. (This would be analogous to a rabbi asking, "What difference would it make if one million more Jews studied Torah every day?") In my mind's eye, I saw the beautiful sanctuary of the synagogue I belong to, mentally scanning the issues that consume most of our attention as a congregation. With the awareness that people are killing one another all over the world, how much of our activity would meet Wesley's penetrating challenge?

The question continued to resonate in me. By the end of the meeting, I realized that I had been changed by the experience. Two months later, I talked about this encounter with my congregation on Rosh Hashana (the Jewish New Year). Like many of the people in my synagogue, most of my friends are Jewish. I have traveled in other countries, but my perspective on the world has always had the Jewish people and Israel squarely at its center. In Geneva I had had a glimpse of what the world looks like through the eyes of Buddhists from Sri Lanka and Thailand, Hindus from India and Trinidad, Muslims from Egypt and South Africa, and Christians of several different races and nationalities.

It was a simple and life-changing realization: the world is much larger than the needs of my own people. I thought of the question, "Is it good for the Jews?"—our standard (if only half-serious) touchstone for judging political issues. Suddenly I knew more deeply than before that this question is far too small for an age in which the world is in such peril.

I examined the angry, adversarial reaction I had had upon first hearing my colleagues discuss conversion, instinctively feeling that I could not trust them to understand what I knew. I had reacted from a place of deep Jewish historical memory. But my colleague's powerful question, "What difference would it make?" challenged my own comfortable, lifelong particularist Jewish perspective, according to which every issue is approached from the unique perspective of the Jewish people. Surely, history has taught us all too well that if Jews do not speak from our own collective experience, we can by no means count on others to do so on our behalf. But the primal goal of defending Jews from harm was suddenly revealed to be too narrow a preoccupation.

In fact, from within Jewish theology, according to which Jews are called to serve as a "light unto the nations" (Isa. 42:6), it is essential for Jews to develop the capacity to see the world as others see it, as well as through the lens of our own experience. If we never fully open ourselves to global perspectives, how can we serve the nations? If we can never believe that we are safe enough to listen calmly and respectfully to other perspectives, we cannot discern intelligently how to use our own beliefs and experiences for the betterment of the world.

That week in Geneva, something fundamental changed in the balance of two aspects of my identity: as a passionate leader in the Jewish community, on the one hand, and as a citizen of the world, on the other. I had watched the millennia-old "us vs. them" perspective arise in me from a deep place of collective memory. Continuing to honor that perspective, I also knew that I could let in people whose reality was fundamentally different from my own. A set of new, precious relationships had allowed me to meet the religious "other" not as an enemy to be feared and distrusted, but as a treasured person to learn from, work with, and embrace.

Questioning the Axiomatic

The following summer, Debbie Weissman—an old friend, renowned Israeli educator, international interreligious leader, and a long-time participant in the group—was present at the proceedings. No longer the only Jew in the room, free of my internal need to serve as the voice of the entire Jewish people, I was thrilled to have an opportunity to further develop my identity as a citizen of the world, expanding my perspective and stretching my heart and mind. This happened in a surprising way.

Since the topic was conversion, we expected that challenging moments might arise in conversation between the proselytizing religions represented at the table (Christianity and Islam) and those religions that tend not to seek converts aggressively (Judaism, Buddhism, and Hinduism). To our surprise, this year our attention was drawn to a different fault line in the group. The challenge of conversing across deep divides of belief arose among the monotheists (Jews, Christians, and Muslims), those from nontheistic traditions (Buddhists), and those that recognize multiple manifestations of the Divine (Hindus).

In my opening remarks on Jewish perspectives on conversion, I had sought to articulate why seeking converts has not been a prominent part of Jewish practice over the centuries. I emphasized that Judaism seeks to serve as a "light unto the nations" (Isa. 42:6) to help bring the world to God and to justice, but not to persuade the peoples of the world to live as Jews. In the course of exploring that point, I cited beloved texts that are central to my own prayer life, such as, "On that day God will be one and God's name one."[5]

When I finished my introductory talk to the group, my Hindu colleague, Anant Rambachan, offered some appreciative words about what I had said.

---

[5] Zech. 14:9, quoted in the daily *Aleinu* prayer.

Then, very gently, he said that my remarks on bringing people to the one God and my reference to the prayer for the recognition of God's oneness were difficult for him. "Such texts," he said, "remind me of times when, growing up in Trinidad, people would break into our Hindu temples and destroy the *murti* [sacred images]."

Anant is a brilliant and gracious man, who commanded great love and respect in the group. The room fell silent as he spoke. I was mortified that I had offended someone whom I hold in high esteem. I rushed to tell him that I was sorry to have caused offense, that that had certainly not been my intention. He made clear that he had not been personally hurt, but something important had transpired. We had encountered a profound difference between the self-described monotheistic traditions of Judaism, Christianity, and Islam, on the one hand, and Hinduism, on the other, with its rich teachings of the many different names and manifestations of the Divine in the world. Monotheists at the table were forced to wrestle with the ways in which belief in one God can give rise to exclusivism, a conviction that ours is the only truth, an orientation that too often results in violence against "the other."

This was a stunning moment for me. In my work, I have spent a good deal of time and energy seeking to help Christians understand that some of the ideas, language, and images that are most precious to them resonate painfully for Jews, evoking memories of nearly two millennia of oppression at the hands of Christians. I have asked Christians to examine their liturgy and sacred texts and to take the empathic leap of imagining how these words might look from a Jewish perspective. As an heir to the profound Jewish historical memory of persecution (and worse), I have argued that Christians have a responsibility to look self-critically at their own tradition and history, to see how it has done harm, and to consider the implications for Christian practice in our own day.

Suddenly, my own religious language—words that I have known since I was a small child and recited daily for many decades—was a source of pain to another, who had himself been on the receiving end of religiously motivated violence. The concept of monotheism lies at the epicenter of Jewish tradition and Jewish self-understanding. How could this concept possibly be a source of harm to others? Yet here was my treasured colleague, challenging me to contemplate the damage that had been done in the name of my own cherished belief.

These were the very moments for which the "Thinking Together" project was created, moments when each of us might enter into an entirely new understanding of our own tradition by seeing it through the eyes of "the other." In relationship with people of different religions and from different parts of the world, we were forced to consider hitherto unimaginable questions. Our relationships of respect and affection led us to examine unthinkable thoughts and consider our most beloved convictions from multiple perspectives, each of us seeing our own worldview as but one among many imperfect human attempts to make sense of a world far beyond our understanding.

In such moments, one has another option. One can say, explicitly or implicitly, "No! I am right, and so you must be wrong![6] My truth is simply correct, and I have no interest in considering your perspective on it!" We all see this kind of behavior modeled every day in the public square and too often in our personal relationships as well. But for thoughtful people who desire to understand more about human life and to respond to the sacred call to make peace in our world, we must listen to "the other," even when he or she challenges beliefs that are axiomatic for us.

Since I experienced this conversation, what is my obligation? Do I need to stop saying the offending words in my daily prayer? Do I need to reconstruct my whole theology to excise monotheism from my beliefs about God and the world? Certainly not. If two parties to intergroup dialogue do not both bring their deeply held truths to the table, the encounter is not dialogue but monologue, with only one side speaking authentically. The purpose of dialogue is emphatically not for either side to abandon its beliefs.

But in dialogue we do change as we come to understand how others see us. We grow by learning how the beliefs that are embodied in each of our religions, all imperfect human constructions, can have adverse impact on others. With these newly gained understandings, we can make conscious

---

[6] This phrase is inspired by the title of Brad Hirschfield's wonderful book, *You Don't Have to Be Wrong for Me to Be Right: Finding Faith without Fanaticism* (New York: Three Rivers Press, 2009).

decisions about how to minimize hurt to those beyond our group. We are no less faithful to our own religious commitments, but with the benefit of the other's perspective we can carry our religious commitments in ways that are truer to our desire to be a force for good in the world.

This kind of learning requires deep concern for the other and a willingness to learn from others. In this work, we practice the skills of listening deeply to truths different from our own, grappling with these perspectives, and allowing them to affect the way we think about our lives. In the process, we stretch our minds and hearts beyond our own comfortable truths, an essential ingredient of peacebuilding, one conversation at a time. The work also requires a measure of humility: we need to remember that we cannot possibly know everything there is to know about life. When we transcend arrogance and listen to different perspectives without defensiveness, we can enter into a deeper partnership to work together to address issues of both local and global concern. Thus, interreligious dialogue embodies the essential skills of peacebuilding among people and can contribute to the cause of peace in the world.

The Diversity of Creation

In the ancient *beit midrash* (study hall), the Rabbis played an interesting game. Though they honored every word of the Torah text as divine wisdom, they nonetheless asked one another: "What is the most important principle in the Torah?" The responses of two great Rabbis are recorded, and their disagreement is profound and enlightening.[7]

Rabbi Akiva replied, not surprisingly, that the most important verse in the Torah is Leviticus 19:18, "Love your neighbor as yourself." I sometimes ask Jewish audiences their answer to this question, and there are always people in the group who reach for this verse. After all, love of neighbor is arguably the foundation of ethical life, the basis for all interpersonal relations, and the ground on which a healthy and moral society is built.

This cardinal principle has been variously interpreted by commentators both ancient and modern. Many commentators understand the

---

[7] *Sifra Kedoshim Parasha* 2, 4:12. The *Sifra* is a collection of midrash on the book of Leviticus, edited late fourth century.

commandment to be telling us that the "other," whoever that may be for us, wants the same things that we do: good health for ourselves and our families, a life in which our needs are provided for, basic human dignity and freedom, and support and compassion in times of pain. From this perspective, the verse gives rise to the "Golden Rule," present in so many religious traditions. As formulated by the ancient sage Hillel, this minimally and pointedly means, "Do not do to the other anything that would be hateful to you."[8] Or in a perhaps more expansive formulation, "Offer to the other what you know you yourself would desire." In either case, this reading understands the verse to premise caring for the other on our own intimate knowledge of our own needs and the assumption that others' needs and wants are much like our own.

Other commentators emphasize the fact that we are to see the "other" as one who is like ourselves.[9] Every person I encounter is a mortal, fragile human being, just as I am, subject to the many challenges of life, doing the best he or she can in any given moment. Such a mental intention, if consistently practiced, would lead us to offer the other the benefit of the doubt, as we do to ourselves, when he or she errs.

He said a harsh word? Maybe he has a sick child at home and is doing all he can to get through the day. She insulted me, disappointed me, even betrayed me? She must have been acting out of old, deep pain, locked inside her, that causes her deep suffering and, despite her best efforts, sometimes hurts others as well. The commandment thus reminds us that the other is just like us: imperfect, fallible, prone to fall short of our own aspirations. The other can't help it: like you, she is doing the best she can at any given moment.

Strikingly, Rabbi Ben Azzai disagrees. I am certain he did not fail to grasp the profundity of Leviticus 19:18. Yet he offers a different verse as the foundation of the Torah. For Ben Azzai, the central verse is, "This is the book of the generations of humanity" (Gen. 5:1). Ben Azzai must have believed that the command, "Love your neighbor as yourself," was too tenuous a basis for the imperative to treat every human being with

---

[8]   BT *Shabbat* 31a.

[9]   Moses Mendelsohn, *Biur Commentary to the Torah*, ed. Perez Sandler (Jerusalem: R. Mas, 1940), 44.

absolute dignity. Leviticus 19:18 grounds the practice of love of other in our knowledge of our own needs, desires, and hurts. But what of a person with little capacity for self-awareness or self-love? How is he or she to know what the other would and would not want? How can a person who has been deprived of the experience of being loved know how to treat others with empathy and compassion?

Rather, Ben Azzai believes that it is the fact of createdness in the divine image that is the unassailable foundation for the principle of human dignity and the practice of compassion. There can be no exceptions to this principle, since there is no human being not created in the image. This, then, for Ben Azzai, is the basis upon which the entire Torah is built.

I find myself returning to this debate regularly in the course of my interreligious work, for both views offer deep insight into the process of opening to the other and what may block that process. On the one hand, most religions honor some version of the "Golden Rule," the fundamental imperative to treat others as we would like to be treated. This principle unquestionably applies to rejecting bigotry, stereotyping, and discrimination about those with beliefs different from our own. Yet as we know all too well, pain, fear, threat, and wounding regularly lead us—both individually and collectively—to forget this universal truth. For such times, we may need to ground ourselves in Ben Azzai's view, the existential reality that all human beings, even those who have hurt and threatened us, are human creatures like ourselves, worthy of the same respect and dignity we demand for ourselves.

This appeal to the imagery of createdness suggests a radical theology of diversity in the human family. To contemplate creation is to be filled with wonder at the stunning variety of beings in our world. We instinctively know that the wide range of creatures in the animal world is a beautiful thing. We know that a garden is far lovelier for the variety of species contained in it. Mountains and craters are more exquisite for the multifaceted impact of water and wind, affecting different areas differently, creating a spectacular array of colors, shapes, and forms.

The creation image reminds us as well that the fact that the other appears to be unlike me is not a mistake or an outrage. Why did God create people of different religions, ideologies, and national origins? Because God wanted the human race, like the floral world, to be a world of endless, exquisite diversity. The point is not to fight to force the other to become like me (as if that were possible). The challenge of human life is to open to diversity as a gift, an invitation, an opportunity for mutual learning and enrichment.

Interfaith Road Trip

Early in the sabbatical year that was to be devoted to writing this book, an irresistible opportunity came my way. The invitation came from my colleague Rabbi Gerry Serotta, whom I knew in his role as founding chair of Rabbis for Human Rights, an organization I have long been proud to support. I knew that Gerry had recently created Clergy Beyond Borders, an organization devoted to empowering religious leaders to promote interreligious understanding, as an expression of our shared, religiously grounded passion for peacebuilding. Gerry, whom I know to be a person of great integrity, courage, and good-heartedness, was inviting me to join in the organization's Caravan of Reconciliation, gathering clergy of three faiths to travel around the country together, beginning on September 11, 2011, to promote interreligious dialogue. I knew this invitation was a gift I should not refuse.

The caravan began in Washington, DC, on a fifteen-day road trip, traversing three thousand miles, addressing some five thousand people at university campuses, synagogues, churches, and Islamic centers in fifteen cities. Jewish, Christian, and Muslim clergy traveled in the caravan together, stopping for two or three public events each day, where we offered teachings from our three traditions in support of active, respectful engagement with people of other religions. We spoke of the dangers to American democracy posed by rising trends of religious intolerance, particularly against American Muslims. We shared our own personal stories of passionate engagement between and among religious communities, and we offered prayers for peace in many languages.

Central to my experience of the caravan was the co-founder of Clergy Beyond Borders, Imam Yahya Hendi, the well-known and widely beloved Muslim chaplain at Georgetown University, the first Muslim ever to hold such a position on an American university campus. Brother Yahya (as he is affectionately known) is a force of nature, a person of boundless energy, enormous charisma, and a heart as loving as any I have known. Yahya, a Palestinian American, has studied both Christianity and Judaism on the graduate level and speaks fine Hebrew. He has advised four presidents on matters related to the American Muslim community and has brought his infectious message of peace and reconciliation to scores of countries around the world.

Yahya is a large man, with a big sense of mission about this sacred work. Not a shy bone in his body, he thinks boldly about possibilities for bringing people together across boundaries of religion and national origin. He was constantly planning how to promote our next engagement, how to engage more media, and how to expand the work throughout the country and around the world. I could not even approach his level of physical stamina, but being in his presence evoked inspiration and hope.

The caravan experience was also defined by the loving friendship shared by Rabbi Gerry and Imam Yahya. There were many wonderful stories about the work they had done together, places they had visited together, and the loving things their children had said about one another. My personal favorite: When Gerry had told his twin children that he would not serve as rabbi for their *bnei mitzvah*[10] so that he could be fully present at the ceremony as their father, he asked them which rabbi they would like to invite to officiate. Their first choice was a beloved family friend, a rabbi in Jerusalem. If he was not available, their second choice was to ask Yahya to officiate as the rabbi at their bar mitzvah! Being in Gerry and Yahya's presence, one could not help but be moved by the love, admiration, and sheer inspiration that bound these two great religious leaders, working together for peace within and beyond their own religious communities. Their affection, respect, and deep sense of partnership with one another infused our experience together.

Each morning, before setting off on the day's adventures, Yahya would sit in stillness for a moment in the driver's seat, then call us to prayer in our respective languages of prayer. One morning I chanted the biblical words, "*Ma gadlu ma'asecha Yah*," "How great are Your works, O God, your thoughts are very deep" (Ps. 92:6) expressing my reverence for the awesome beauty of this inspired group of people setting off for a day of

---

[10] Plural of "bar mitzvah," a celebration of religious majority at the age of thirteen for a boy and twelve for a girl.

sacred work, ready to travel many miles for the sake of peace.

Steve Martin, our Evangelical pastor, began to pray spontaneously in the characteristic cadence of Evangelical Christians. At first his inflection struck a negative chord in me, instinctively reminding me of televangelists proclaiming their exclusive truth. But I soon grasped that Steve was prayerfully offering an intimate articulation of what we were all experiencing. In a tone both eloquent and conversational, he thanked God for the pleasures of friendship, camaraderie, and mutual appreciation in our relationships, and for the blessing of important work to fill our days. In a moment, my visceral response of clenching against the sound of the religious other's voice had turned to deep appreciation and love.

Finally, Yahya chanted the opening verses of the Koran: "*Bismillah Ar-Raḥman Ar-Raḥim . . .*," "In the name of God, the Most Gracious, the Most Merciful. Praise be to Allah, Cherisher and Sustainer of the Worlds; Most Gracious, Most Merciful; Master of the Day of Judgment. It is You that we worship and Your help that we seek."[11] These words have become dear to me, having so often heard Muslim colleagues begin meetings by calling us together into prayerful awareness with this text. The words and descriptions of God all have exact parallels in Hebrew, evoking in me a visceral sense of familial connection. The chant, beautiful and contemplative, filled our small van, consecrating our common space and time. It was sure to be a blessed day.

On the morning of September 12, we met with a group of Egyptian imams touring the United States on a cultural exchange program. As our two groups converged, I fell into conversation with a professor of Arabic literature at Al Azhar University in Cairo. His English was halting, but his warmth and desire to connect unmistakable. The two of us fell into step together, walking toward our photo op on the Capitol steps.

I sensed that we both felt the power of the encounter—beyond the spoken word—Egyptian imam and American rabbi, walking together toward the Capitol steps. He began to offer what I can only describe as a spontaneous ode to peace. "It's such a wonderful thing to be walking together, to be working together," he said. "We can make a difference; we can make peace." "This is what we need to do. This is what God wants of

---

[11] Holy Qur'an 1:1. Translation adapted from Abdullah Yusuf Ali, ed., *The Meaning of the Holy Qur'an* (Beltsville, MD: Amana Publications, 1999).

us." Here was an Egyptian imam expressing the very same deep, religiously based yearning for peace that guides my own life and work. I drank in his precious words, wanting to remember the moment of deconstructing old stereotypes and fears of "the other," praying to be able to convey to others the hopeful sensation I felt as we walked together and spoke of peace.

We stood on the Capitol steps—twelve Egyptian imams and eight caravan members, and received a blessing from the Reverend Patrick Conroy, chaplain of the House of Representatives. Paul Monteiro, of the White House Office of Faith-Based and Neighborhood Partnerships, offered President Obama's blessing in words that revealed a deep understanding of our purpose. Monteiro is a youthful citizen of the world, conveying his blessing on our work.

Rabbi Gerry sounded the *shofar* (ram's horn), expressing a Jewish call to justice and righteousness, the sacred sound echoing across the Capitol plaza. We showed Paul Monteiro the large scroll on which people we had met had already begun to write their own heartfelt prayers for peace. We knew that the scroll would soon be filled with moving prayers, both liturgical and personal, from young and old, from people of many religions and in many languages. Gerry and Yahya asked to meet with the President upon their return to share the precious peace scroll with him.

Before leaving DC and setting out on our way, I had asked that we stop for a few moments of prayer at the newly opened Martin Luther King National Memorial. We spoke words from Jewish, Christian, and Muslim traditions, but the deepest inspiration for our journey came from the Reverend King's own words, inscribed on dramatic black slabs of granite arranged along the length of the Memorial: "Darkness cannot drive out darkness, only light can do that. Hate cannot drive out hate, only love can do that." "If we are to have peace on earth, our loyalties must become ecumenical rather than sectional. Our loyalties must transcend our race, our tribe, our class, and our nation; and this means we must develop a world perspective." "Injustice anywhere is a threat to justice everywhere. We are caught in an inescapable network of mutuality, tied in a single garment of destiny. Whatever affects one directly, affects all indirectly." "We shall overcome, because the arc of the moral universe is long, but it bends towards justice."[12]

---

[12] Wikipedia article on Martin Luther King National Memorial, http://en.wikipedia.org.

It seemed that Dr. King was blessing us on our journey, for we too, in our own way, sought to bring light to the darkness of prejudice, to bring love to places where hate still lives in the hearts of Americans. We too longed to develop a global perspective, deeply honoring our own religious uniqueness, but also widening our gaze to consider the well-being of all. We too were on a journey to confront the injustice of judging all members of a religious community by the actions of a few, working every day to inspire a recommitment to equal opportunity for all. King's prophetic words fortified us as we went on our way.

Honoring Every Life

Therefore the human race was created from a single person, to teach that one who destroys a single soul[13] is considered by Scripture as if he [or she] had destroyed an entire world; and whoever saves one soul is considered by Scripture as if he [or she] had saved an entire world. And for the sake of peace among people, that one should not say to his or her fellow, "My parent is greater than yours. . . ." And to declare the greatness of the Holy One, blessed be God, for a human artisan stamps out many coins with one model, and they are all alike, but the King, the King of kings, the Holy One, blessed be God, stamped each person with the seal of Adam, and not one of them is like his [or her] fellow. Therefore each and every one is obliged to say, "For my sake the world was created." And lest you say, "What do we need with this trouble?" Has it not already been said, "He being a witness, whether he has seen or known, if he does not utter it, then he will bear his sin" (Lev. 5:1).[14]

---

[13] Many versions of this teaching say here "of Israel," suggesting that only Jewish lives are of ultimate value. I have long been convinced that the original mishnah, rich with universalistic creation imagery, must have intended to remind us of our kinship with all of humankind. I suspect that experiences of persecution led later Jewish editors to limit the scope of the mishnah's majestic teaching. I recently learned that Professor Efraim E. Urbach has conclusively shown that "of Israel" is a later addition, not the original reading: *Tarbitz* 40 (5731): 268–84, with thanks to Professor David Golinkin for this reference.

[14] Mishnah *Sanhedrin* 4:5.

Always one of my favorite rabbinic texts, I especially love teaching this passage in the presence of Muslims. Since the first part of it also appears in the Koran, this text evokes a collective gasp of delight, one of those moments when we are reminded of the truth that Jews and Muslims are family, and that we revere sacred texts that teach shared beliefs and values.

In its original context in the Mishnah, this passage is a set of instructions given by judges to the witnesses in capital trials. The witnesses are instructed sternly about the elemental value of every human life. They are to carry out their duties with rigorous honesty, purity of heart and intention, and reverence for the weightiness of their task. Nothing less than an infinitely valuable human life hangs in the balance.

This text, beloved by Jewish teachers both ancient and modern, is applied in many contexts in which the essential principle of human dignity is evoked,[15] and I can think of no more compelling rationale for the requirement to reach out to the religious other. The mishnah offers four different aspects of the assertion that every human person is imbued with ultimate value.

1. The human race began with a single person. Once again, evoking the story of creation, the mishnah recalls that in the beginning, one human person (Adam, followed by Eve) was the whole of the human race. As such, the destruction of any single person, from the perspective of creation, is equivalent to the destruction of all of humankind. It is a radical and challenging thought experiment for us, living in a world populated by some seven billion people, to imagine that the entire human race constitutes one—and then two—people. Yet this image brilliantly highlights the boundless value of every human life. From this perspective, the destruction of any human life is an earth-shattering catastrophe, and disrespect to any one person is itself a tragedy of global proportions.

2. We all descend from a single pair of ancestors. The mishnah traces all human lineage to a single pair of parents, Adam and Eve. This image suggests

---

15   E.g., Melissa Weintraub, "*Kvod Ha-Briot:* Human Dignity in Jewish Sources, Human Degradation in American Military Custody," T'ruah: The Rabbinic Call for Human Rights (formerly Rabbis for Human Rights–North America), http://www.truah/org. Rabbis Elliot N. Dorff, Daniel S. Nevins, and Avram I. Reisner, "Homosexuality, Human Dignity and Halakhah: A Combined Responsum for The Committee on Jewish Law and Standards," Rabbinical Assembly, http://www.rabbinicalassembly.org.

both an intimate kinship tie and complete equality of value among all human beings. The fact that we all descend from the same pair of parents means that we are literally members of the same family, back to the very beginning of time. Further, the fact of common lineage equalizes. No human being can claim descent more worthy than another's; no person can claim superiority to another by virtue of noble ancestry. We are all made of the same stuff, all the same at our core.

3. The miracle of human diversity. The mishnah lauds the Creator's wondrous act of creating the entire human race in the image of God. Unlike the human craftsman, whose copies of a single image are identical, each human person created in the image is inimitable and inestimably valuable. Every human person shares the seal of the first human being, sharing the characteristics that make us human, yet each of us is distinctive and irreplaceable.

Here again we find the compelling theology of diversity that arises from creation imagery. Contemplating creation, we marvel at the beauty and wonder of all things, including—perhaps especially—their diversity and variety. Although we may prefer one variety of flower to another or one color to another, we easily recognize the magnificence of a garden containing many different species. The human heart naturally rejoices at the sight of many diverse species of flora and fauna, quickening at the beauty and range of creations in our world. So, too, the creation image suggests that human diversity is not a mistake of creation, but an essential aspect of its beauty.

The marvelous act of creation of humankind is a tribute to the Creator but also an indication of the incalculable worth of every person. Since each of us comes from the stock of Adam, we carry within us the DNA of the entire human race. The world was created for us, for all human beings throughout time. We are exhorted to know our own identity as the handiwork of the Holy One, Creator of heaven and earth, the master Designer of all. The same is true of every member of the human family, without exception.

4. Why bother? The instructions to the witnesses conclude with a penetrating challenge to human nature. The question, "Why do we need this trouble?" originally addressed the fear, apathy, or laziness that might tempt witnesses to a crime to evade their responsibility to testify. The mishnah insists that sharing what one knows with the court for the sake of justice is a basic obligation of membership in society.

But we may apply the same question to the broader implications of this majestic sacred text. Why bother cultivating awareness of the infinite worth of every human life? Developing such consciousness is a lot of work, and acting on its implications even more so. To treat every person we meet as one entitled to the reverence due to the Creator imposes great demands on us. Couldn't we just forget, and succumb to the "natural" tendency to judge rather than extol the diversity of the human family?

The mishnah exhorts that maintaining such high standards of human dignity is a basic existential responsibility. The very nature of our existence mandates that we recognize the kinship and ultimate worth of all human beings, created just as we are, matchless and boundlessly precious. To fail to do so is to violate the very intention underlying our creation, and dishonor the One who brought us to life.

As we all know, there are times when primal instincts lead us to violate these deepest human principles that lie at the heart of all interpersonal and intergroup relations. When the thinking mind is engaged, these immortal images and concepts have the power to help us override our baser instincts. Particularly in times of conflict and threat, we may need repeated reminders from holy texts and sacred community to return us to the commitments we hold most dear.

Why Interfaith?

Each time the caravan rolled into another town and addressed another audience, I was asked to articulate the basis for positive interreligious engagement from within Jewish law and theology. Among the many principles I could have reached for in the corpus of Jewish text, three central images continued to arise for me: (1) the teaching that all human beings are created in the image of God, (2) the Torah's relentless reminder to defend the needs of the stranger, remembering our own experience as a persecuted minority in Egypt, and (3) the pursuit of peace as a central preoccupation of Jewish prayer and theology.

Created in the Image of God

This teaching has always served as a foundational principle in Jewish law and theology, providing the basis for Judaism's rigorous teachings on human dignity. Teaching this concept in an interreligious context, I began to read these Jewish texts with a Koranic parallel in mind.

> To each of you we prescribed a law and a method. Had Allah willed, God would have made you one nation [united in religion], but [God intended] to test you in what God has given you; so race to [all that is] good. To Allah is your return all together, and God will [then] inform you concerning that over which you used to differ.[16]

That is to say, had the Creator of the Universe wanted for all human beings to be alike, God could certainly have made it so. It was God's desire to create infinite varieties of flora and fauna for the sheer beauty of it and, dare we say, for our enjoyment.

So, too, the Universe has given us diverse peoples, religions, ethnicities, and beliefs. This is not a terrible flaw of creation, as if God really should have created everyone to look and think like ourselves. Diversity is not a cosmic deficit to be corrected, not a problem to be solved. Rather it is only because our brains' ancient instincts associate difference with threat that we are prevented from responding to human diversity in the same way that we appreciate a garden—with curiosity, wonder, and gratitude.

You Know the Soul of the Stranger

The second foundational Jewish teaching that must move us to positive interreligious engagement is the memory of Israelite slavery in Egypt. The Torah teaches no less than thirty-six times (more than any other single imperative) that the Jewish people is to champion the needs of the "stranger, the orphan and the widow." The Torah tells us this again and again, knowing that we will forget, evade, and subvert this teaching. "Do not wrong or oppress a stranger, for you were strangers in the land of Egypt" (Exod. 22:20–23). "Do not oppress a stranger, for you know the soul of the stranger, having yourselves been strangers in the land of

---

[16] Koran 5:48.

Egypt" (Exod. 23:9). "God upholds the cause of the orphan and the widow, and loves the stranger, providing him/her with food and clothing. You too must love the stranger, for you were strangers in the land of Egypt" (Deut. 10:18–19). "You shall not subvert the rights of the stranger, the orphan; you shall not take a widow's garment in pawn. Remember that you were a slave in Egypt and that Adonai your God redeemed you from there; therefore do I enjoin you to observe this commandment." (Deut. 24:17–18).

At the very heart of Jewish self-understanding is the memory that we were formed as a people in the cauldron of slavery and in our redemption from a land of totalitarianism, where we suffered persecution and dehumanization. This story could have been told and carried through the ages with a very different moral conclusion. The message could well have been, "Thou shalt never again allow yourselves to be oppressed. Always be strong so that you can defeat the tyrant who seeks to destroy you." Nowhere does the Torah draw this conclusion from the Exodus story. Quite the opposite, as in the stunning verse, "Do not hate the Egyptian, for you were a stranger in his land" (Deut. 23:8). We are absolutely not taught to hate the Egyptian who enslaved us. Rather, we are enjoined to draw on our own memory of oppression for the benefit of all peoples.

The Torah insists that the lesson to be learned from this paradigmatic historical experience is that the people of Israel is always to stand with and work for those on the margins—for the poor, the vulnerable, the marginalized, and the stranger. Perhaps the Torah knew that we would at times become embittered by traumatic history and grow weary of standing in the moral vanguard for all peoples, with energy only for our own self-protection. Again and again comes the clarion call, *not* "Fear the stranger, for he may hurt you," but "Love the stranger."

We now know why these commands needed to be repeated so relentlessly. Instinctively, the human spirit narrows in the face of danger and hurt, allowing us to forget even our deepest beliefs and commitments. When we are sick, we have energy only for our own pain. When we feel threatened, attention becomes constricted, and we focus more narrowly on personal concerns. We need to be reminded again and again that acts of loving-kindness and justice are the best way—if not the only way—to preserve that which is most precious to us.

Seek Peace and Pursue It

For me, the most powerful impetus to interreligious engagement is the Jewish imperative to seek and pursue peace. Multiple prayers for peace punctuate and conclude every prayer service. Rabbinic literature abounds in odes to peace, as if the very word opens floodgates of religious passion. It is said that "Peace" is among the many names of God, and that peace is the essential blessing from which all other blessings flow. Undoubtedly, the pursuit of peace is a central preoccupation in the Jewish imagination and a central imperative in Jewish life. The command to "seek peace and pursue it" (Ps. 34:15) has become the central imperative of my life.

In my own journey, interreligious work has become a powerful way to respond to the imperative of peacebuilding. As an American rabbi, living in a diverse metropolitan area in a time in which religious intolerance is a potent reality, I have ample opportunities to serve the larger cause of peace by working to create relationship and increase understanding among people of different religions. Lacking the means to effect international peacemaking through political and diplomatic channels, it is my work to help build peace right where I live, teaching people how to calm fear of the other in order to bridge isolating boundaries between communities. By serving the cause of peace right where I live, I support the reality of peace everywhere.

Fellow Travelers

At the end of the first day of our caravan journey, we spoke to a small group in the majestic chapel at Duke University in Durham, North Carolina. Father Adam Bunnell had changed his civilian clothes to don the floor-length brown habit, simple belt, and sandals of the Franciscan order. He spoke reverently of the life of Saint Francis of Assisi who, in the midst of the violence and hatred of the thirteenth century, took off his opulent clothes and put on the peasant's habit to live among the people and to serve them.

At first, Adam told us, Saint Francis thought that the only way to encounter Islam was to convert its followers. In fact, he set out on the violent journey of the crusaders to Egypt. But in the course of the journey, he crossed the battle lines to engage the Sultan and embraced him humbly. The encounter transformed him, and he taught his students a new theory of interreligious dialogue. "Go and serve the people and submit, and *only if you are asked*, tell them about the faith that is in your heart."[17]

In a courageous act of public self-critique, Adam offered powerful words of remorse for Christianity's historical sins of arrogance and persecution of religious others, and urged us to emulate Francis's model of humility and genuine desire to know the other. Adam's vivid portrait of his spiritual guide touched a yearning in all of us to actively cultivate a mind and heart spacious enough to appreciate truths different from our own.

Next morning, we spoke with a group of students at Duke Divinity School. Something about this group of emerging leaders inspired us all to be especially honest and self-critical about challenges within each of our communities. Yahya taught with particular passion about the centrality of compassion in Islam. Islam, he said, teaches that God named the womb after woman,[18] suggesting that the best manifestation of divine mercy is woman. "If you want to know mercy," Yahya taught in the name of Islam, "you must know woman."

This led him to express deep pain about the abuse of his faith by Muslim extremists. He began to cry as he contemplated "the crazy imams in Afghanistan who pour acid in the faces of women who do not wear the *burqa* [the garment worn by many women in some Muslim countries, covering the entire body and the face]." In anguish, he asked, "Where is the *Rahma* [mercy]? How do we [Muslims] become a voice of compassion in the world?"

At lunchtime, we were hosted by Imam Abdullah Antepli, the Muslim chaplain at Duke University. Among friends, Abdullah speaks in quiet understatement, with gentleness and humility. Yet he could not mask his pride at hosting us for lunch at the beautiful new Muslim student activity center, the first such center at an American university.

Abdullah had been offered several different positions at prestigious American universities, but only Duke had agreed to build such a center, conveying the university's full support for vibrant Muslim student life

---

[17] Father Adam Bunnell's interpretation of chapter 16 of the nonapproved Rule of St. Francis from the year 1221 (personal communication).

[18] In Arabic, as in Hebrew, the word for "compassion" comes from the same root as the word for "womb."

on campus. Abdullah walked us out to show us the sign, visible from the street, announcing "Muslim Life at Duke." "What that means to the Muslim heart," he said, touching his heart with deep feeling. The term "Muslim heart" was new to me, but I could easily translate the phrase into my Jewish context, knowing how the Jewish *neshama* (soul) was moved and strengthened when American institutions first began to accept us as full members of American society.

He told us, however, that not everyone in Durham had been pleased by the sign. A nearby FBI office had called Abdullah to ask what kinds of activities the center sponsored. The office had received a large quantity of email suggesting that the center was an Al Qaeda recruitment center. Abdullah laughed softly at the absurdity of it. "If we were recruiting for Al Qaeda, would we really post a sign on the street?"

And so it went, from one engagement to the next, from one city to the next. Back on the bus together, there were countless moments of spontaneous prayer, hilarious exchanges of self-deprecating religious humor, strategy sessions about pedagogy, media relations, and electronic gadgetry, hugs, and loving laughter. Traveling hundreds of miles a day in a small, crowded van, we were a microcosm of the world we seek to build, in which people of different religions connect deeply with one another and join their particular religious commitments to work together for justice and peace.

Come Shabbat, at the Temple in Atlanta, after a warm and joyful evening service, our friend Imam Yahya Hendi rose to deliver the sermon. He looked around the sanctuary, where two hundred and fifty Jews greeted him with an air of welcome and expectation. Deeply moved to be received so warmly, as a Palestinian American imam addressing a Jewish congregation, he said tearfully, "My sisters and my brothers," he said, "I love you all. We are one family."

Sprinkling his sermon with references to Jewish liturgy, he spoke of the unity of all people. "*Shema Yisrael*," he said, "Hear O Israel," referencing the most beloved prayer in all of Jewish liturgy, "*Adonai Eloheinu, Adonai Echad*," "The Lord our God, the Lord is One." "We are one," he asserted: "Jews and Muslims, Christians, Hindus and Buddhists, Israelis and Palestinians, Muslims and Westerners, old and young, black, brown, white, red, and yellow. All of us come from dust and to dust we will return. We are in this predicament of life together. We have hurt one another in the past.

Let us not allow the bitterness of yesterday to dictate the possibilities of tomorrow. We must build a better world together."

His sermon was greeted by a resounding ovation, rounds of hugs and many tears. The imam had won the hearts of this community of Jews, and the synagogue was luminous with joy.

On Saturday evening, as darkness fell, my colleagues and I headed for Al Farooq, the largest mosque in Atlanta. It was a magnificent house of worship, the most beautiful Islamic center I had ever seen in this country. The deep, reverent silence of the prayer hall moved me deeply, and the audience of one hundred men and women listened with rapt attention, hushed by the momentousness of the occasion. We gave our presentation, "From Fear to Faith: Advancing Religious Pluralism," and were greeted with fervent applause, a round of encouraging, thoughtful questions, and much engaged conversation after the formal session ended.

My colleagues then headed into Tennessee, where a debate raged about enacting "anti-shariah" legislation, prohibiting Muslims from following their own religious law, just as many Jews turn to *halacha* (Jewish law) to govern their religious lives. This was sure to be a challenging and fascinating leg of the trip, but it was time for me to go home to attend to other obligations.

It was bittersweet to leave my treasured friends and our sacred mission of peace education, after many precious hours of love, laughter, and prayer together. We had lived together for many days, on and off the van, creating for ourselves and modeling for others a world in which difference is not only tolerated but embraced and celebrated. Each of us had brought our whole self to the experience, including fierce loyalty to our own religious traditions, openness to exploring areas of strong disagreement, and delight in our common commitments. Most powerfully, we had been nourished by our shared mission to demonstrate to others the practice of loving the religious other as ourselves. Even in those moments when disagreement demanded difficult conversation, we moved through it without compromising our love for one another

It had been a joy and a privilege to participate. We had stimulated those we met along the way to commit to interreligious work in their own communities, and we had elicited many beautiful prayers for peace in many different languages on a sacred scroll that we took with us as we went on our way. I had tasted the rich blessing of living as one family across religious lines. I wish everyone could have such a blessed experience.

A Reluctant Prophet

The biblical Jonah is such a strange character that it is challenging to think of him as a prophet. Jonah is called by God to exhort the people of Nineveh to repent of their sinful ways. Jonah's immediate reaction is to jump on a boat, as if to flee from God. In addition to the theological absurdity of it, he also completely disregards the safety of all those on the ship with him, exposing them to God's displeasure with him.

He eventually accedes to God's command. After just one day of Jonah's preaching in the streets of Nineveh, all the inhabitants of the city, "from the greatest of them to the least" (Jon. 3–5), immediately enter into a profound process of repentance. This would be a wonderfully happy ending from God's perspective, but Jonah, for his part, is extremely angry. "Please, God, wasn't this what I said when still in my own land? This is why I fled to Tarshish, because I knew that You are a gracious God, compassionate, long-suffering, and abundant in kindness, repenting of evil. Now, O God, please take my life from me, for I would rather die than live" (Jon. 4:2–3). The text tells us that God is puzzled over Jonah's anger, and so, as readers of the text, are we.

Why did Jonah object so strongly to the idea that God would have mercy on a repentant people? I have often read the text to mean that Jonah's protest was based on his own ego needs. He knew that if he urged the people to repent and they did so, God would forgive them, thus invalidating Jonah's prophecies of doom. Simply put, Jonah was afraid that God's act of forgiveness would make him look foolish. In the ambiguous ending of the book, God seems to rail at Jonah's small-mindedness, "Should I not have mercy on Nineveh, that great city of twelve thousand people?" (Jon. 4:11).

But there is another possible explanation for Jonah's remarkable objection to God's act of compassion. Whereas most Biblical prophets of doom were assigned to implore the Israelites to repent, Jonah was sent to the capital of Assyria, the enemy of the Israelites. Jonah knew that God was sending him to Nineveh in the hopes that the people of the city would change their ways and God would grant them mercy.

Perhaps on behalf of his own people, Jonah would have been willing to risk harm to his own reputation, but not on behalf of "the other," to whom he could not imagine extending compassion. God's final challenge to Jonah can thus be understood to mean, "Do you think I should be compassionate only with the Israelites? The people of Nineveh are also the work of my hands!" Jonah's position seems absurd according to this interpretation as well. How could anyone possibly think that, from the perspective of the Creator of the universe, one group of people is more valued than any other?

We should pause a moment before too quickly condemning Jonah's ethnocentrism. How often do we fail to respond with empathy to people of different religions, nationalities, or even ideologies? How often, if the truth of our minds be known, do we actually wish ill for "the other side"? Even if we do not actively rejoice at their failures or their suffering, how often do we deeply call to mind the fact that they, too, are works of the divine hand?

Surely, it is natural, even necessary, to attend first to the needs of our own families, and by extension, our own community. In Hillel's immortal words, "If I am not for myself, who will be for me?"[19] For the Jewish people, history has borne out this truism with painful regularity, so it is understandable that the Jewish people has needed to elevate this truth to the level of a sacred command.

But, of course, Hillel's wisdom does not stop there. "If I am for myself alone, what am I?"[20] I am one of many Jewish leaders of this generation who have come to believe that isolationism and a predominant focus on survival issues no longer serve the Jewish people. Although Jews have been represented disproportionally in many social justice movements, one still finds in many Jews of my generation and older an assumption that we can never fully trust non-Jews. We know in theory that we owe them human caring, but our habitual responses at times still keep us from fully letting the other into our hearts.

Embracing the religious other requires stepping beyond our long-rehearsed history of victimization (as true as it may be) and instinctive self-protectiveness. It does not require us to weaken our identity or passion

---

[19] Mishnah *Avot* 1:13.

[20] Ibid.

as Jews or to stand passively in the face of real danger to our people. But it does ask us to let go of outmoded habits of suspicion of the other. It requires us to stretch, to question our own fears and assumptions, and to extend curiosity and compassion to those we have come to believe may be threatening to us. It calls us to consider inviting the religious other into our lives as a friend.

In this chapter, we have seen how interreligious engagement can function as a sacred laboratory for the work of grassroots, person-to-person relationship-building across religious lines. In interfaith work, one sees the primal fear of difference manifesting as avoidance, suspicion, stereotyping, and discrimination against religious groups. One also regularly sees how readily the development of personal relationships dissolves misinformation and alarming generalizations about other communities, so that the religious other becomes a treasured conversation partner and friend.

In interreligious work, countless people around the world practice the ability to calm apprehension and suspicion in order to consider religious others as real, lovable human beings. Once the brain's warning systems cease scanning for danger, the relationships are guided by the reflective mind. Then these encounters can be a place to explore both human commonalities and fascinating differences among religious groups. Interreligious encounter becomes a tool for building stronger communities and for contributing to peacebuilding efforts in conflict regions around the world.

3

Peace among Jews

Rabbi Abba said in the name of Sh'mu'el: For three years
the House of Shammai and the House of Hillel debated [a
matter of ritual purity]. These said, "The law is according
to our position," and these said, "The law is according
to our position." A divine voice came and said, "These
and these are the words of the living God, and the law is
according to the House of Hillel." But if these and these
are both the words of the living God, why was the law
set according to the House of Hillel? Because they [the
House of Hillel] were gentle and humble and they taught
both their own words and the words of the House of
Shammai. And not only this, but they taught the words
of the House of Shammai before their own.

— *BT Eruvin 13b*

The foundational sacred texts of Judaism are filled with records
of disagreements. The Mishnah, the Talmud, and the books of
midrashic exploration of biblical texts regularly record multiple
responses to any question and diverse understandings of earlier
texts, including the name of the teacher who offered each view.
Many explanations have been offered as to why the literature is
constructed in this way. Is it to model respect for all the scholars
who have offered their teachings? To preserve multiple views in

case one that is rejected in one generation becomes essential at a later time? To demonstrate that in the world of ideas, as in the natural world, diversity is an intentional gift from the Creator? Or perhaps to anticipate what an argumentative people the Jews will become?

A Tradition of Debate

Whatever the reason, virtually every page of these ancient texts contains disagreements, often between specific pairs of rabbis. In particular, Hillel and Shammai were known to differ with each other about almost every matter that arose in the academy, and the disputes continued with their intellectual descendants, the "House of Hillel" and the "House of Shammai." (In Jerusalem "Hillel Street" and "Shammai Street" are parallel. In a city planner's joke for those with knowledge of rabbinic literature, they never meet.)

This particular text is beloved by many, a classic rabbinic affirmation of the reality of a multiplicity of truths in God's world. In order to understand the text's often quoted "punch line," however, it is essential to grasp that this was no trivial difference between the House of Shammai and the House of Hillel. The two schools were engaged in a years-long, passionate debate about a matter of Jewish law that was of great importance both theoretically and practically. The text's account of the debate invites us to imagine both interpretive schools holding their positions forcefully and urgently. Hence the surprise of the divine voice suddenly breaking into the human argument to declare that both sides of the argument are correct, saying, "These and these are the words of the living God."

But for our purposes, the final part of the text is even more important. The Talmud asks, if both sides of the debate are equally correct in their content and logic, why is the law according to the House of Hillel? On what basis is one side's view chosen if the other side's reasoning is equally valid? The startling answer is that the law is set according to the House of Hillel in this matter (and presumably, in many other cases in which these schools' viewpoints diverge) not because of superior analysis, but based on the House of Hillel's tone and style of communication, their way of carrying themselves in the midst of conflict.

The text tells us that the students of the House of Hillel, like their mentor, Hillel, were "gentle and humble" in their conduct, even as they engaged in debate with their colleagues. Not only did they articulate their own view gently and respectfully, in order not to offend or demean those on the other side, but they affirmatively taught both their own view and the view they rejected, to communicate that both views contained an aspect of truth. Not only this, but when they taught the two perspectives on the issue at hand, they taught their opponents' position first, to explicitly acknowledge its value and to give honor to those who thought that way. Only after teaching their opponents' view—with understanding and appreciation—did they proceed to explain why their own opinion was more compelling.

Imagine rhetorical exchanges in the contemporary news media being conducted in this way, in accord with basic Jewish (and humanistic) values of respect and dignity due to all people. Sadly, it's virtually impossible to imagine cable news commentators, or even many of our own favorite political leaders, conducting themselves in this way. This would be a radically different social world than the one in which we live. Even more seriously, it may be just as difficult to envision political discussions[1] at our own family dinner table being conducted with this exquisite practice of giving honor to those holding views at odds with our own.

It seems clear to me that there are relatively few people to whom this way of conducting oneself in the midst of contentious conflict comes naturally. I don't believe that all of Hillel's students naturally defied the human tendency to escalate, polarize, and dehumanize around conflict. Hillel must have taught his students that communicating respect to their colleagues was always more important than winning the argument. Nothing was more important than relating to others with the kindness and honor naturally due to every human being.

For most people, this does not happen unless we work at it diligently, in a lifelong spiritual practice of stretching to see the human dignity, or the image of God, in one's conversation partner, no matter how heated

---

[1] The root meaning of the word "discuss" is from the Latin *discutere:* "to shake, strike asunder, or break up" (Online Etymology Dictionary, http://www.etymonline.com). Is this what we want to be doing to our families, our community, and our society when we have "discussions"?

the argument gets. I know a few people who make it look easy, but that's only because they have worked at it, cultivating the capacity to respond with reverence to another human being even if that person represents the "other side" of a rhetorical chasm.

Thus Hillel and Shammai stand as an ancient and eternal example of the possibility of engaging in vibrant, honest disagreement about highly important matters with those with whom we passionately disagree. Many Jewish leaders have suggested that the tradition of Talmudic debate is evidence of the fact that we are an innately argumentative people, doomed to perpetuate patterns of contentious communication even when these patterns harm the fabric of community. I disagree. Rather, the Talmud models on virtually every page the art of living with difference and conducting passionate debate on vital issues without violating the most basic Jewish and humanistic values of dignity, respect, and reverence for all of God's creatures.

In this chapter I turn my attention from interfaith engagement to one example of entrenched intracommunal conflict. At first, one would think that the work of interreligious dialogue, particularly in our age of rampant prejudice and violence across faith lines, would be particularly difficult. Most of my colleagues, however, agree that interreligious dialogue frequently reveals far deeper chasms of disagreement within religious communities. When I tell a Christian colleague that intra-Jewish dialogue is more difficult than our interfaith work, this generally brings a laugh, followed by a sober smile of recognition. Passionate discord within a community is often experienced as more painful and more dangerous than disagreement with the religious other.

Why is this so? I have come to believe that intracommunal conflict is particularly difficult precisely because of the hardwired reactions we bring to experiences of sameness and otherness. When we discover that we strongly disagree with the religious (or political or ideological) other, this may be disturbing but not all that surprising. There is no shock in learning that our worldviews are very different; this matches our expectation.

But when we discern that someone "within the family" holds a view very different from our own, our circuits are crossed. A spike of outrage easily arises in us, as if to say, "You're supposed to be like me! How could you possibly think that?" Just yesterday, I was startled to learn that a close

Muslim colleague and friend holds a political view quite different from my own. I teased, only partly in jest, "I thought you were my friend!" In more serious situations, this shocking difference of view may give rise to accusations of betrayal of the group.

This instinct of shock at recognizing divergence of viewpoint with someone whom I consider to be "like me," by virtue of one or another marker of identity, doubtless comes from the same ancient part of the brain that is alarmed by the appearance of "the other." How could you possibly think that way? I thought you were "one of us."

This all sounds lighthearted, but the experience of it is quite distressing. As I write these words, Israel and Hamas are once again shooting bombs at one another. I am dismayed but no longer as surprised as I once was that ferocious blog posts, emails, and facebook postings dart around Jewish media and cyberspace, with words sharpened into weaponry. Encountering profound difference with "one of our own" is almost too painful to bear.

In the preceding chapter, I interpreted the sense of existential threat we experience in response to the religious other as a matter of primal fear of difference. That fear may express itself similarly within religious (or communal, ethnic, or national) groups, when the one presumed to be "like me" turns out to be "other." In addition, intracommunal conflict threatens one's core sense of identity. If another from my own group believes differently than I do, then who am I? Who is this group around which I construct my life? If I am alienated from members of my own group, then where do I stand in the world?

Such deeply destabilizing identity questions awaken the same neurological warning bells we may feel when encountering external difference, only the surprise is more primal and hence more frightening. Thus the conflict can easily explode in heartrending and destructive ways.

In this chapter, I explore one example of intractable intracommunal conflict, the one I know best, concerning discussions of Israel within the American Jewish community. It is but one example of how communities and societies navigate the turbulent waters of strong religious and ideological diversity in their midst. This example will include many negative illustrations of how polarized communication around contentious issues can damage the fabric of relationship in communities. It will also point the way toward a wiser and more fruitful way of living with difference.

A Synagogue at War

When violence erupted in Israel and the West Bank in the fall of 2000, my congregational home was torn with conflict. I was not the rabbi of the synagogue, but, as one of many devoted members, it was my spiritual home. It was a no-nonsense and low-ego place, with large numbers of Jews conversant in Jewish prayer and text, and many opportunities to study and pray together with fervor. A real community in the best sense of the word, it was a place where people truly cared for one another. We showed up for one another's bar and bat mitzvah celebrations and funerals and brought meals to homes that had just welcomed a new baby or lost a loved one. The rabbi, Shelly Lewis, was an extraordinary spiritual leader—loving, humble, learned, and authentic. I loved him and loved this place, where I had lived through many important years of my life and where I had raised my daughter.

I watched with horror as a verbal firestorm erupted within the congregation when, during the Second Intifada, Palestinians launched attacks on Israeli civilians, and Israel retaliated with powerful military interventions. All of us were wracked with pain, following the news obsessively, bracing ourselves for reports of the next attack on our friends and family in Israel. Some of us agonized about whether Israel's military responses, however understandable, contributed to the cycle of violence in harmful ways.

Somehow, in the midst of the pain we all felt, we turned on each other. The congregation's new electronic mailing list became a battleground, as community members vented their anguish about violence in Israel by waging rhetorical war on one another. The listserv was young at the time, and we had not yet learned how divisive email communication could be when community members had the ability to attack one another's logic and loyalty with quick, unreflective strokes of the "send" key.

Harsh words were spoken on both the right and the left. Community members holding right-of-center viewpoints reacted with fury at any suggestion of Israel being anything but innocent victim, engaging in the most morally justified acts of self-defense. Left-leaning congregants, aware of the imbalance of military and economic power between Israel and the Palestinians, were critical of what they considered to be Israel's disproportionate use of power in responding to attacks. The activity on the list came to be increasingly dominated by extreme views, expressed with harsh disregard for the possibility that any sane and devoted Jew could think differently.

The congregational leadership intervened, reorganizing the email list to protect middle-of-the-road congregants from the disturbing spectacle of belligerent and accusatory messages. Still, the exchanges had torn the social fabric of the synagogue, ending some relationships and straining others. People on both sides felt silenced and unsafe to discuss this most important of issues except with those with whom they were already in agreement. The echo chambers began to operate, as each side consumed and shared only those sources of information that confirmed their own certainties, not those that might raise important questions, shed light on unsettled matters, or further understanding among differing perspectives.

This experience was formative for me, launching me into a years-long exploration of the distorted communication process by which words and logic were used as weapons within the Jewish community, doing great harm to people, relationships, and the fabric of the community itself. I wracked my brain about how anyone—left, right, or center—could think that these confrontational exchanges could contribute to Israel's well-being. I connected with colleagues around the country who, like me, were anguished by the violence in Israel and the Palestinian territories and also sensed the urgency to change "the Israel conversation" in the Jewish community before further damage would be done. I ached to learn what caused these destructive communication patterns and what could transform them.

Two Jews, Three Opinions

The day I began work on this chapter, the columnist Bradley Burston published the following words in Israel's liberal Haaretz newspaper:

> We're a people that can appreciate nasty, us Jews. Chalk it up to survivor guilt or oppressor guilt, put it down to a legacy of Talmudic and tribal disputation, to a legacy of abuse, or to a tradition of stand-up, the evidence is clear: Two Jews, Three Zingers—barbed, caustic, and intentionally so.[2]

---

[2] Bradley Burston, "At Last, 'Occupation Zionists' and Israel-loathing U.S.

The startling phrase, "Two Jews, Three Zingers," is funny and poignant because the phrase, "Two Jews, Three Opinions," is so often used to describe Jewish conversational style.

The phrase, "Two Jews, Three Opinions," gets a laugh whenever I use it. The belief that Jewish dinner tables are naturally argumentative is held with a certain sheepish pride. (Everyone says, "We're Jews. That's how we talk," with a wink and a shrug of the shoulders.) Perhaps this is evidence of linguist Deborah Tannen's "aha factor,"[3] meaning that members of a culture instantly recognize a description of their own communication patterns, especially those regarded disapprovingly by the surrounding culture.

In her fascinating study of "New York Jewish Conversational Style,"[4] Tannen enumerates characteristic features of "New York Jewish" speech (though she acknowledges that some of these apply to non-Jewish New Yorkers, to Jews not from New York, to American blacks, and to people throughout the Middle East!).[5] These include, among others, "persistence (if a new topic is not immediately picked up, reintroduce it, repeatedly if necessary),"[6] rapid pacing of speech, swift turn-taking (no pauses between speakers), and what she calls, "cooperative overlap and participatory listenership" (a pattern of starting one's own comment before the other has finished theirs, not viewed as rudeness but as active engagement).[7]

Linguist Deborah Schiffrin offers a similar analysis of speech patterns of American Jews with Ashkenazic (Eastern European) background, in which she suggests that argument among Jews is a "vehicle of sociability."[8] She

---

Jews Can Agree," *Haaretz*, November 29, 2011, http://www.haaretz.com.

[3] Deborah Tannen, "New York Jewish Conversational Style," *International Journal of the Sociology of Language* 30 (1981): 146.

[4] Ibid., 133–49.

[5] Ibid., 147.

[6] Ibid., 137.

[7] Ibid. See also her articles, "Don't Just Sit There—Interrupt! Pacing and Pausing in Conversational Style," 75, no. 4 (2000): 393–95, and "When Is an Overlap Not an Interruption: One Component of Conversational Style," in Robert J. Di Pietro, William Frawley, and Alfred Wedel, ed. (Newark: University of Delaware Press, 1983), 119–29.

[8] Deborah Schiffrin, "Jewish Argument as Sociability," *Language in Society* 13, no. 3 (1984): 332.

asserts that friendly, non-antagonistic conversation among Jews is frequently expressed in the form and cadence of argument.[9] The challenging tone of the conversation, she says, is playful and paradoxical, "designed to show that the interactants' relationship is close enough to withstand what would be considered by outsiders to be verbal assaults."[10] The "sociable argument" is based on a "taken-for-granted level of intimacy of the relationship."[11]

Anecdotally speaking, American Jews do not need to study linguistic research to confirm that Jews love to argue. In fact, many assume that this trait is traceable to the very beginnings of our national history, making us a congenitally contentious people.

There are some good reasons for this view. After all, our founding leaders, Abraham and Moses, argued with God on multiple occasions. Our very name as a people, *Yisrael*/Israel, identifies us as a people who wrestles with God.[12]

Further, as we have seen, the Talmud's sixty-three volumes rigorously record debates about every imaginable issue in Jewish life, including minority views as well as the opinions that became legally authoritative. As Talmudist David Kraemer puts it, "Something in the nature of traditional Jewish discourse allows (or, perhaps more accurately, *encourages*) us to disagree passionately with one another, sometimes so passionately that the fabric of our community appears in danger of unraveling."[13] The pattern continues through the ages, as the pages of the *Shulkhan Arukh*[14] record the divergent views and practices of Ashkenazic and Sephardic[15] Jews side by side.

Our people's central sacred documents undoubtedly accept, even celebrate, the coexistence of diverse views without insisting that disagree-

---

[9] Ibid., 329.

[10] Ibid., 331.

[11] Ibid.

[12] "Your name will no longer be 'Jacob' but 'Israel,' for you have struggled with beings divine and human and prevailed" (Gen. 32:39).

[13] David Kraemer, "Disputes That Unite," *Sh'ma: A Journal of Jewish Responsibility* 28, no. 543, (December 12, 1997): 1.

[14] *Shulkhan Arukh* (literally, "Set Table") is the most authoritative code of Jewish law, written by Rabbi Joseph Caro, sixteenth century.

[15] Jews with family roots on the Iberian Peninsula and later, after the expulsion of Jews from Spain, the Middle East and North Africa.

ments be resolved. The Talmud sometimes declares after an inconclusive debate, "*Teiku*," literally meaning, "let it stand," colloquially understood to be an acronym signifying, "Elijah the Prophet will settle questions and difficulties."[16] That is to say, in this world the matter will remain unresolved. Only in some messianic future time will such arguments be settled. Rabbi Barry L. Schwartz puts it succinctly: "Judaism not only maintains a great respect for debate; one could readily argue that debate is central to its religious expression."[17] Rabbi Daniel Roth, of the Pardes Center for Judaism and Conflict Resolution in Jerusalem, teaches that the medium of the Talmud is one of its core messages: the necessity of understanding divergent views, even on the most important of issues, and the essential need to live wisely in the presence of difference and discord.[18]

I have long been skeptical of the widely held view that the tradition of Talmudic debate has written a strident conversational style into our collective DNA, such that this communication pattern is both normative and unalterable. After all, relatively few contemporary American Jews have intimate knowledge of Talmudic discourse, such that its cadences and rhetorical styles would define their everyday speech. Is it really plausible that the conflict-tolerant nature of ancient Jewish scholarly texts has produced an irreversibly antagonistic speaking style for all Jews throughout time?

To my surprise, the Israeli communication scholars Shoshana Blum-Kulka, Menahem Blondheim, and Gonen Hacohen, make this theory more compelling by suggesting that it is not only the dispute-filled character of the ancient texts, but the living tradition of argumentative speech among students of Jewish texts throughout history, that reinforces this style of speech among all kinds of Jews.[19]

---

[16] Rabbi Judith Abrams, "*Teiku*: Seeing All Sides of an Issue," *Makom: A Place for the Spiritually Searching, A School for Adult Talmud Study*, http://www.maqom.com.

[17] Rabbi Barry L. Schwartz, *Judaism's Great Debates: Timeless Controversies from Abraham to Herzl* (Lincoln: University of Nebraska Press, 2012), xi.

[18] Rabbi Daniel Roth, "Talmudic Mediation: Conflicting Interpretations of the Talmud as Conflicting Needs in Society," at "Text and Texture" blog of "Tradition," http://text.rcarabbis.org.

[19] Shoshana Blum-Kulka, Menahem Blondheim, and Gonen Hacohen, "Traditions of Dispute: From Negotiations of Talmudic Texts to the Arena of Political Discourse in the Media," *Journal of Pragmatics* 34 (2002): 1569.

These scholars did a linguistic analysis of the conversations of *ḥevruta* (dyadic study) partners in contemporary Israeli Talmudic academies, in comparison to a television political talk show. The two conversations showed remarkable linguistic similarities, despite the fact that the talk show paired secular political leaders with serious political differences, whereas the Talmudic debate was the stylized "superficially adversarial format"[20] of conversation in Orthodox study halls. Perhaps, after all, because Talmudic-style debate has been kept alive through the ages in the *yeshiva* (traditional study hall), it has continued to influence even everyday secular Jewish speech.

Renowned Israeli author and journalist Amos Oz offers a different (and equally unprovable) theory about why Jewish arguments tend to be so fierce and constant. He suggests that the Jewish people, including the large branch of the family in Israel, suffers from a

> troubled conscience and our soul-searching and our self-flagellation and our alternating fits of apocalyptic rage and visions of salvation: "We shall be a light to lighten the nations even though all the nations are threatening to close in on us tomorrow or the day after and annihilate us."
>
> In what other country in the world does a noisy parliament assemble every morning at every bus-stop, in every queue, in every grocer's shop, amid the violent crush and sweaty pushing and jostling, discussing and arguing and quarreling about politics, religion, history, ideology, metaphysics, the meaning of life, the true will of God, furiously, sarcastically, while all the time the participants in the debate elbow their way to the head of the queue or rush to grab a free seat.[21]

Oz, in poignant albeit essentialist style, argues that the collective Jewish psyche gives rise to a quarrelsome conversational style because of the conflicting, but equally passionate, desires that define us as a people. If, as

---

[20] Ibid.

[21] Amos Oz, *Under This Blazing Light*, trans. Nicholas de Lange (Cambridge: Cambridge University Press, 1995), 108–9.

he suggests, we alternate between fits of fear and anger, on the one hand, and hopes for the redemption of the world, on the other, how could we possibly stop arguing? To put it differently, Oz incisively expresses how ideological discussion touches at the very core of identity in the Jewish community, so that debate of religious and political matters quickly activates the hypersensitivity of existential threat.

Whatever the historical source, it is clear that there is a recognizable cultural pattern of rapidly paced, highly interactive, and playfully contentious conversational style among many North American Jews. Nonetheless, there is a great difference between high-energy, fast-paced discussion of issues and the phenomenon of "raised voices, personal insults, and outrageous charges"[22] that have become so common in American Jewish public life, particularly in discussions about Israel[23] in recent years.

Many Jewish leaders have recently decried the increasing prevalence of ferocious public diatribes, character assassination, public shaming, and accusations of speakers' disloyalty to the community.

> In recent years, however, we have been witness to an increasing challenge in general society and in our own community. There is greater political and socio-economic polarization, the deterioration of civil interaction, decreased sense of common ground among individuals with divergent perspectives, greater tension around global issues and their impact on American society. . . .
>
> As differences devolve into uncivil acrimony, dignity is diminished and people holding diverse viewpoints cease listening to each other, it becomes more difficult if not impossible to find common ground. We are experiencing a level of incivility, particularly over issues pertaining to Israel, that has not been witnessed in recent memory. Where such polarization occurs within the Jewish community, it tears at the fabric of *Klal Yisrael* [the unity of the Jewish

---

[22] JCPA Civility Statement, website of Jewish Council for Public Affairs, http://engage.jewish publicaffairs.org.

[23] Israel is not the only subject that inspires rigorous debate in the twenty-first-century American Jewish community. Examples of other passionate contemporary debates are analyzed in Samuel G. Freedman, *Jew vs. Jew: The Struggle for the Soul of American Jewry* (New York: Simon and Schuster, 2000).

community]—our very sense of peoplehood—and is a cause for profound concern.[24]

Some observers have even compared the current toxicity of discourse within the Jewish community to what the ancient Rabbis called *sin'at ḥinam*, "baseless hatred," a pattern of acrimony among Jews that was said to be responsible for the destruction of the Second Temple in the year 70 C.E.[25]

Some suggest that there is nothing new in today's debates, that Jews have argued fiercely with one another throughout our history.[26] But this theory is flawed for two important reasons. One is that while Jewish culture may encourage an outspoken style of speech, Jewish tradition is filled with sources that mandate the highest regard for the dignity of all people, openness to learning from others, vigilance about hurtful use of language, and the value of humility.

Do not hate your kinsman in your heart. (Lev. 19:17)

Who is wise? One who learns from every person.[27]

The value of human dignity is so great that it supersedes a negative commandment of the Torah.[28]

Whoever shames his neighbor in public is like a shedder of blood.[29]

Just as it is our duty to reprove another when we are likely to be heeded, so is it our duty to withhold from reproof when we are not likely to be heard.[30]

---

[24] "Resolution on Civility," Jewish Council on Public Affairs, http://engage. jewish publicaffairs.org.

[25] BT *Yoma* 9b.

[26] There are certainly many examples of passionate debate among Jewish leaders and among groups of Jews throughout our history. A listing of ten such debates is explored in Schwartz, *Judaism's Great Debates*.

[27] Mishnah *Avot* 4:1.

[28] BT *Berachot* 19b–20a.

[29] BT *Bava Metsi'a* 58b.

[30] BT *Yevamot* 65b.

One who rebukes a colleague—whether because of a [wrong committed] against him or because of a matter between his colleague and God—should rebuke him privately. He should speak to him patiently and gently.[31]

These are but a few examples of such principles.[32] One simply cannot overemphasize the importance of the values of human dignity, love of neighbor, and createdness in the image of God in Jewish tradition. To suggest that Jews insulting one another in ideological arguments is a Jewish way to be is simply absurd.

Just as important, contrary to popular belief in the Jewish community, it turns out that uncivil debate about highly contentious issues is by no means a uniquely Jewish trait, to be enjoyed as a marker of Jewish identity. As we have seen, for many different people, by no means only Jews, an interactional pattern characterized by hostile attack and polarization is a typical feature of entrenched high-conflict disagreements. It may simply not be true that the reason we have been arguing with one another is because this is how Jews talk. There are deep human dynamics at work.

Public Conversations Project

Years into my exploration of these issues, I participated in a workshop with the Public Conversations Project, a national leader in analyzing and facilitating public conversation around highly polarized issues. The project began in late 1989 after the social worker Laura Chasin observed a ferocious televised debate between "pro-choice" and "pro-life" spokespersons, in which "the moderator either made ineffective moves to interrupt the accusations or sat helplessly, apparently unable to slow the verbal escalation or promote genuine dialogue."[33] Chasin engaged a group of fellow

---

[31] Maimonides, *Mishneh Torah, Hilchot De'ot*, 6:7.

[32] Fine overviews of Jewish principles of speech appear in David A. Teutsch, *Ethics of Speech* (Wyncote, PA: Reconstructionist Rabbinical College Press, 2006), and in Rabbi Joseph Telushkin, *Words That Hurt, Words That Heal: How to Choose Words Wisely and Well* (New York: William Morrow, 1996).

[33] Chasin and Margaret Herzig, "Creating Systemic Interventions for the Sociopolitical Arena," in *The Global Family Therapist: Integrating the Personal,*

Boston-based family therapists to explore how their expertise in addressing toxic communication patterns in couples and families might apply in the sociopolitical arena.

This connection was itself revelatory to me. As a trained clinical social worker, and a person who has lived through divorce, it was illuminating to think about the relationship between the tortured pattern of communication in troubled marriages and the toxic patterns of interaction I saw in my community. I daresay that anyone who has been in couples therapy knows the qualities of entrenched, conflict-soaked communication: "broken record" repetition of long-rehearsed fights, laundry lists of ancient past hurts, serial speeches rather than attentive listening, accusation as a primary mode of address, and a strange sense of being stuck in an obviously harmful dynamic, with no possibility of exit.

The family therapists, who later founded the Public Conversations Project,[34] called together a group of prominent national pro-life and pro-choice spokespersons for a series of private, confidential meetings. The purpose of the meetings was neither to reach consensus nor to identify common ground between divergent perspectives. Rather, the facilitators worked to change the nature of the conversation, allowing participants to relate to one another as whole human beings, with real human stories and convictions, rather than as unidimensional straw people characterized only by their position on a particular ideological issue. The project grew into a nationally renowned facilitation, training, and resource center on polarized conflict in communities and in society.

I was already quite familiar with PCP's materials, having used them in my own teaching and facilitating on the Israel issue in the Jewish community. But one of the training videos used in the workshop was transformative for me.

In the video, two animated humanoid characters appear to be engaged in a conversation that grows increasingly heated. As the level of tension rises, other figures join the primary characters on each side of the conversational divide. Then a large, menacing black arrow traverses the screen, suggesting

---

Professional, and Political, ed. Benina Berger Gould and Donna Hilleboe DeMuth (Boston: Allyn and Bacon, 1994).

[34] Public Conversations Project (henceforth PCP), http://www.publicconversations.org.

the threat of danger hovering over the conversation between the two groups. As the threatening presence grows more ominous, large groups of people join both sides of the argument and a chasm opens between them and then widens further, so that direct conversation between the two sides becomes literally impossible. With human conversation blocked, communication continues only through the media, with its own distorting spin mechanisms contributing to ever greater alienation and estrangement.

One person in the workshop called out in recognition, "That's right! That is exactly what is happening in the Catholic Church!" I was dumbstruck, for, of course, I thought that the presenter was offering an astute and knowledgeable analysis of the conversational crisis in my own community. I had thought that this set of dynamics was our own unique twenty-first-century Jewish problem, that, as many people affirm, "The Israel conversation just makes people crazy." I was stunned to learn that the all-too-familiar pattern of belligerent and dehumanizing communication was by no means unique to our community. Rather, this is how human beings react in entrenched, high-stakes religious, ideological, or political conflict, particularly in the presence of fear. The problem is as deep as the most ancient structures in our brains, but the solution is well understood.

Many-Chambered Room

> One may say to oneself, "Since the House of Shammai says 'impure' and the House of Hillel says 'pure,' one prohibits and one permits, why should I continue to learn Torah?" Therefore the Torah says, "These are the words" [Deut. 1:1]: All the words were given by a single Shepherd, one God created them, one Provider gave them, the Blessed Ruler of all creation spoke them. Therefore make your heart into a many-chambered room, and bring into it both the words of the House of Shammai and the words of the House of Hillel, both the words of those who forbid and the words of those who permit.[35]

As in our previous text, the Rabbis continue to puzzle over the example of the House of Hillel and House of Shammai, who found themselves on opposite sides of almost every issue but remained in caring relationship

---

[35] *Tosefta Sotah* 7:12.

with one another. I imagine the author of this text telling the Hillel/ Shammai story as instruction to his students, exhorting them to emulate the example of the ancient masters, perhaps too often violated in their day as well as our own.

The author of this text imagines a student growing exasperated with the constant controversies, saying, as it were, "What kind of sacred literature is this, anyway, that doesn't give me clear answers about anything?" The reply: the book of Deuteronomy begins with the words, "These are the words" (Deut. 1:1). This is God's way of telling us that *all* of the words—the opinions we agree with and those we find ridiculous or abhorrent—were created by the same Source of truth, by the same living God. "Therefore," the text exhorts true students of wisdom, "make yourself a heart of many rooms,[36] and bring into it both the words of the House of Shammai and the words of the House of Hillel, both the words of those who forbid and the words of those who permit."

I love this image of the heart of wisdom as a many-chambered organ. This metaphor suggests that Rabbinic works record debate in order to remind us repeatedly (and counterintuitively) that it is a mark of wisdom to actively work at expanding our heart's capacity to hold multiple views. "Stretch your heart," it encourages, like a wise and gentle yoga teacher, "and now stretch it some more and explore what that feels like." Expand your heart and mind so that you have space for your own worldview and also for those of many others, for they may contain an aspect of divine truth that eludes you.

I find it important that the image is not of a "melting pot" chamber, in which divergent views melt into one another. Rather, each view has its own integrity and its own truth to be explored and respected. The essence of wisdom, by this definition, is neither to grow ever more attached to our own opinions nor to jettison all views into a relativist stew. The path of wisdom is to continually enlarge our capacity for respect and understanding so that we have room in our hearts and minds for many legitimate sides of an argument.

---

[36] This translation of the Hebrew phrase is from David Hartman's book, *Heart of Many Rooms: Celebrating the Many Voices within Judaism* (Woodstock, VT: Jewish Lights Publishing, 1999).

We all know how hard this is. It is so much easier to speak and listen only within the echo chamber of our own choosing, not to "get into it" with people who hold the opposing view. But again and again the Jewish texts remind us: these, too, may be the words of the living God, and so we are commanded to listen for their wisdom.

Now, to be true to the integrity of this text, we must remember that the Rabbis did not mean to suggest that all words spoken in the world are equally true. The Rabbis of the Talmud were most certainly not relativists. These texts refer to the internal deliberations within the Rabbinic *beit midrash* (religious academy), a community in which all opinions emerged from a common religious worldview and a shared system of religious practice.

However, at this dangerously embattled time in the history of the world, I suggest that we must thoughtfully apply this spiritual practice of pluralistic debate beyond the walls of the traditional study hall. Surely, there are immoral and dangerous outlooks in the world today. But there are many beliefs that are within the realm of plausibility, just far from our own. The Talmud's doctrine of the multiplicity of truth applies to many views of well-intentioned people that we would prefer to dismiss. We must rigorously ask ourselves whether we have closed our mind to a particular argument because it is undeniably evil or because we prefer not to have our own thought system challenged. Again and again we must remind ourselves that our own understandings are necessarily limited and that perspectives far from our own may also contain a measure of divinity.

That is, to be true to the tradition's own teachings on living with disagreement, we have no choice but to engage in the regular spiritual practice of introspection. We must regularly question our own assumptions about which views are truly evil and dangerous. We must consider whether we are responding with arrogance or competitiveness to another's legitimate point of view. We must remind ourselves again and again of the finitude of our own knowledge and vision, cultivating humility in the presence of views widely divergent from our own.

Multiplicity of Truth

Can one not raise a doubt about the need to say that it all comes from the mouth of the Master of all deeds? . . . The meaning is that just as the multiplicity of creatures is from God, may God be blessed, just as all creatures are separate and some are even complete opposites, nonetheless all are from the Name, may God be blessed, Who is One, and in all of them there is a dimension of truth. Just as we say that God acts in truth, and God's work is truth. For in its own way, water is truth in the way of its creation, and fire also, which is opposite in the character of its creation, is also truth. Likewise the multiple views in themselves are all from God, blessed be God. . . .

Just as among all who exist, each has a unique dimension of truth. Nonetheless at times one of them may be found to be closer to truth than another, and it is the most complete truth. . . .

Similarly, among differences of opinion, there is one that is closer to complete truth and becomes the *Halachah* [the law]. Yet until the *Halachah* is established, that which is not the complete truth should not be dismissed before the other view. Just as among creatures that nonetheless exist and are complete and bear a dimension of truth.[37]

The Maharal further develops the now-familiar rabbinic examination of the phenomenon of intellectual debate. In a question as contemporary as it is classic, he asks how one can possibly say that all views, even those decisively rejected in a particular generation, originate in the mind of God. Once again we imagine a student in the study hall expressing incredulity at the apparent call for relativism. How can you say that all views are equally valuable, even equally divine? Don't you believe that good is good and that there is real evil in the world? What happened to our collective clarity about morality and truth?

Professor Earl Schwartz, a beloved teacher in my own community, once rose to present the Jewish view of religious pluralism on an interfaith panel. He began in a stunning way, saying, "There is only one thing I know about God. That is that God is unknowable." Like the author of our text and many other venerable Jewish teachers through the ages, Earl was teaching epistemological humility—an awareness of the limits of our knowledge of the truth.

---

[37] Rabbi Judah Loew ben Bezalel, Maharal of Prague, sixteenth-century rabbi, talmudist, moralist, and mathematician. *D'rush Al Hatorah* 42a, with thanks to Rabbi Shelly Lewis for sharing this text with me.

In my own experience, many religious liberals are comfortable with the limits of their knowledge of God (whatever they may mean by that word), but they are utterly convinced that their political or ideological view on a particular issue is the only possible position for a sane person to take. Members of my own family (myself included!), for whom strong political opinions are a multigenerational tradition, frequently rage at how right-minded people could possibly believe in the other side of the latest policy debate (i.e., the side opposed to our own). How could the other side possibly have any legitimacy? Why should I even consider what dimension of truth may reside in the opposing perspective? It is so much more satisfying to deride and denounce the other side, to once again strengthen our belief that our way of thinking is the only sane way possible.

The Maharal once again answers this question with an appeal to the imagery of creation. He asks us to consider the infinite range of creations in God's universe. Each being is unique, some radically different from one another, yet all of them are works of God's hands and therefore "true." It would be absurd to say that the lion is a true element of God's universe but that the mosquito should not exist, that roses are godly but dandelions are mistakes of nature. In all creations "there is a dimension of truth," even those that apparently negate one another, like fire and water, black and white, or male and female.

So, too, he reasons, "among all [human beings] who exist, each has a unique dimension of truth." All opinions emerged from the mind of God, just as surely as all of creation is God's handiwork. All rightly belong here, all are in some sense "true." All are part of the grand, blessed Oneness that is God. He then demurs, acknowledging that "at times one of them may be found to be closer to truth than another."

In a now familiar leap of theological reasoning, he applies the natural metaphor to the world of ideas, saying that among the various points of view debated in the rabbinic academy, a particular generation may judge one view to be "closer to the complete truth" and deem it legally binding on the community. But still, the rejected view should not be dismissed, for, like the less beloved phenomena in the created universe, this view, too, contains a measure of truth, otherwise God would not have placed it here among us.

As we have seen, the appeal to the imagery of the natural world is powerful. It seems to me that human beings must be hardwired to appreciate the natural world, finding earth, sky, mountains, clouds, and the variety of creatures to be wondrous and beautiful. We naturally gasp at the splendor of a garden containing many different shapes and colors. We would never rage at a certain color of rose, denying it a place on earth.

To appeal to that part of our mind and soul that naturally loves and reveres diversity is a kind of visualization exercise, as if to say, "Imagine how much you love the wide range of flora and fauna in the natural world. Now, try to hold onto that feeling as you contemplate people whose beliefs are very different from your own." Retraining our minds and bodies to respond in this way to the religious or ideological "other" would represent nothing less than a dramatic shift in human consciousness.

Yet some readers may respond to this text with resistance, asking whether it suggests an attitude of relativism, regarding all ideas as equally valuable. Others may jump to the ultimate challenge: "All human beings are equally good? What about Hitler? What about Osama bin Laden?"

Again, we must remember that the Maharal, and the earlier rabbis whose reflections he is developing, are talking chiefly about disputes within the relatively narrow context of the rabbinic *beit midrash* (study hall), among a group of people who share an all-encompassing worldview and community of practice. It is within this community that the premodern rabbis whose words we have studied argue for the legitimacy of all views.

Yet we must carefully consider whether these teachings may legitimately be applied more broadly in our own day. Surely, there are many viewpoints and attitudes that have no place in moral discourse, that nearly all would agree lack any dimension of truth or legitimacy. But with the blessing of an open society and a mutually connected world, we must do the rigorous work of challenging ourselves to distinguish between those ideas and persons that are truly illegitimate and those that are simply wrong from our own point of view.

Quite obviously, the answer to the question, "Does this apply to Hitler?" or "Does this apply to truly evil people?" is a resounding "no." But the truth is, very few of us interact with genocidal psychopaths during the course of our lives. These teachings invite us to broaden the range of ideas whose veracity we can at least examine, particularly ideas held by people in our own neighborhoods and communities. Hitler does not live here. To refuse to expand the horizons of our thinking because there have been and still are some truly evil people in the world is, to borrow Emil Fackenheim's phrase, to grant Hitler a posthumous victory,[38] staying permanently imprisoned in our own comfortably familiar but partial systems of meaning.

Rather, the universality of the Maharal's creation image invites us to think as expansively as we can, stretching to appreciate a wide expanse of different human beings and different thought systems in the world. Refusing to do so, according to this theology of creation, would be to reject the vast world that is God's creation and assert instead that we would rather live in a different, much more limited world, one of our own creation.

Wars of Words

The Gaza war of December 2008–January 2009, known in Israel as "Operation Cast Lead," was one of those terrible times when bloodshed in the Middle East generated rhetorical warfare among American Jews. Gazans presumably allied with Hamas or Islamic Jihad had launched several thousand rockets over the preceding years toward civilian targets in southern Israel. Although the primitive Kassam rockets caused blessedly few physical injuries, they succeeded in their goal of terrorizing the civilian population. After an extended period of restraint, in December 2008, the Israeli government declared that it would no longer tolerate the attacks on its population. Israel launched a military campaign to uproot terrorist infrastructure responsible for the rocket fire.

Israeli Jews, usually a fractious society, were remarkably united in their support of the operation, some outraged that their government had not reacted sooner with military force to protect its southern communities, living within range of Kassam rockets. Most of Israel's friends in the United States mirrored this view, arguing that no sovereign nation would endure such attacks on its civilian population without responding militarily.

Left-leaning Jews, even those deeply pained by the unimaginable trauma inflicted on citizens of southern Israel, tended to be anguished by Israel's use of overwhelming military force, resulting in between 1,100

---

[38] Emil L. Fackenheim, *The Jewish Return into History: Reflections in the Age of Auschwitz and a New Jerusalem* (New York: Schocken Books, 1978), 22.

and 1,400 civilian Palestinian deaths by the end of the war,[39] contrasted with 13 Israeli deaths over the three weeks of the war. On the left, calls for a ceasefire were desperate and urgent.

Some two weeks into the war, my interfaith colleagues and I became aware of a number of collaborative calls for a ceasefire issued by multifaith leadership coalitions in various American cities. The documents had obviously been painstakingly negotiated and edited, in an attempt to frame them in ways that could resonate for Jewish, Christian, and Muslim leaders.

Trusting my own intuition of what kind of language my centrist colleagues would need in order to consider the document, I spent a great many hours working with Christian and Muslim colleagues, hoping to serve as a bridge between centrist Jewish and non-Jewish leaders. I knew there could be no perfect document, no collective statement whose every word would work for everyone. But after insisting on many changes to the language to accommodate Jewish sensibilities, I thought I had a draft worth bringing to a national group of rabbinic colleagues for their consideration. I could not bear to imagine that an interfaith call for a ceasefire would be blocked because my rabbinic colleagues rejected it.

I was surprised and dismayed by my colleagues' response to the letter. Some responded with uncomfortable silence and some respectfully articulated their objections to aspects of the letter, but none indicated support. One rabbi, a man I have known for many years, sitting beside me at the meeting, shouted his objections to my assertion that we needed to acknowledge that there were, in fact, two narratives about this war—one Israeli and one Palestinian. "What you call 'narratives,'" he pronounced, "are for some of us deeply held religious truths." I felt I'd been assaulted, and my relationship with my colleague was severely damaged.

---

[39] As with so many dimensions of the Israeli–Palestinian conflict, the numbers are disputed, with Israelis and Palestinians disagreeing on how many of the Gazan deaths were civilians and how many military personnel. See, for example, "Counting Casualties of Gaza's War," BBC News website, January 28, 2009, http://news.bbc.co.uk; "Rights Group Names 1417 Gaza War Dead," MSNBC website, March 19, 2009, http://www.msnbc.msn.com; "The Gaza War in Numbers," Arutz Sheva Israel National News website, January 19, 2009, http://www.israelnationalnews.com.

Shortly after the war ended, I placed an opinion piece in a Jewish newspaper, expressing what I considered to be mild, nuanced critique of Israel's conduct of the war, interwoven with deep pro-Israel sensibilities, bred and cultivated in me over a lifetime. Days later I received a call from the editor of the paper, asking how I wanted to respond to the flood of highly critical mail he was receiving in response to my piece.

In the days and weeks that followed, I received many letters, some published in the newspaper, others sent to my personal email account. A few expressed strong, substantive critiques of my position. But most could only be characterized as hate mail, telling me I was responsible for the deaths of Israeli children at the hands of terrorists and that I was unfit to be a rabbi. It took me months to recover from these assaults. Only with the passage of time did I learn to hear them as the expression of their writers' fears that my views would actually endanger them, their families, and their own deepest convictions.

On Fear and Conflict

As we have seen, strong, rigorous exploration of different perspectives can be fruitful, even redemptive, both in relationships and in communities. Disagreement is not necessarily a problem, unless disagreement degenerates into polarization, with its attendant dynamics of belligerent rhetoric, personal attack, rupture of relationship, demonization of the other, suppression of doubt, and obstruction of curiosity and creative thinking. What turns ordinary disagreement into dysfunctional diatribe, specifically in intracommunal conflict?

In a word, fear. This may be counterintuitive, as ideologues locked in cycles of serial tirades tend to look and sound more fierce and angry than vulnerable and frightened. But in the dialogue field, it is widely held that at the core of hostile communication across ideological lines is fear, as symbolized by the ominous black arrow in the Public Conversations Project's impactful video.

But what are the two sides in this debate afraid of? For great numbers of American Jews, particularly those born in the 1950s or earlier, primal Jewish fear of persecution, and Holocaust fear in particular, animates all conversation about Israel. For Jews middle-aged and older, including many of those in positions of American Jewish communal leadership, the State of Israel represents essential psychic protection against the threat of anti-Semitism. As long as Israel is secure, we need never again fear the day when we will have no place to go, no country to shield us from genocide.

For such people, every conversation about Israel is a matter of life and death. Every attack on Israel, whether physical or rhetorical, evokes the primal fear of annihilation bred in Jews throughout our history. Hence the hypersensitivity to even mild criticism of the State of Israel, and the rapid escalation of conversation across political lines from difference of opinion to red-faced, high-decibel exchanges.

As Peter Beinart and others have observed,[40] demographic survey data reveal that younger generations of American Jews are less afflicted with the ancient Jewish fear of extermination, less persuaded that we are an "endangered species," and less connected to a narrative of the Jewish people as persecuted and victimized. For increasing numbers of younger Jews, at least in non-Orthodox communities, the primary narrative of meaningful connection to Judaism and the Jewish people is not the story of threatened extinction and heroic survival. Rather, for such people the most meaningful dimension of Jewish connection is engagement in *tikkun olam* ("world repair"), deeds of social justice and compassion, and defending victimized people against the kind of persecution that we have so often known in our own history.[41]

It is clear, then, why security-conscious Jews are profoundly frightened by criticism of the State of Israel. But what of *tikkun olam* Jews, those animated by their association of Jewishness with commitment to social justice? If fear underlies the fierceness of their engagement in Israel conversations, what are they afraid of?

Some of my closest friends and beloved family members are progressive activists. In defending their views about a range of issues—be it international human rights abuses or unequal distribution of wealth in America—

---

[40] Peter Beinart, "The Failure of the American Jewish Establishment," *New York Review of Books*, June 10, 2010, and *The Crisis of Zionism* (New York: Times Books, 2012).

[41] A different view of the concerns of young Jews appears in Jack Wertheimer, "Generation of Change: How Leaders in Their Twenties and Thirties Are Reshaping American Jewish Life," Avi Chai Foundation website, http://avichai.org.

they can be forceful, even ferocious, in their indictment of perpetrators of injustice and in defense of their own analysis of the problem. If pressed to name the emotion beneath their rhetorical battles, they would say they are righteously indignant, not fearful.

Growing up in the Jewish community, they were taught to love Israel as an expression of the Jewish people's mission to serve as a "light unto the nations," an exemplar of justice and compassion. The gap between that high expectation and current realities now registers as a betrayal. Suspicion arises that perhaps the love of Israel bequeathed to them in Jewish summer camps and day schools was a whitewash for Zionism's "original sins," and this is infuriating to them.

Other Jews on the left say that their anger stems from their exclusion from the communal conversation. When they perceive that left-wing organizations are refused a place at the table at Jewish communal and campus organizations and synagogues, they feel silenced and frustrated in their desire to have their voices heard. When silenced, people frequently respond with anger.

Still others say that they are incensed at being regularly attacked as "self-hating Jews" or traitors to the Jewish people simply for holding views that are ubiquitous in Israeli newspapers. The more security-conscious Jews accuse them of evil motives, the angrier and more provocative they become. Each side's anger intensifies the other's, and the cycle of rageful communication continues.

I found compelling insights on the sometimes hostile, accusatory tirades of the political left in Parker Palmer's classic volume, *The Courage to Teach*.[42] In exploring that which blocks the educator's open, creative, and relational use of self in the classroom, Palmer writes, "We fear encounters in which the other is free to be itself, to speak its own truth, to tell us what we may not wish to hear. We want those encounters on our own terms, so that we can control their outcomes, so that they will not threaten our view of world and self."[43] That is, for Palmer the answer to the question, "What is the fear that animates your rage?" is the very encounter with difference.

---

[42] Parker Palmer, *The Courage to Teach* (San Francisco: Jossey-Bass, 1998).

[43] Ibid., 37.

The Frightening Encounter with Difference

Palmer enumerates four distinct ways in which encounters with "the other" generate fear. First, Palmer writes, is the fear accompanying the realization that ours is not the only truth.

> As long as we inhabit a universe made homogeneous by our refusal to admit otherness, we can maintain the illusion that we possess the truth about ourselves and the world—after all, there is no "other" to challenge us! But as soon as we admit pluralism, we are forced to admit that ours is not the only standpoint, the only experience, the only way, and the truths we have built our lives on begin to feel fragile.[44]

I can be so sure of my own view when I am completely surrounded by others who think as I do. There is something affirming and reassuring about living in such a univocal universe, in which every email, every radio program, every dinner conversation communicates that which I believe to be right and true. Challenges to our exclusive truth claims may evoke a deep sense of vulnerability, as our construction of reality is the ground on which we build our lives.

Second, according to Palmer, we may fear that the meeting of differing truths may generate conflict. So many of us, despite our conscious beliefs about the fruitfulness of open inquiry, carry personal fears about the destructive impact of conflict on relationships. Thus, being in the presence of potential conflict can be frightening.

A third level of fear in encountering diverse points of view, for Palmer, is fear of loss of identity. "Many of us are so deeply identified with our ideas that when we have a competitive encounter, we risk losing more than the debate: we risk losing our sense of self."[45] More than simply fearing criticism of our convictions, we may be so attached to our beliefs that an attack on our opinions represents a peril to our very self. Deprived of the beliefs around which our identity is constructed, we know that we would no longer be the same person.

---

[44] Ibid., 38.
[45] Ibid.

Thus, an attack on my ideas represents no less than a threat on my life. No wonder the debate is so threatening, on all sides. Fear then gets expressed as powerful anger, an emotion oddly more comfortable to feel than fear and vulnerability, and the ferocious rhetorical cycle continues to escalate.

Palmer articulates a fourth layer, suggesting that "live encounter with otherness" may challenge us to transform our lives, and this, he suggests, may be "the most daunting threat of all."[46] For some, he asserts, it may be terrifying to contemplate changing, expanding, and recreating our identities. When an encounter with an ideological "other" asks us to do this, we stand on the edge of a chasm of change. We have no idea whether we will survive the leap to the other side, and who we will be if and when we get there.

Exploring fear of otherness in the context of his inquiry into education, Palmer sheds much light on the dynamics at work in the American Jewish "Israel conversation." Although the source of danger is different for people at different points on the ideological spectrum, many are gripped by fear. Some are terrified by mortal threats to the Jewish people and some most alarmed by the prospect of losing their own sense of self. In either case, danger is in the room well before the conversation begins. Thus, the slightest reference to the conflict may trigger powerful fears, which readily erupt into embattled communication.

Such psychological analysis of the fear of otherness may suggest that conversational opponents across ideological divides are doomed to endless rounds of fear-fueled vitriolic interaction. But Palmer also offers a vision of moving beyond fear as a primary experience of difference. "If we dare to move through our fear, to practice knowing as a form of love, we might abandon our illusion of control and enter a partnership with the otherness of the world."[47]

What would it be to "practice knowing as a form of love," which could help us "enter a partnership with the otherness of the world," rather than instinctively associating difference with danger? I think this is akin to Buber's vision of the I-Thou relationship, in which being in

---

[46]   Ibid.

[47]   Ibid., 56.

intentional connection with another human being is a sacred act, a way of encountering the divine. Turning toward such relationship—precisely because the other is different from ourselves—is a way of expressing love of God's creation. Cultivating genuine curiosity about another human life is a way of giving thanks for the gift of life and appreciation for the many creatures God has invited us to encounter.

"Though the [spiritual] traditions vary widely in the ways they propose to take us beyond fear, all hold out the same hope: we can escape fear's paralysis and enter a state of grace where encounters with otherness will not threaten us but will enrich our work and our lives."[48] Palmer envisions a transformation of the deeply embedded association of otherness with danger, a re-education of the oldest regions of our brain that trigger instinctive fight or flight responses when the stranger crosses our horizon. Palmer asks us to conceive of a world in which human beings instinctively recognize "the other" as a source of learning, joy, and personal enrichment rather than as a source of danger.

Rebuke with Love: A Strange and Critical Concept

Just prior to what is perhaps the best-known verse in the Hebrew Bible is a little-known set of commandments, critically important and immensely challenging.

> Do not hate your kinsman in your heart. Admonish your kinsman but incur no guilt because of him [or her]. Do not take vengeance or bear a grudge against one of your people. Love your neighbor as yourself. I am Adonai.[49]

Whole treatises have been written on this passage, containing core instructions for righteous living. Most essential to our inquiry, it is striking that the Torah not only permits but commands an individual who has been wronged by another community member, or who observes the other

---

[48] Ibid., 57.

[49] Lev. 19:17–18, translation adapted from *The Torah: The Five Books of Moses: A New Translation of The Holy Scriptures according to the Traditional Hebrew Text* (Philadelphia: Jewish Publication Society, 1962).

behaving inappropriately, to admonish the other on his or her behavior. Subsequent rabbinic interpretation specifies that the rebuke must be carried out with great sensitivity, or the rebuker is to be held accountable for his or her sin of hurtful speech.[50] Further, the critique must first be expressed in private,[51] so as not to violate the Jewish norm that shaming another in public is akin to murder.[52]

This text offers profound Jewish wisdom about how to conduct ourselves in relationship in the presence of conflict, guiding the wounded party, within Jewish tradition's strict norms of sacred speech, to gently and honestly communicate how the other's behavior has been hurtful. More broadly, the concept of *tocheḥa* (rebuke) is proving to be an important focus of reflection in conversations on Jewish intracommunal debate. The command to rebuke expresses sacred norms of speech and raises important questions: Are we permitted, even obligated, to criticize other Jews for the public positions they take that we consider to be harmful to the Jewish people? If we are unable to offer our critique without shaming the other, must we refrain from offering our view?

Two Talmudic sages reflected on the profound difficulty of performing this mitzvah. "I wonder whether there is anyone in this generation who accepts reproof, for if one says to him: 'Remove the mote from between your eyes,' he [the other] would answer: 'Remove the beam from between your eyes'! Rabbi Eleazar ben Azariah said: 'I wonder if there is one in this generation who knows how to reprove!'"[53]

This mitzvah, difficult to perform in Talmudic times with the sacred intention and skillful practice that the Torah intended, is surely no less challenging in our own day. Who among us is able to listen nondefensively when another tells us how we have hurt them, or how our words or actions have harmed the community? And how many of us can offer such admonishment, whether personal or communal in focus, in a way that preserves the other's dignity and strengthens rather than damages the relationship between them?

---

[50] BT *Arakhin* 16b.

[51] Maimonides, *Mishneh Torah, Laws of De'ot/Personality* 6:8.

[52] BT *Bava Metsi'a* 58b: "One who embarrasses another in public, it is as if that person has shed blood."

[53] BT *Arakhin* 16b.

A remarkable text in the Zohar[54] adds another layer of meaning to this practice.

> "Do not hate your kinsman in your heart. Admonish your kinsman ..."
> It is a *mitzvah* [imperative] to admonish one who has sinned, to show one's great love by admonishing him [or her]. For one who offers rebuke[55] demonstrates love for the other. . . . As it is said with reference to the Blessed Holy One, "God rebukes those that God loves, as a parent rebukes a beloved child" [Prov. 3:12, my trans.]. Just as God admonishes those that God loves, we are to learn from God's way and admonish those we love.[56]

Counterintuitively, the Zohar presents the practice of *tocheḥa* as a practice of love. While it may often feel that offering or receiving criticism is an act of rejection or attack, sure to damage the relationship, the Zohar asserts that, just as God admonishes only God's beloved ones (a troubling theology, but that's another matter), we should follow God's example of offering loving, honest critique to those we love.

Think about it: we generally do not bother to give critical feedback to those for whom we have no affection or respect. We have already shut them out of our hearts and minds. Since we do not expect them to behave in thoughtful and respectable ways, we do not take the time and trouble to correct them at all, much less in the painstaking, mindful way that Jewish norms of speech require. To consider thoughtfully when to offer rebuke and how to offer the criticism so that it can best be heard, and to do all of this in a tone of tender love and respect—this is surely a labor of love.

More deeply, the text asserts that loving criticism is an essential aspect of intimate relationship, an investment in the other person's well-being and in the health and depth of the relationship itself. Not only must admonishment be offered and received in a loving spirit; it is a necessary

---

[54] The Zohar (literally, "Radiance") is the preeminent work of Jewish mysticism, authored by Spanish kabbalist Moses ben Shem Tov de Leon, who died in 1305.

[55] I use the words "admonish" and "rebuke" interchangeably. The Hebrew text uses the same word, "*lehochi'ach*," throughout.

[56] Zohar, *Kedoshim* 85b, translation mine, with thanks to Rabbi Sheldon Lewis for sharing this text with me.

component of loving relationship. In the words of the ancient midrash, "Rabbi Yosi ben Ḥanina said, 'A love without reproof is no love.' Resh Lakish said, 'Reproof leads to peace; a peace where there has been no reproof is no peace.'"[57]

The implications for intra-Jewish dialogue are profound. First, the mitzvah of rebuke demonstrates that Jewish tradition views critical feedback to be not only permissible but obligatory and potentially sacred in human relationship. While rebuking another for a political or ideological view may or may not be what the Torah intended, it seems very much within the spirit of Torah's teaching to criticize another's view as harmful. The stark statement of the midrash that there is no true love without rebuke powerfully expresses a view of loving relationship that includes struggle, critique, and rigorous honesty.

Second, the responsibility to confront another honestly about questionable behavior is rooted in a conviction that one's fellow Jew (I would say, one's fellow human being) is someone to whom we are deeply connected. Our lives are interdependent, and this profound bond between us requires us to call attention to another's error, as we understand it. At the same time, we are required to offer our feedback as we would to a beloved person—someone whose presence in our lives we treasure, whose well-being we desire as our own.

Third, this assumption of deep connection carries the implication that we and the one we challenge share basic Jewish (or human) values. From this perspective, it becomes impossible to demonize another; we must remember that the other is us. So, too, we cannot assume the other to be dishonest, nefarious, or hopeless. Unless we have specific evidence to the contrary, we must assume the other person to be essentially good and well-meaning, a person from whom we have much to learn—at the very least, to learn how another person could come to conclusions so different from our own.

Finally, Jewish teaching on admonishment demands a rigorous standard of speech on the part of the person offering reprimand. We must absolutely guard the dignity of the other, refrain from public shaming, and keep the importance of the relationship in mind as we choose our words, our tone,

---

[57] *Genesis Rabbah* 54:3.

and the timing and mode of the reprimand. The tradition is quite clear that if we cannot offer the rebuke in a way that will not shame or harm the other, we must be silent.

When we have been wounded by another or when we witness public speech that deeply offends us, it is extremely challenging to live up to these rigorous standards. In the midst of conflict, we feel compelled to counterattack without stopping to weigh the morality of our own speech and actions. But Jewish tradition insists on another road: a way of self-reflective, mindful, and loving speech that can only be the fruit of a lifetime of practice.

Understanding and Healing Polarization

The human world is today, as never before, split into two camps, each of which understands the other as the embodiment of falsehood and itself as the embodiment of truth. . . . Each side has assumed monopoly of the sunlight and has plunged its antagonist into night, and each side demands that you decide between day and night. . . . Expressed in modern terminology, he believes that he has ideas, his opponent only ideologies. This obsession feeds the mistrust that incites the two camps.[58]

In battles between right and left, between ultra-Orthodox and secular, between Israelis and Palestinians, each side is quick to cast the contest in terms of good and evil, to both simplify and exaggerate its nature. Before we know it, we have convinced ourselves that the opposing force is malevolent to the core, and our triumph over it an existential imperative. Though we may somehow sense that the causes and remedies for these clashes are complex and, at some level, unknowable, we covet a simpler story of victim and villain, of right and wrong.[59]

---

[58] Martin Buber, "Hope for This Hour," in *The Human Dialogue: Perspectives on Communication*, ed. F. W. Matson and A. Montagu (New York: Free Press, 1967), 307.

[59] Tal Becker, "Zero Sum Logic and Its Perils," Shalom Hartman Institute Website, January 5, 2012, http://www.hartman.org.

Writing in 1967, Buber offers a description of polarized discourse as contemporary as it is classic. In this description, Buber names the central problem of conflict interaction and hints at the healing needed to transform it. In so doing, he anticipates the work of the best theory and practice in the contemporary fields of conflict studies and communications. Tal Becker's characterization of polarized rhetoric in contemporary Israel is a perfect illustration of the problem that Buber described decades ago.

In a generative article on polarized public discourse, family therapists Richard Chasin and Margaret Herzig write that "sociopolitical systems, like families, experience times of struggle."[60] Some such struggles, they assert, are developmental crises in the society's evolving history, as in the period after a declaration of independence. Others erupt during a time of acute trauma in the life of the group, as in the aftermath of war. Chasin and Herzig focus on "a third type of sociopolitical struggle, one that resembles families stuck in chronic conflict."[61] In such struggles, spokespersons and supporters of each side

> believe they hold the high moral ground and are prey to unpro-voked attacks from the other side, which they see as power hungry, self-centered, destructive, and perhaps even deranged. Each side enlists bands of allies to support its own interpretation of history. The opponents' interactions are almost ritualized, and their strife, though costly, resists resolution. Such patterns of interaction often resemble couples engaged in acrimonious divorce litigation. As embattled spouses review their shared history of accusation and defense, they each find "proof" of their own innocent victimhood and of the other's unwarranted attacks and wrongdoing.[62]

Having witnessed divorce many times, I readily recognize the descrip-tion of the divorcing couple. Although there are blessed exceptions, all too frequently partners in a dying marriage regard one another as malevolent, stupid, and/or deranged. The history of hurt is so entrenched that every new exchange or incident is seen through the lens of past offenses. If one

---

[60] Chasin and Herzig, "Creating Systemic Interventions."

[61] Ibid.

[62] Ibid.

partner says that the sky is blue, the other argues that this claim is nonsensical, accusatory, and manipulative. The history of unresolved past traumas is so close to the surface and the pattern of adversarial communication so deeply embedded in the relationship that communicating even about simple matters has become impossible.

When stuck in the midst of entrenched conflict, combatants tend to think that their dispute is utterly unique. This husband, this wife, this work partner is experienced as the most outrageous, crazy-making person on the planet, and the conflict as uniquely intractable. From a communications perspective, however, these patterns of polarization are common to virtually all cases of chronic conflict.

Remember the televised public service announcement in the anti-drug campaign, "This is your brain on drugs?" The first stage in changing dysfunctional conflict interaction is to recognize the common characteristics of such discourse, or, as I have come to call it, "This is your brain on conflict."

Drawing on their expertise in healing family conflict, the Public Conversations Project (PCP) applies the insights of family therapy to the transformation of toxic communication in the sociopolitical realm. The project has studied "what happens to people when they engage in or witness conversations on polarized public issues. How do they speak and listen? What parts of themselves do they open or shut down?"[63] In group conflict as in individual conflict, what is needed is to "lead participants away from deadlock and toward authentic dialogue,"[64] away from stuck, adversarial positioning to authentic conversation in which individuals can see one another as whole human beings, each with his or her own compelling life experiences, personal needs, and perspectives.

Like other conflict specialists, PCP observes that underlying the claims and counterclaims in a particular ideological conflict are common and predictable patterns that typically arise in chronic, polarized conflict, be it interpersonal or intergroup, regardless of the content of the conflict. These patterns include the following:

---

[63] Carol Becker et al., "From Stuck Debate to New Conversation on Controversial Issues: A Report from the Public Conversations Project," *Journal of Feminist Family Therapy* 7, no. 1/2 (1995): 143.

[64] Chasin and Herzig, "Creating Systemic Intervention," 1.

- Complex issues are defined in dichotomous, "win-lose" ways, with nuances and intermediate positions suppressed.
- Conversation partners are divided into two distinct camps defined as "allies" and "opponents."[65]
- There is little genuine listening to perspectives from the "other side."
- Questions from one side to the other are rhetorical and prosecutorial rather than genuine requests for information or understanding.
- Those on the "other side" are seen as all alike and completely negative and those on "our side" are seen as unified, strong, sure, and praiseworthy.
- Self-critical thinking is rare, as each side seeks to put forth its strongest argument in the antagonistic discourse.
- Opinions are strong and emphatic; personal authenticity is sacrificed, as doubt, ambiguity, complexity, and inner value conflicts have no place in the dichotomous schema.
- There is little or no openness to other views or perspectives, since "our side" is completely right and the other side is not trustworthy.
- The contentious mode of conversation encourages rhetorical "winners" to "fear losing disputed territory," and "losers" to "feel they must retaliate to regain lost respect, integrity, and security."[66]

To make matters worse, in public debates, the media play an important and all-too-often destructive role in the perpetuation of polarized communication patterns. Since it is widely believed that the viewing public prefers stories of conflict and violence to nuanced wrestling with ideas, the media tend to report on polarized issues in ways that accentuate simplistic, dichotomous thinking. Although well-meaning journalists may wish it were otherwise, they often succumb to media spin, exaggerating the

---

[65] Carol Becker et al., "From Debate to Dialogue: A Facilitating Role for Family Therapists in the Public Forum," *Dulwich Centre Newsletter* (Australia) 2 (1992): 1.

[66] Becker et al., "From Stuck Debate," 145.

conflict between the "two sides" of multifaceted issues in order to respond to the presumed preferences of the market. The media's repeated framing of issues in extreme, adversarial ways reinforces the public perspective that there are exactly two diametrically opposed sides to the conversation, hopelessly locked in combat with each other.

The dichotomous, oppositional framing of the issues comes to seem increasingly true, if only by dint of repetition, and parties to the conversation think there is no way out of the endless rounds of vitriolic debate. But conflict specialists know that, with skillful intervention, people can step out of high-conflict communication patterns and learn to speak with genuineness, listen with respect and curiosity, and see both self and others as whole, complex human beings.

Conflict interveners facilitate a different kind of conversation, free of the noxious patterns of polarized conflict. In this new conversation, individuals speak for themselves rather than for whole groups, and speak to one another rather than to unseen constituencies. Setting aside the agenda of proving the other side wrong, they share their own unique personal narratives and passions as well as doubts, uncertainties, and areas of inner conflict, rather than reciting fully formed canned positions. The conversation shifts from an exchange of diatribes to an encounter between real human beings, who become curious about how those on the other side construct their worldview. They discover a sense of human connection with those who see life differently than they do and engage in an opportunity to see the world from a very different perspective.

This kind of dialogue is, contrary to popular belief, not an attempt to suppress expression of strong, passionate beliefs. Neither is it a covert attempt to convert all participants to a particular way of thinking. Rather, it is a way to replace repetitive, dysfunctional pseudoconversation with respectful inquiry between real human beings who live in the world together. In the course of such communication, individuals learn a great deal about how the "other"—a real person, not a stereotype or mythic enemy, thinks, feels, and lives. At the same time, participants have the opportunity to reflect deeply on their own views and the life experiences that created them, rather than simply repeating battle-worn talking points.

It becomes clear that the villain in the situation is neither the other side nor the content of the disagreement. The problem—the common enemy to both sides and to the community or society of which they are a part—is the polarized communication pattern. This pattern, when left unaddressed, can destroy communities and fray the fabric of a democratic society. When discussants can see the damage being done to people and communities they treasure, human connection can be reestablished. Polarized discourse can be transformed into honest, creative, and respectful disagreement.

What distinguishes diatribe from dialogue is the habit of stereotyping, demonizing, and dehumanizing the other.[67] The rift between "us" and "them" can be healed and a sense of human connection restored, for the sake of building a civil and compassionate society, even as vibrant and passionate debate continues across a range of perspectives.

Healing "The Israel Conversation" in the Jewish Community

One of the great challenges to Israel's democracy today is not from the so-called "religious" parties but from the right. By the "right," I do not mean the political Right, but those who are certain that they are right, and in no need of voices of dissent.[68]

We produce a shrill, unhealthy debate in which opposing sides demonize each other by essentially arguing that, since we are on a knife's edge, the standard rules of respectful and pluralistic debate cannot apply.[69]

In these striking statements, two scholars from the Shalom Hartman Institute (a pluralistic Orthodox research and leadership center in Jerusalem) offer penetrating critiques of the state of dialogue within the Jewish community in the United States and in Israel, picking up on key themes

---

[67] A chart demonstrating the differences between debate and dialogue appears in the appendix. "Distinguishing Debate from Dialogue: A Table," Public Conversations Project Website, ©1992, http://www.publicconversations.org.

[68] Donniel Hartman, "The Danger of Stability and the Challenge of the 'Right,'" Donniel Hartman Blog at Shalom Hartman Institute website, November 11, 2011, http://www.hartman.org.

[69] Tal Becker, "The Audacity of Nope," From Our Scholars Blog at Shalom Hartman Institute website, December 20, 2011, http://www.hartman.org.

from our review of the field of communications and conflict studies. For Donniel Hartman and for Tal Becker, our people's greatest challenges today include the illusion of certainty (the "right"), the pattern of mutual demonization within the Jewish community, and the distorting impact of fear on the intracommunal conversation.

The problem seems intractable, as every day's news contains abundant evidence of polarized rhetoric, suggesting that far too many Jewish leaders still harbor the illusion that they can destroy their ideological opponents. Opposing views cannot be destroyed, nor should they be, for they represent the real, vibrant, and necessary range of views within the American Jewish community. What can be destroyed is Jews' sense of connection to one another and to the venerable tradition of Jewish teachings on human dignity and sacred speech. Perhaps most urgently, the ferociously contentious tone of conversation among organizational leaders alienates many young American Jews, who have little desire to invest time and life energy in a community that is so fiercely embattled.

Becker dares to question the collective wisdom, suggesting that the presence of fear and danger does not justify the suspension of rules of "respectful and pluralistic debate,"[70] nor, I might add, the abrogation of thousands of years of Jewish wisdom on human dignity and the ethics of speech. I reject the "two Jews, three opinions" theory of Jewish conversation, at least the simplistic version of that theory that rationalizes ad hominem attacks, character assassination, and demonizing of ideological opponents. Instead, I am persuaded by the following creative twist on the aphorism: "If there are only two Jews, why are there three opinions, not two? Perhaps because out of the conflicting individual opinions, a third one emerges—one that is best for the Jewish community *and* closest to the truth." That is to say, "Truth emerges out of the clash of conflicting ideas."[71]

Pioneering Efforts

In recent years, gifted professionals around the country have begun to address the issue of incivility in the Jewish community. Encounter, an award-winning conflict transformation organization, brings high-level

---

[70] Becker, "Audacity of Nope."
[71] Murray J. Laulicht, "Shared Vision," *Sh'ma* 28, no. 543 (1997), 3–4.

American Jewish leaders to meet with Palestinians in Bethlehem and other West Bank cities to grant them "access to Palestinian perspectives and claims on the ground."[72] In the process, Encounter draws Jewish leaders from across the religious and political spectrum and engages them in sophisticated conflict transformation training. The Jewish Dialogue Group is "a grassroots organization that works to foster constructive dialogue within Jewish communities across the world about the Israeli-Palestinian conflict and other challenging issues,"[73] offering workshops, publications, and facilitation training on intra-Jewish dialogue throughout the American Jewish community.

The Jewish Council for Public Affairs, whose mission "is to serve as the representative voice of the organized American Jewish community in addressing the principal mandate of the Jewish community relations field,"[74] has created a "Campaign for Civility,"[75] including widely disseminated public education materials and leadership trainings, as a prelude to a multifaceted national campaign. Top leaders of the agency have worked intensively with numerous North American Jewish communities to address destructive rhetorical dynamics as they arise in particular locales.

A local exemplar of this work is the Year of Civil Discourse Initiative, a collaborative effort of the San Francisco Jewish Community Relations Council, the Northern California Board of Rabbis and the Jewish Community Federation of San Francisco, the Peninsula, Marin and Sonoma Counties "to elevate the level of discourse in the Jewish community when discussing Israel"[76] in the wake of serious intracommunal discord. The year-long pilot program in 2010–11 included public education programs,

---

[72] "What We Do," Encounter website, http://www.encounterprograms.org.

[73] Jewish Dialogue Group, http://www.jewishdialogue.org.

[74] "About," at Jewish Council for Public Affairs website, http://engage.jewishpublicaffairs.org.

[75] JCPA Civility Statement, at JCPA website, http://engage.jewishpublicaffairs.org.

[76] Year of Civil Discourse Initiative, Jewish Community Relations Council of San Francisco, the Peninsula, Marin, Sonoma, Alameda and Contra Costa Counties, http://www.jcrc.org.

text study sessions, training programs for rabbis and Jewish professionals, intensive trainings of cohorts of community members in four area synagogues, as well as study materials in the local Jewish newspaper. Program evaluations suggest that these interventions resulted in a sea change in communal conflict dynamics.

Rabbis and Jewish communal leaders now have tools and resources at their disposal as they seek to name and change the destructive communication patterns prevailing in so many places in the Jewish community. Yet the work of restoring respect, even human decency, to the Israel conversation, is still challenging to say the least.

This chapter has explored several kinds of resources that may be helpful in efforts to transform one community's ability to live with internal difference. First, theological bases for the work of respectful, engaged dialogue within the classical Jewish tradition and in the work of Martin Buber have been considered. Second, the role of fear in ideologically charged conversation has been explored, with the suggestion that self-reflection can loosen the grip of fear so that individuals and communities may return to using speech in ways truer to their personal and collective morality. Third, this chapter has looked at the work of systems-oriented communication scholars, whose theory and well-established practice prescribes a way forward in work with communities torn by polarized conflict.

Most powerfully, I have offered a treasure trove of classical Jewish texts that describe the spiritual practice of recognizing wisdom and holiness in the other even in the midst of high-stakes conflict. As I read them, these texts do not prescribe a quick or easy fix for the ancient neurological pattern that catapults us into fight-or-flight response when we are challenged by another's views. Rather, the texts provide a standard of speech to which we are to aspire and images and mantras that can inspire us to pause before responding instinctively to rhetorical threat. The tradition's sacred reflections, cultivated over a lifetime of study and practice and honored in community, plant within us an imperative to do better and reach higher than our ancient instincts lead us to do. In this way, our speech and relationships are more likely to be infused with the desire to know and revere the divine within and among us.

A Brief Manual for Sacred Conversation

Ben Zoma says:

> Who is wise? One who learns from every person.
> Who is heroic? One who conquers one's own impulse to evil.
> Who is rich? One who is happy with what one has.
> Who is respected? One who respects all beings.[77]

This deceptively simple text is rightly beloved, as it names essential attributes of righteous living, at the same time hinting at the more common default assumptions by which we too often conduct our lives. For our purposes, it can also serve as a brief but penetrating instruction manual for sacred conversation.

Who is wise? One who learns from every person. In Jewish culture, book learning and intellectual acumen are highly prized. The sages of old are called "*Ḥachamim*," the wise, referring primarily to their scholarship. Those steeped in the wisdom of the tradition are esteemed above all.

But Ben Zoma's teaching turns this set of values on its head, defining wisdom as humility, willingness to learn, and openness to the truth that may reside in the "simplest" of people. The wise person is the one prepared to suspend his or her own assumptions in order to make room for that which has been revealed to another, even one with less education or apparent intellectual ability. By this logic, erudite and well-spoken community members who arrogantly refute positions different from their own lack basic wisdom. The wisest person may be the child, the one who articulates his or her views tentatively, who asks more than proclaims. (Whereas the traditional Passover Haggadah idealizes the "wise child," who wants to know every detail of religious law related to the observance of the holiday, in our family, it is the "simple child" asking "What is this about?" who seems the wisest.)

A story was told of Elisabeth Kübler-Ross, when, early in her work with hospice patients, she labored to learn how to work more effectively with people facing the dying process. While she believed she was exploring

---

[77] Mishnah *Avot* 4:1.

important territory, she felt that the interventions she was using were not making a difference in reaching her patients.

> Then one evening Dr. Kübler-Ross went back after hours to visit a man who was dying of cancer. She stopped short of entering the room because she noticed that he was talking to someone. She couldn't see who that person was. As she eavesdropped she heard this man pouring out his deepest thoughts and feelings. Kübler-Ross said she was stunned. The patient was doing what she had for weeks unsuccessfully tried to get him to do. She waited at the door to speak to this amazing counselor/facilitator and learn his or her techniques. After a while, and much to her amazement, out stepped the cleaning lady! . . .
>
> Kübler-Ross took her aside and asked her how she got that man to talk so freely. The cleaning lady responded quite simply, "Honey, I didn't do a thing. I guess he just knew I was willing to listen. And when he started to talk I just sat there, held his hand and listened to him. The good Lord did all the rest!"[78]

The wise person in dialogue is the one who listens more than she speaks, asks more than advocating for his truth. Wisdom is found in hearing the spaces between the spoken words, recognizing and honoring the life experience in which a particular view is grounded. The wise dialogue partner extends a sense of hospitality, caring, and safety so that truths often left unspoken can find expression. Relational wisdom, by this definition, is characterized not primarily by erudition but by empathy, not by cleverness but by compassion, not by persuasive argument but by gracious, expansive listening.

Who is heroic? One who conquers one's own impulse to evil. As I write these words, I find myself in a café in downtown Jerusalem. For all too many Jewish Israelis, whose lives are profoundly shaped by experiences of army service in young adulthood, then punctuated by months of army reserve duty over the course of their adult lives, military images of heroism are

---

[78] Nancy Flam, Janet Offel, and Amy Eilberg, *Acts of Loving-Kindness: A Training Manual for Bikkur Holim* (Visiting the Sick) (San Francisco: Ruach Ami: Bay Area Jewish Healing Center, 1992), 19–20.

all too present. In this culture, physical prowess and strategic boldness are seen as valiant. In American society, judged by the media attention they attract and salaries they command, it is sports figures, film stars, and the political heroes of the moment that are, absurdly, honored as heroic.

In sharp contrast to these superficial images, our text defines heroism as an inside job. The hero is one who attains a measure of success in learning his own interior landscape deeply enough to resist the powerful pull of long-practiced destructive habits. Heroism here is defined as self-knowledge and awareness, rigorous honesty and the courage to face the darkest places within. The hero has developed a space between the match and the fuse,[79] coming to recognize which situations and modes of expression tend to become triggers to anger and insult. According to this logic, owning one's vulnerabilities, apologizing for wrongdoing, and entering into conversation with those who threaten our sense of well-being are all acts of courage.

In conversation, the hero is not the loudest or most prolific speaker. Rather, "hearing others into speech," to use Nelle Morton's phrase,[80] or helping others feel safe enough to own their own truths, is heroic. Entering into highly conflictual subjects, choosing to "sit in the fire," as Arnold Mindell puts it,[81] is bold. Daring to speak one's own unpopular truth can be an act of courage, as is breathing deeply rather than exploding when an accusatory rhetorical assault comes our way. The conversational hero is present, active, and honest, but also compassionate, curious, and empathic.

Who is rich? One who is happy with what one has. In the same paradoxical way, the text rejects the literal meaning of wealth, pointing instead to qualities of gratitude and acceptance. The one who appreciates whatever life gives is prosperous. The person who accepts exactly who he or she is at this moment of life lives in abundance. Riches are to be found in the gifts of the present moment, in loved ones and "simple" pleasures.

---

[79] I thank my colleague Alan Morinis, the master teacher of Mussar, for this illuminating metaphor, offered in teaching retreats for the Morei Derekh program for Jewish Spiritual Direction.

[80] Nelle Morton, *The Journey Home* (Boston: Beacon Press, 1985), 202.

[81] Arnold Mindell, *Sitting in the Fire: Large Group Transformation Using Conflict and Diversity* (Portland, OR: Lao Tse Press, 1995).

In relationship, one can easily recognize the person who lives in abundance and gratitude. It is not by the visible signs of fine clothing or jewels, but by a depth of presence and compassion, a sense of being at home in the midst of one's own life. Such a person lives and converses with a quality of grace and graciousness. Having everything he needs, he is happy to let the other speak first, grant others their needs and acknowledge their gifts. She doesn't need to dominate the conversation or be acknowledged as right, but can also speak painful truths in ways that others can hear.

Who is respected? One who respects all beings. Likewise, in its reflections on respect, the text beautifully inverts the usual assumptions and addictive patterns that afflict so many lives. Just as wealth is not to be found in possessions, honor is not to be found in public praise, enthusiastic reviews, or job promotions. Rather, honor is defined as the ability to offer affirmation to another, to recognize that which is sacred and beautiful in another human being.[82] The admirable person needs no accolades or effusive introductions, and prefers to praise others rather than receive acclaim. She is the one who greets everyone equally, regardless of social status, communicating that there is no one in the world she would rather be with right now than you. The worthy person is the one who sees the good in everyone, drawing out the best in people by his gentle encouragement.

In dialogue, honor is due to the one who, like the sage Hillel, can speak respectfully and insightfully of views different from one's own and can speak across ideological lines in ways that others can hear. The truly impressive conversational partner expresses real interest in all sorts of perspectives, responding to alien views with genuine curiosity rather than judgment or aversion. He is enlivened by the opportunity to learn about a hitherto foreign worldview and excels in exploring not only the details of the belief but the life experience that informs it. She would rather help those in conflict converse respectfully with one another than find an admiring audience for her own rhetorical skills. The exemplary dialogue partner is the one who inspires all parties to both speak and listen, to feel safe, heard, even treasured.

This beautiful text offers a glimpse of the spiritual work of dialogue, sketching the values and traits that are needed if we are to engage respectfully

---

[82] The root meaning of the Hebrew word *kavod*, or honor, is related to the words "weighty" or "substantial."

in highly charged conversations within our own communities, when our listening abilities are sorely tested. As I explore in chapter 5, Jewish tradition offers great wisdom on the qualities of soul that must be cultivated over a lifetime if we are to resist the emotional brain's pull toward polarizing speech. In the view of this text, it is the practice of humility, self-reflection, grateful awareness, and respect that can allow us to navigate the most difficult exchanges with dignity. Only when guided by these principles can our communal discourse rightly be called "Jewish conversation."

4

Peace between Israelis and Palestinians

The award-winning Encounter program was created to give emerging Jewish leaders a chance to learn another side of the Israeli–Palestinian reality. Without any political perspective or agenda, the program appealed to participants' curiosity and desire to expand their perspective by meeting Palestinians on the other side of the separation barrier. There was no expectation of what conclusions anyone would draw, only that their experience would be broadened. In an early measure of success, participants from across the denominational and political spectrum flocked to Encounter's thirty-hour programs, which included meetings with Palestinian civil society leaders in Bethlehem and a home stay with a Palestinian family. Back in Jerusalem, the participants, diverse groups of Jews, used their newly practiced listening skills to share their reactions with one another.

Split-Screen Viewing

Back from Bethlehem, the group in which I participated—all of us mentally and emotionally exhausted—took refuge in the home of one of the facilitators in the Jerusalem neighborhood of Talpi'ot, just minutes inside the Green Line. There was a sacred tone to our debriefing session, as people listened to one another with gentleness and respect, sharing deep feelings of pain and confusion about what we had seen and heard. For some participants, hearing the Palestinian perspective was completely new and intensely painful. For others, the information was familiar, but hearing Palestinians criticize Israeli policies in strong and compelling ways was still deeply distressing.

As for me, I had a familiar headache. I had often felt this way in my early meetings with Palestinians, whose perspective on the reality of Israel is so different from my own. My friend Susan Cobin, a master Jewish educator from St. Paul, Minnesota, who was there with me in the group, reflected on the process of absorbing a different narrative on the conflict while holding on to our own lifelong perspective, saturated with deep love of Israel. Susan said, "You know how sometimes news programs place two different videos on the same screen, and you have to watch two different realities at the same time? That's what this was like." I have never heard a more perceptive description of the challenging process of learning a narrative that deeply challenges our own. When we choose openness to learning over the easy course of rejecting an alternate view, we must hold the two realities in parallel, contemplating both side by side. It makes the head and soul ache, but it is the only way to deepen understanding of an immensely complex situation.

Listening to Both Sides

> Do not carry false rumors; do not join hands with the guilty to act as a malicious witness. (Exod. 23:1)[1]

To the casual reader, the verse appears to be a self-evident warning not to engage in slander. Delving more deeply into the text, one is drawn into multiple layers of meaning. The linkage of the first part of the verse—apparently related to individual ethics of speech—with the second part—related to court testimony—is intriguing. With his exquisite eye for language and context, Rashi comments, "'You shall not bear a false report.' [For the individual, this is] a prohibition against hearing slander or gossip. [For a judge the verse dictates that] he should not hear the plea of one litigant until his opponent arrives."[2]

---

[1] Translation adapted from *The Torah—The Five Books of Moses, A New Translation of The Holy Scriptures according to the Traditional Hebrew Text* (Philadelphia: Jewish Publication Society, 1962).

[2] Rashi on Exodus 23:1, s.v. "You shall not carry," based on BT *Sanhedrin* 7b.

The judge is cautioned not to hear a case involving two litigants unless both are present, lest he formulate an opinion based on the persuasive personal story of one side of the conflict before hearing the other's account. Read in this way, the verse is declaring that the truth of the conflict is always larger than one person's view of it, and justice can emerge only from the broadest possible view. The judge can gain an unbiased appreciation of the whole of the story only if he (or, in our day, she) looks into the eyes of both litigants, hears both of their narratives, and observes their reactions to one another's claims. The judge must look into the face of the conflict from multiple perspectives, taking in the pain, hurt, and anger of all those involved.

Another commentary draws an additional layer of meaning out of the same verse, saying that the text also adjures each litigant to refrain from telling his or her own story to the judge until the opponent arrives.[3] It is clear why the Torah must issue a directive about this, for the temptation to try to gain the judge's sympathy, to claim exclusive truth for one's own view, is strong. The more significant the conflict, the more powerful the temptation. Indeed, in cases of long-standing, entrenched violent conflict, it seems impossible to imagine that the "other side" can speak any truth at all.

As the listener, as we "judge" or form our own opinions, it is so much easier just to listen to the version of the story told by "our people," by those seen to be like us and therefore credible. The more important the issue is to us, the harder it is to take in the reality of a person who sees the matter from a radically different perspective, based on different life experiences and core assumptions. Listening to the version offered by "the other side," our heart may pound, blood may rush through our veins, and our head may explode with angry retorts. It is hard work to learn to listen to the other's narrative, to take in the full humanity of those on "the other side," even to recognize some truth in the other's view. But this kind of listening is the very essence of the pursuit of peace.

In this chapter I explore the practice of transformative listening and conversation in the context of one of the world's most intractable disputes, the Israeli-Palestinian conflict. These conversations include experiences of third parties seeking to bring sacred listening to the

---

[3] BT *Sanhedrin 7b.*

Middle East and Diaspora Jews working to heal rifts in relationship caused by the conflict. I also present portraits of gifted and courageous grassroots Israeli and Palestinian peacebuilders who dare to believe that real human relationship can contribute to the transformation of even the most difficult of conflicts.

Throughout this chapter, I express my deep belief in the value of "Track Two Diplomacy,"[4] the role of nondiplomats—civil society leaders and ordinary citizens—in any international peace process. Obviously, only professional diplomats can negotiate peace treaties. But only the people on the ground can make peace among people. Local conflict specialists, dialogue activists, and civil society leaders, in particular, have two enormously important roles to play: (1) helping to create a national consensus to encourage governments to enter into political agreements and (2) preparing the ground for diplomatic resolution by weaving webs of relationship that will eventually give life to peace treaties. I have come to know countless "Track Two" diplomats, whose work I deeply admire and very much want to amplify.

In the portraits presented throughout this chapter, we will see again how fear of difference and fear of loss of identity can perpetuate conflict. Here we have two additional elements: real history of historical wounds and the structural power differential between the primary adversaries. Israelis and Palestinians are not only frightened of the other as different from themselves; their fear is a fear of annihilation by the other. In recent memory, children and families have been killed and terrorized and communities destroyed. Trauma and injustice is a present reality on both sides. It is not surprising that many people have despaired of all hope for peaceful relationship.

Yet the portraits offered here demonstrate the counterexample of reconciliation work that goes on every day among people on the ground. Such people work every day to hear and befriend the other, learning to

---

[4] The term, now widely used among conflict analysts and activists, was coined by Joseph Montville, then a State Department employee, according to Charles Homans, "Track Two Diplomacy: A Short History," *Foreign Policy*, July/August 2011, http://www.foreignpolicy.com. Marc Gopin has coined a similar concept, "Citizen Diplomacy," in *To Make the Earth Whole: The Art of Citizen Diplomacy in an Age of Religious Militancy*" (Lanham, MD: Rowman and Littlefield, 2009).

respect viewpoints very different from their own, and transcending natural feelings of hate and vengefulness in order to give peace a chance.

The Compassionate Listening Project

Early in my personal search for a way to serve the cause of peace, I found The Compassionate Listening Project.™[5] Based in Seattle, the project trains people in harnessing the transformative power of listening for the sake of peace. In particular, the project has been bringing delegations to Israel and the Palestinian territories since 1990. The goal of each delegation is to teach groups of listeners to sit attentively and hear the stories of people on all sides of the conflict. I knew that in the past delegations had met with extremists on all sides—with settlers who advocate the "transfer" of all Arabs out of Israel, members of Hamas still committed to violence, and many in between.

Knowing that many of the various positions we would encounter would be abhorrent to many of us, the group leaders asked us to listen deeply to our own internal reactions and to commit not to speak out of our own anger, horror, or self-righteousness. As aspiring peacebuilders, we were to practice refraining from the attempt to debate, criticize, or persuade the speaker of our own point of view, although we knew we would strongly disagree with some of what we heard. Our task was to seek to understand the person behind the sometimes-repugnant belief, bringing our shared conviction that grassroots relationship-building is at least as important to any peace process as the agreements created by governments.

Our technique was first to simply listen to the person's story, silently and mindfully noting our own inner spikes of emotion as they spoke. We would then go around our circle, inviting participants to express what they had appreciated about the person's story, inviting the speaker to silently listen to moving expressions of caring and understanding. Only then, having established what project director Leah Green called "a force field of love," we would ask challenging questions to deepen our own understanding of the speaker's perspective, but only if we could ask the question without insult, criticism, or judgment. In all of this, we

---

[5] The Compassionate Listening Project website, http://www.compassion-atelistening.org.

developed our capacity to put our own judgments on hold in order to recognize the humanity of people on all sides, even in the presence of fierce disagreement.

A Note to the Reader

During the coming pages, there may be moments when you notice emotion rising in you: anger, horror, even outrage. Perhaps you already feel angry about things I have said or have been tempted to slam the book shut. When you notice such reactions arising, I invite you to conduct your own experiment in compassionate listening.

When you notice your heart beginning to race or pound, when you hear the verbal monologue in your mind growing loud and combative, or whatever other reactions you may have, take a moment and bring some attention to what is happening inside you. Notice that for a moment war is raging in your mind or heart, as stress hormones course through your body. See what happens if you try to fully acknowledge your reactions but choose not to feed the internal energy of war. Consider the possibility of listening calmly, just for a few moments, to a view you find deeply objectionable. If you can call on the higher parts of the human brain to soothe the limbic upset, might you discover that there is something new for you to learn in this new territory?

Prying the Heart Open

Min hamaytzar ka-ra-ti Yah
Anani bamerchav Yah.

Out of narrow straits I've called out to God;
God answered me with wide expanse. (Ps. 118:5)

I have long loved this verse from the Psalms, used liturgically in *Hallel*, the Psalms of Praise added to the Jewish liturgy on festival days. But the verse rooted itself deep inside of me when my daughter was a little girl and her teacher in Hebrew day school taught the children hand and body movements to the melody we used to sing the verse. With the words, "*Min hamaytzar,*" "Out of narrow straits," the children would bring their hands together toward their eyes, with little heads bowed and bodies hunched inward. On the words, "*Anani bamerḥav Yah,*" "God answered me with wide expanse," arms would be spread outward, bodies opened, and young faces turned upward in joyous expectation. For years we sang the song together at our family Seders. I thought I was doing it for the children. Eventually, the verse became a body prayer for me.

In times of narrowness and constriction, we are tight and clenched, gripped by fear. We remember past hurts and are convinced that suspicion, if not outright hostility, is the only sensible response. We hold tightly to our mental narratives, certain that our frightened version of "the facts" is the only one. Trust seems foolish or impossible; all we can see is danger. Somehow, rehearsing the risks feels like it will keep us safe.

When we are blessed with moments of openness, fists unclench, and the heart and mind relax. Things look startlingly brighter, as if our surroundings had been washed clean. There is light and promise. We can consider new thoughts, entertain the possibility that things may change, or even recognize that the truth is larger than our own perspective. Like Hagar, who feared for the death of her son Ishmael in the wilderness until God spoke to her (Gen. 21:19), we can open our eyes and see the source of living waters that was there all along to nourish and sustain us. We can open to possibilities beyond our ability to know, even dare to hope.

To be honest, I live in the "straits" much of the time, focused on narrow concerns and familiar perspectives. I have to be startled out of this constricted way of living—by an undeniably true human encounter, an unexpected gift of new insight, or travel to faraway places. Then I realize that the world is much larger than my own mental constructs, and I want to know more.

In recent years I have been given a powerful image that God is prying my heart open. I don't mean this on any literal level, for I don't believe that God has hands or is a "Someone" at all. But I have experienced a quiet yet commanding summons to open wider and more often—to invite new people and perspectives into my life, to question beliefs long presumed to be true simply by force of repetition, and to actively seek out experiences and relationships that will broaden me. It seems clear that this is what God is asking of me. Actually, the Torah requires this of all of us, lest our hearts be closed to neighbors in need of compassion. To be faithful to this command requires an often-challenging struggle with habitual patterns of fearful thinking. It is the work we are all called to.

Healing Fear

From the very first day, the Compassionate Listening trip began to work on me, moving me to think deeply about the dynamics of fear. Our group was staying at a charming Christian hostel in the Muslim quarter of the Old City of Jerusalem, a Palestinian neighborhood, and I felt unsafe. Entering the Old City through the Damascus Gate (which, like most Jews, I had never done), I wondered whether people would watch me with suspicion, even desire to harm me. I chose not to say my morning prayers, wrapped in *tallit* and *tefillin* (traditional Jewish prayer shawl and phylacteries), on the beautiful rooftop terrace of the hostel, for fear that someone would shoot at me.

But with each passing day the place became more familiar, and my fears began to feel silly, or at least exaggerated. I had no desire to be cavalier. Tensions were surely real between Palestinians and Israelis. But fright had fed on itself, leaving me locked in a sense of mortal danger, when in fact, I should just be sensible, as I would anywhere. I had been suffering from my own fear of the other, which produced its own mental realities: I don't know those people; perhaps they hate me; perhaps they wish me harm. But, becoming more familiar with the area, I came to appreciate the charm of this magical part of the Old City, with the playful aggressiveness of the storekeepers, the feel of the ancient stones underfoot, the smells of freshly baked goods, and the sights of colorful wares displayed everywhere. The area had become a place where I could feel safe. I was coming to know "the other," and this stranger no longer seemed quite so frightening. I felt a palpable sense of liberation from the painful and burdensome structure of fear in my own mind and heart.

Listening with the Heart

As much as I thought I knew about the "Jewish side" of the conflict, there was much for me to learn from some extraordinary encounters we had with Jews on my trip with the Compassionate Listening Project.[6] To name just a few: We met with Hagit Ra'anan, who turned to peace activism after her husband was killed in Lebanon in 1982. She now conducts peace rituals and creates peace curricula for Jewish and Palestinian children throughout Israel. We met with Ester Golan, a survivor of the Kindertransport,[7] who, well into her eighties, made frequent trips to Germany to teach her message of compassion and acceptance, even as she tells her own Shoah (Holocaust) story.

We met with two of the university students who had led the efforts to prevent the disengagement from Gaza, who shared both their passionate opposition to the withdrawal and their sense of personal devastation when they found themselves confronted by fellow Israeli soldiers. We spent time with a member of Maḥsom (Checkpoint) Watch, which stations Israeli civilians at checkpoints to document occasions when human rights abuses occur.

But unquestionably, I learned the most from our encounters with Palestinians. I am not proud to say that I had never had a deep or extended dialogue with a Palestinian until I came to know Maha El-Taji, the co-leader of our trip. Maha told me of her own journey from a childhood of hating Jews, since her family had been evicted from their family home in 1948, to her first friendship with an Israeli. Today she is a woman with an enormous capacity for love and a profound understanding of the Jewish sensibilities that must be attended to before peace can come.

We met with the leaders of Bil'in, a Palestinian village that had been conducting weekly, unarmed demonstrations against the route of the separation barrier, which cut the village off from its fields, thus denying villagers access to their lands and livelihood. One of these men brought us to his spartan home for tea, where we met his family, listened to his poetry, and shared heartfelt prayers for peace.

---

[6] See Carol Hwoschinsky, *Listening with the Heart: A Guide for Compassionate Listening* (Indianola, WA: Compassionate Listening Project, 2001).

[7] The Kindertransport was a rescue mission through which some 10,000 Jewish children were transported without their parents from Nazi Germany, Austria, Poland, and Czechoslovakia to safety in Great Britain between 1938 and the start of World War II. http://www.kindertransport.org.

We spent the night in Al Aroub, a Palestinian refugee camp near Hebron, where we were hosted by Jamil Roshdy, one of the national leaders of a grassroots campaign called the Popular Campaign for Peace and Democracy, which had collected 500,000 signatures—on both sides—on a document outlining the contours of a final peace agreement. This was for me a life-changing night, which began when we entered the camp, finding ourselves in the midst of a frightening demonstration honoring the first anniversary of Yasser Arafat's death. By the end of the visit, I had fallen in love with Jamil's beautiful children and shared family photos with his mother, with whom I shared not a word of common language. I had slept on the floor of his living room and been awakened in the morning by his young children exploring their unfamiliar guest—all without common language—and my heart had been pried open.

On our way out of the camp, exuberantly making use of my few words of Arabic, I greeted people, young and old, who lined the street. When I had entered the town, these people had looked threatening; now I felt love for them, as extensions of the family who had opened their home and their hearts to me. As we left, Jamil asked me, the first rabbi he had ever met, to pray for his efforts. The fear I had felt when entering the camp had dissolved. I now knew these people, having eaten at their table, slept on their floor, and played lovingly with their children. Enemies had become friends.

Strange Commonalities

Beyond the stories of the people we met and the heartening things they said, one striking feature of the trip stayed with me. In our listening sessions with Palestinians, as they described some of the basic realities of their situation, I consistently heard laments that were difficult to hear yet sounded uncannily familiar. Again and again, I heard Palestinians say things like the following:

1. There is no one for us to talk to on the other side. If only we had a partner for peace. *(At first, an angry voice in my head shouted, "What?! Israel has been seeking peace and the Arabs have been rejecting it for over sixty years!")*

2. We never know when one of our loved ones may be suddenly taken from us. *(This one made my heart race with righteous anger. After all, it is they who have been killing our children. But I began to hear that, although the circumstances are very different on the two sides, the unpredictable injury and loss of loved ones has been a real part of Palestinian life, as well as Israeli life, for many years.)*

3. Why can't they understand that we are not going anywhere? They cannot wipe us out. *(This one made me ponder how ready we, both Israeli and American Jews, are to give up our deep wish that the Palestinians would just somehow go away.)*

4. Why do they teach their children to hate? *(How could they possibly think this of us? I thought, instinctively outraged. Slowly, I began to understand that, truth be told, there is hate on our side as well.)*

5. How can they fail to understand that the lives of our children are more precious than land? *(I flashed to media images of Palestinian communities celebrating children "martyred" in acts of violence. Is it just possible that those images are media spin, that their values are not so different from ours after all?)*

6. Among some in our community, you're a traitor if you advocate peace with the other side. *(I was accustomed to thinking that Palestinian peace activists would immediately be murdered by their own people. Clearly, though that has sometimes happened, there is today a well-developed Palestinian peace camp. It has become all too clear that Jewish peace activists also face condemnation from some quarters of the Jewish community, both in Israel and in the United States.)*

7. The American media is against us. *(This one almost made me laugh out loud the first time I heard it, so convinced was I that the American media is biased against Israel! But they were serious, which led me to an extended reflection on the claims and counterclaims of bias in the media. Feeling passionately right and deeply wronged in a conflict, both sides will instinctively insist that a particular report has misrepresented their position.)*

I spent years reflecting on this strange set of mirror images of life experience on the two sides. Surely, the two sides are not equivalent. The Palestinians have long used suicide bombing, then rocket bombing, specifically targeting civilians in order to terrorize Jewish Israelis. Yet, from the Palestinian side of the barrier, Israel is seen as a military superpower that frequently uses overwhelming military force, often with the effect of terrorizing a civilian population.

Having moved back and forth between two peoples with radically different life experiences and perspectives, what began to emerge was that "they" are not so different from "us" after all. We heard two very different narratives of suffering, but beneath these contrasting stories, there is much human similarity. On both sides of the conflict, all of the people we met shared the same primal longing: to live in peace and security, freedom, and dignity. The people we met said that virtually everyone they know simply wants to live in peace, free to care for their families and go about their lives.

Taking in these painful narratives took real effort on my part, challenging a lifetime of conditioning about how to view the people on the other side. My instinctive response would have been to debate them in my head if not in person and reject their stories as dangerous lies that threatened my people. But having entered into their world in order to enlarge my understanding, I had to work to contextualize and, in some ways, deconstruct my former views. Entering into relationship with real Palestinians, I knew there was truth here that I had not yet understood.

In the end, I found myself deeply encouraged by the perplexing commonality of experience between the other and my own people. Having discovered the others as human beings (rather than the monstrous creatures I had been educated to expect), I recognized the possibility that peace-loving people on all sides of the conflict could unite at the level of common yearning that lies beneath the past history of hate, violence, and trauma.

Helping Your Enemy

In my own journey, I have found the study of peace texts in our vast tradition to be deeply nourishing, encouraging, and inspiring. They are precisely the balm my soul needs at times when the world seems especially beset by violence and hate.

Some years into my work of teaching and writing about these texts, however, I had to admit that not everyone responded to the peace texts in the same way that I did. Some people assumed that I taught texts about peace as only a dimly veiled form of advocacy for a particular political position. Others rolled their eyes, as if to say that talk of peace was pie-in-the-sky, naïve reflection, utterly divorced from the real world in which we live. Still others looked at me with sadness in their faces, indicating that life experience (whether personal or international) had destroyed their ability to hope for peace anytime before messianic times.

Somewhere along the line I discovered that teaching Torah texts on "the enemy" could allow for a fresh and less embittered approach to the issues of peace and conflict in our lives and in our world. At first, I had resisted such texts, fearing that talk of "the enemy" would encourage the closed-minded and closed-hearted view of "the other" that I sought to challenge. Eventually, I learned that studying what the Torah says about one's adversaries, whether personal or national, opens a window onto the Torah's profound and realistic understandings of what impedes peaceful relationship and what promotes it.

> When you encounter your enemy's donkey wandering, you must take it back to him. When you see your enemy's donkey sagging under its burden and would refrain from raising it, you must nevertheless raise it with him. (Exod. 23:4–5)

Some years ago my colleague Rabbi Ed Feld offered a wonderful commentary on this passage that opened up the human experience beneath the surface of this law. Encountering my enemy's animal wandering far from its owner, how could I return it if not by working to locate my enemy, risking my personal safety and comfort by entering his or her territory or home, thus creating a face-to-face meeting with a person I would rather avoid? The situation in the second verse is even more striking. If I came across my enemy himself struggling with a large animal on the ground with its load scattered all around, "raising it with him," as the text commands, would require that I roll up my sleeves and do sweaty, backbreaking work side by side with my opponent. The Torah is commanding far more than a detached, grudging willingness to help. What is required of me is that I offer my time, my comfort, and my physical strength, working collaboratively with my adversary for the purpose of helping her in her moment of need.

What might this mitzvah look like in our world? It might be helping dig a hated ex-boss's car out of a snowbank, being the parent who runs to the field to take one's enemy's injured child to the emergency room, or extending real compassion to someone who has hurt me when she experiences her own loss. Imagining these contemporary equivalents makes me appreciate the Torah's brief phrase, "would refrain from raising it." The Torah knows that I will likely resist the call to help my foe. My heart will clench. I will want to turn the other way, to let someone else help, to rationalize my unwillingness to come to this person's aid. The Torah responds, "I know you will want to avoid helping, but you must help anyway."

Then I wonder what might happen after this incident. After I had transcended my instinct to refuse to help, might the other person's attitude toward me have changed? What of mine toward her? After being through this experience together, the force field of adversarial feeling between us may have weakened. Surely that is precisely what the Torah has in mind.

I have come to love the honest realism of this text. For nearly everyone I know, there are those in our lives that we dislike, resent, avoid, and even hate. We do not move around our lives with perfect equanimity, exuding loving-kindness to all who cross our path. There are people we can't stand. The Torah accepts this reality and uses a real-life misfortune to facilitate transformation in a conflict-ridden relationship, as becomes clear in the following text.

Two donkey drivers who hated each other were traveling along the same road. The donkey of one of them fell down. The other saw it but passed him by. After he had passed by he said, "It is written in Holy Writ, 'if you see your enemy's donkey . . .'" Forthwith he went back to help him with the load. The other began to think things over and said, "So and so is evidently my friend and I didn't know it." Both went into a roadside inn and had a drink together. What led to them making up? One of them looked into the Torah.[8]

---

[8] *Midrash Tanhuma, Mishpatim*, 1. (*Tanhuma* is a ninth- to tenth-century aggadic—nonlegal—collection of midrashim on the Torah.)

Graced Moments

For many years, I traveled to Israel at least once a year, each time creating opportunities to hear the stories of more Palestinians and to strengthen my relationships with some who had become friends. At first, I would be easily angered by their negative commentaries about Israeli policies. Even with a strong intention to listen with compassion and respect and open myself to new perspectives, it was challenging to take in their stories. But over the years, this perspective became more familiar to me, and I found myself able to hear such arguments more calmly and connect with the human being who held this view, with which I disagreed. Eventually, I realized that I had worked so hard to absorb the Palestinian perspective, assuming that the Jewish perspective was in my bones, that I had lost my ability to listen to Jews with a right-of-center perspective. Now I needed to seek out opportunities to listen again to their side of the story.

Sometimes it was hard, very hard. At times I felt angry and incredulous, with the powerful energy of righteous indignation filling my mind, so that it would be very difficult to listen with inner stillness, empathy, and respect. And then there have been graced moments when somehow, mysteriously, an encounter that could have been excruciating instead yielded blessing and learning.

Such a moment came when I visited two of my oldest friends in Israel, people I have loved for over thirty years. They are among the kindest and most generous people I have ever known. They live in an area that many Jewish Israelis consider part of Israel, and that the Palestinians and the international community consider to be a settlement.

We lit Hanukah candles together, said prayers, and sang songs in a tone both gentle and reverent, as if we were wrapped in a velvet cushion of our shared sacred practice. They treated me to a lavish dinner, where there was much talk of upcoming weddings and new grandchildren. In passing, one of their children (younger than my own) mentioned something in passing about his time in Gaza during the recent war.

My friends know very well how different my politics are from theirs, as we have discussed the issues on each of my visits. After everything I had read and heard about the recent campaign in Gaza, here was a rare opportunity for me to hear from a soldier who had been there. I suspected his politics would be much to the right of mine, and yet I felt an almost maternal sense of protectiveness toward their child. I wanted to listen deeply to his experience, foreign and even offensive as I suspected it would be for me.

Not wanting to pounce, I waited through a few more moments of conversation before turning to the young man and saying gently, "I don't know if you can answer this question, but I wonder: Is there anything you can tell me about your experience in Gaza?" He began to talk, and he went on for over an hour.

Without revealing classified information, he spoke of the experience of being called up, of the fear of wartime, of times of waiting, tension, and boredom. He spoke of the spiritual realities of war and the different experiences of religious and nonreligious soldiers. He spoke of his gratitude for the clear sense that the people of Israel were with him. I hardly had to prod him with questions. He spoke fluidly, eloquently, and with self-awareness as he articulated the view that the Israeli army had done everything possible to minimize civilian Palestinian casualties, without unduly endangering our own soldiers. After listening for nearly an hour, I asked tentatively, "Did you see anything that you had questions or moral doubts about?" He responded in the same even tone that he had not.

Remarkably, there was no shouting in my head. No argument and counterargument, no internal gathering of evidence, citing of facts and figures or memory of this or that critical commentary I had read in the press. He was articulating a position that was indefensible from my own perspective. But I simply wanted to know this young man, to get inside his experience of the war, to practice listening to a person who in that moment was "the other" to me. And it worked.

On that occasion I was so calm and genuinely curious about this person that I was able to bracket my own very different view and take in his experience without judgment, debate, or inner struggle. The loving warmth of my encounter with my friends encircled us, and I instinctively avoided harming it, not wanting to endanger our friendship in any way. Although this young man's political views remained very different from my own, he was not the enemy; his parents were my lifelong friends.

It also helped that he was younger than my own children. As neuroscientists have begun to document, parental instincts can overpower the mechanism in the brain that reacts to an opposing ideological view in much the same way that it reacts to a lethal attack. Though surely we get angry with our children at times, the instinct to reconcile and reconnect is deeply embedded in us. I wonder what it would take for us to mobilize that parental instinct more often (for everyone we speak with, after all, is someone's child). Seeing our interlocutors in that way, we would have many more people in our hearts, regardless of disagreement, and many fewer enemies.

Shabbat in a Settlement

Another such moment came when I chose to spend Shabbat in a West Bank settlement, in the home of a friend's sister, an Orthodox Jew. I knew that my friend adored her sister, even though there were significant religious and political differences between them. My friend expressed concern that spending Shabbat with her family might be more of a stretch than I imagined. Still, I jumped at the opportunity. Here was a unique chance to be in the presence of people very different from me religiously and politically, to experience their home, pray with them, and listen to them, as I had frequently done with their Palestinian neighbors in the West Bank.

The routes among the Jewish settlements were unfamiliar to me, and it was an adventure finding the home of my friend's sister that Friday afternoon. From the moment Leah opened the door, I could see my friend's face and feel her gentle mannerisms in the strong sisterly resemblance between them. I immediately saw that Leah took pleasure in hosting me. We were connected, because I was connected to her beloved sister and could share delight in her American nieces' growth. I could instantly feel why my friend loved and admired her sister's genuine piety and deep capacity for love. The hustle and bustle of the last hour of preparing the kitchen and the house for Shabbat were completely familiar, and my hosts could not have been more hospitable.

After showering and changing for Shabbat, I came out to the living room to join in Shabbat candlelighting and heading off to synagogue with my hosts. I gasped inwardly (and hopefully not too obviously) when I saw how they were dressed. David wore the garb of a Hasidic rabbi, including a large black hat and long black robe. Leah was beautifully dressed, with a regal white and gold headscarf wrapped elaborately over all of her hair.

I wondered how they felt about their guest, dressed modestly but obviously reflecting the norms of a very different community. They saw the *kippah* (head-covering, traditionally worn by Jewish men) on my head and knew that I would wear a *tallit* (prayer shawl, also traditionally worn by Jewish males) to their synagogue on Shabbat morning. This was to be a real cross-cultural experience.

I knew to expect soulful, passionate prayer at Friday evening services. I sat in the women's section of the synagogue, feeling very foreign, with my *kippah* and non-Orthodox dress. I wondered how these women might judge my dress and spin mental narratives about my religious identity, obviously so different from theirs. But it quickly became clear that Leah was revered in this community—as the rabbi's wife and by virtue of her own wisdom and piety—so I knew that, as her guest, I was safe and welcome.

Services were beyond beautiful. The entire community sang with powerful focus and intensity, as if the world depended on their raising their voices in praise of God. For much of the time the river of prayer overwhelmed my self-consciousness. I wished that I could join a community like this for prayer every week.

After services, we came back to Leah and David's home, where several of their young adult students joined us for dinner. In the style of Hasidic masters, David, at the head of the table, prayed the *Kiddush*[9]—too often recited by rote in the circles in which I travel—with powerful attention and intention. Between each course of the lavish dinner, he would begin to sing with deep prayerful attention. The rest of us halted our conversation and listened to his ethereal, mystical chants. At first these prayer interludes in the middle of Shabbat dinner, recited by the rabbi alone, seemed strange to me. But eventually I settled into this extraordinary prayer practice. The message was clear: Shabbat dinner includes delicious food and engaged conversation among the guests, but only a few minutes could pass before we would return our attention to God. I was deeply moved.

Much of the conversation centered on the sacred texts the young people were studying and their sense of how transformative this study was for them. It was wonderful to see that the genuine religious passion I had experienced in the community's prayer extended to the study hall. But

---

[9] Literally, "sanctification," the prayer over wine celebrating the sanctity of the Sabbath.

we occasionally drifted into matters of religious politics. I was prepared to listen in a quiet, disciplined way to views that were anathema to me, in order not to offend my gracious hosts. When David turned to me, acknowledging me as an American rabbi, and asked what American Jews thought about a particular issue, I was cautious and measured in response.

There was no explicit talk of news regarding the Israeli-Palestinian peace process. But somehow, the Palestinians were a presence at the table. On several occasions, people spoke in generalized, negative terms about them, implying that all Palestinians were violent and vicious people. These demonizing stereotypes appeared to be shared as a matter of fact by everyone at the table. I felt ill.

I lay awake late that night in their guest bedroom, my head aching with a "split-screen" experience. I admired these people as the real thing: genuinely loving, big-hearted human beings and passionately God-focused Jews. But a portion of the conversation at their table was stereotyped at best, characterizing an entire people as lacking in basic human values and sensibilities. I loved the people they were and admired the depth and seriousness of their practice of Judaism, but their attitudes toward non-Jews were prejudiced, if not downright hateful. How could these two realities exist at the same time, in the same people?

The next morning, Shabbat morning services were again powerful and beautiful. David gave an extended *d'var Torah* (sermon) on the portion of the Torah read that week, in which Jacob and Esau encounter one another twenty years after Jacob left his home in the face of Esau's murderous rage. I have long considered this to be a paradigmatic biblical story of reconciliation, despite the fact that most ancient rabbinic commentaries distrust Esau, denying the possibility that he might have changed enough to desire genuine reconciliation with his brother. In the communities in which I generally travel, the tendency is to give Esau the benefit of the doubt, understanding why Jacob is cautious, but seeing the story as a meaningful first step toward reconciling a tragically broken relationship.

By contrast, David's sermon was about the radical difference between Jacob and Esau and between their descendants. The language was the language of "us" and "them," with the characterizations of "us" always glowingly positive. I heard his words as connected to my experience of the previous evening, in which Palestinians were considered radically "other."

Again I felt ill, and struggled mightily against an instinct to slip out of the synagogue to avoid hearing more of the painful stuff.

I was intent on not sharing my reactions with David or Leah. My responses to his sermon seemed less important than continuing to explore relationship with them. But David asked me about my thoughts on the Torah portion, clearly inviting me into conversation about his sermon. I hesitated, saying that I saw things differently but did not want to offend him. With a tremendously gracious and open demeanor, he persisted in inviting me to share my reactions. Careful to articulate just what I thought I had heard, studiously avoiding accusation or judgment, I told him of my strong discomfort.

What followed was a remarkable conversation. He was genuinely concerned that I had heard his words as judgmental of non-Jews, for he had not intended them that way. We talked about rabbinic sources that supported his view of the story and those that were more in line with mine. I connected my concerns about xenophobia with my work in interreligious dialogue, to which he responded with stories of his own interreligious work. I still believe that there was a chasm between his perspective and mine. But we managed to speak about our different views with great care and respect.

After Shabbat, when it was time for me to go back to Jerusalem, we parted warmly. With Leah, I felt a strong, loving sense of familial connection, and with David, the deep satisfaction of having been able to engage warmly and respectfully across a chasm of disagreement.

Many important things had happened for me during that Shabbat experience. I had applied the dialogue skills I had practiced so diligently with leftist Jews and Palestinians with Jews to my right both religiously and politically. The skills, of course, were the same, but the emotional tenor was different, as I engaged with members of a far-flung wing of my own family. I had experienced deep spikes of judgment and outrage that I had had to attend to internally in order to protect the specialness of our human connection. But the sense of familial bond between us had served as a powerful motivator to cultivate the relationship even in the presence of wildly divergent beliefs.

Perhaps most important, my sleepless night was an exercise in deconstructing stereotypes, in resisting demonization of those with different worldviews, and in living with paradox. I had had to hold two very different images of my hosts simultaneously: they were beautiful, loving, deeply spiritual people—all things that I profoundly admire; and they held views of "the other" that were profoundly troubling. In their home, the simple categories of "like me" and "not like me" dissolved into a perplexing but real human complexity, one that I knew I needed to embrace.

A Month in the Life of an Aspiring Peacebuilder

The sense of impending crisis had been building for days. The press, both American and international, waited in tense anticipation of the arrival of the "Free Gaza" flotilla in late May 2010. There had been prior attempts to break Israel's blockade of the coast of Gaza. In a couple of instances, Israel had actually let a boat through. What would happen this time, with six boats, including several prominent world leaders, and the world watching intently? Would the boats be allowed to land? Would they be diverted for security checks? Was a violent altercation possible?

I felt more than the tension I typically feel when a crisis is brewing in Israel and Palestine (a familiar occurrence, after all). This time, it was personal. My daughter, Penina, long sympathetic to issues of Palestinian rights, was directly involved.

Penina is a child of divorce. From the time her father and I separated when she was five years old through her high school graduation, she lived in the rhythm of joint custody: half a week with me, half a week with her father. Her two homes were equally loving and comfortable, and the alternating rhythm of moving from one home to another became normal for all of us. The two homes had similar values in many areas of life, except for Jewish life.

In my home, Jewish identity was strong, and Jewish practice was a central dimension of our family life. In her father's home, this was not the case. I wondered and worried about how she would eventually construct her own Jewish identity once she was beyond the years of "mom's house/ dad's house," beyond the desire to please both of her parents.

Only years later did I come to understand that this divide of perspectives was especially strong in connection with Israel. In my parenting, in the Jewish day school she attended through fifth grade, in the life of our synagogue, which was a second home for us, and in her high school Jewish youth group, love of Israel was strongly encouraged. In her father's home, Israel was viewed much more ambivalently.

Early in her freshman year in college, Penina found a home with students who were social justice activists, raising funds to build rural schools in Africa, organizing for Darfur, working for environmental justice, and many other progressive causes. In this context, while she studied Hebrew and also made connections with Hillel, she found herself drawn to Students for a Free Palestine.

On her visits home freshman year, I was thrilled by how much Penina had grown—in self-confidence, analytic skill, and political sophistication. But she also brought home increasingly powerful critiques of the Israeli government. She was even asking questions about whether the very foundation of the State of Israel was fair and just. I tried to listen to her perspectives, but it was very difficult for me to hear her articulate such negative views about Israel. For a period of time, we fought about the issue, as she harshly challenged Israel, and I angrily resisted, criticizing the new narrative she seemed to be adopting.

Had this been a faceless group of Jewish college students unhappy with Israel, I might, like many Jewish leaders, have been outraged by this new narrative and critical of the students' estrangement from their Jewish roots. I might have been able to shut out their critiques, even call them names like "self-hating Jew." But this was my daughter, whom I love more than anyone in the world. I could not demonize her, call her names, distance myself from her. I had to do whatever it would take to understand her perspective. My principles as an aspiring peacebuilder demanded it. More deeply, my relationship with my daughter depended on it, and so our conflict became an opportunity to practice resisting polarization in the interest of loving connection.

> Rabbi Hiyya bar Abba said: If a father and son or a teacher and student who are studying Torah in one place become enemies to one another, they should not move from there until their love for one another is restored.[10]

---

[10] BT *Kiddushin* 30b.

Picture the scene: an old-world study hall, with men (yes, just men in the ancient academy) bent over sacred books, mining texts for layers of meaning, quarreling over the meaning of a word or concept. Discussion is passionate, even argumentative. Serious debate emerges about the implication of the text for law and practice. Before long, father and son, or teacher and student, are screaming at one another. "You're wrong!" "No, you're making no sense!" "How dare you talk to me that way?" "I am sick of arguing with you!" I imagine Rabbi Hiyya bar Abba calling out, "Lock the doors. No one leaves this place until we talk this through." With gentle insistence, the senior teacher, as mediator and master peacemaker, sits down with the two, helping them see the other's point of view, helping them reconnect from the heart.

I choose to ignore the hierarchical dimension of this text, privileging relationships between father and son or between teacher and student as those most in need of care. I take this text to mean that when any precious relationship between two people who love each other very much becomes endangered by an argument, all other pursuits should stop until love and connection are reestablished. The relationship is far more important than the content of the debate. Above all, love must be restored. As is so often the case, such restoration requires rigorous self-awareness and clarity of vision in order to resist the powerful temptation to allow the content of debate to damage priceless human ties.

Over time, I began to understand how things looked from Penina's perspective. Some of her points, though very painful to absorb, began to make sense to me. Gradually, her way of communicating her views grew less angry and my own understandings began to shift in response to her perspectives. There were still areas of disagreement between us, but we had both worked hard to weather the tensions. We had engaged in an extended process of trying to hear the other. Our relationship was far too precious to let the issue divide us. So we had talked and talked, reaching a point where the differences that remained between our views no longer challenged the harmony of our relationship with each other.

After college, through a serendipitous connection made by a Palestinian peacemaker who had become a family friend, Penina accepted a job with a nonprofit organization in California that worked on rebuilding homes in the West Bank and Gaza. We both knew that I would be delighted that she was doing important humanitarian work on behalf of Palestinians. We also knew that some of the organization's political views were challenging for me, in some ways more inclined toward the Palestinian narrative than the Israeli view of the conflict. Still, I was thrilled that my daughter had this wonderful opportunity as her first professional job.

Penina, with characteristic astuteness and sensitivity, reflected back to me, "*Ima*, thank you so much for being so happy for me even though you don't agree with everything I'll be doing." Honestly, in that moment, it had not been hard. I was deeply proud of her, and I had learned that I could love and accept her completely even if our views diverged.

The organization where Penina worked was deeply involved in preparations for the flotilla. The group's director worked closely with the staff of a community center in Gaza to assess what kind of building materials and sports equipment the center needed. Those materials would then be sent on the seventh boat of the flotilla, the Irish boat. The boat was named *The Rachel Corrie,* after the young activist who, at exactly Penina's age, had been killed by an Israeli bulldozer as she tried to prevent the demolition of a Palestinian home. Rachel Corrie's mother, Cindy Corrie (a polarizing figure in the mainstream Jewish community), served on the board of the nonprofit where Penina worked.

For weeks, as suspense built about how Israel would respond when the flotilla approached, I heard about my daughter's work coordinating between the Gazan community center and the activists responsible for stocking the boat with cargo they would try to bring in through the blockade. Although Penina worked from her office in the San Francisco Bay Area, for me, the Irish boat was "Penina's boat."

I woke up on the morning of Memorial Day to the news that Israeli naval commandos had boarded the first six ships of the flotilla. (The seventh boat, "Penina's boat," had had engine trouble and, as it turns out, did not arrive till several days later.) On the Turkish boat, the *Mavi Marmara,* physical violence had erupted, and nine activists were reported dead. I felt heartsick as I struggled to absorb the terrible news.

Living in the Midwest, I anxiously waited till 9 A.M. California time on a vacation day to call Penina at her home in San Francisco, wanting to reach out to her, guessing she would already have inside information to share. But her voice was sleepy when she answered her cell phone. "You haven't heard the news yet, have you, sweetie?" I blurted out. Suddenly tense and alert, she asked me what had happened. I replied gently, as I might have told her of the death of a loved one—sorry that I was the one to bear the terrible news to her and also glad that she was receiving the story first, in comforting tones, from me. I told her everything I knew, and she clicked into professional gear and said that she needed to call her boss, who had surely already been on the phones for hours.

The following week was painful in a familiar way. Like the period of Israel's incursion in Jenin in the spring of 2002 and Israel's war in Gaza in December 2008 and January 2009, I felt almost physically ill when Israel was engaged in the use of what appeared to be disproportionate force. I ravenously collected news accounts, opinion pieces, and videos, desperately trying to reconcile the two wildly divergent accounts of what had happened on the *Mavi Marmara*. I watched as the usual two internal Israeli narratives crystallized: one assuming that Israel had boarded the boats entirely in self-defense; another seriously questioning the wisdom of Israel's response to the flotilla.

I spent many hours that week working with a group of rabbis around the country, seeking to create a letter that would criticize Israel's attack while acknowledging Israel's need to defend itself against Hamas rockets. Nearly every day, I exchanged messages or calls with Penina—sending her bits of information and commentary, asking what she had learned and what her colleagues were saying, and commiserating as we lived through the crisis together. That Friday afternoon, as I rushed to prepare Shabbat dinner, the phone rang. It was Penina, calling to say "Shabbat Shalom."[11]

Her call brought tears to my eyes. When Penina left home for college, I had hoped for a regular Friday afternoon phone call, in which I would bless her (as I had at the Shabbat table throughout her childhood) and wish her "Shabbat Shalom." But it had become clear that the rhythm of her week was different from mine, and Friday afternoon was no longer a time for her to connect with family. I no longer expected to reach her before lighting Shabbat candles, and I certainly did not expect her to reach out with Shabbat blessings for me.

Her call was a moment of reconciliation for me, a sweet expression of thanks for my support through a difficult week, but also a marker of how

---

[11] Literally, "a peaceful Sabbath," the greeting used among Jews on the Sabbath.

we had grown in our relationship. She and I had worked our way through many challenging conversations over the years, listened and struggled and listened some more. We had learned to lovingly accept the ways in which we were different as she had established herself as an adult. I had told her how much I had learned from her perspectives, and she had come to respect mine. Her sharing the words of Shabbat greeting was a great gift, and a taste of peace.

A Dialogue Opportunity

As the war of words over the flotilla incident continued, I began preparing for my long-planned trip to Istanbul. Normally I am excited when anticipating such a trip, rich with potential for dialogue. But this time, I was uneasy about the challenging encounters that awaited me at the meeting, convened by the World Council of Churches. I knew it was to be an extraordinary gathering—as it turned out, unprecedented in the history of the World Council of Churches. This was an intra-Christian leadership meeting on the theme "Christian Self-Understanding in Relation to Judaism." There would be some two dozen Christian theologians there to reflect on their own tradition in light of the church's historic relationship to Jews and Judaism.

The meeting took place under the gracious and wise leadership of Shanta Premawardhana, then director of the WCC's Department of Interfaith Dialogue and Relations. At the outset, Shanta resolutely stated the visionary insight at the heart of this consultation. "We know that in the past we have committed terrible mistakes," he said gravely, "by constructing theologies of 'the other' without the presence of that 'other' at the table. We will not make that mistake again." So two Jewish colleagues and I had been invited to serve as participant-observers—to bring Jewish ears and sensibilities to the table, observing the largely intra-Christian conversation and reflecting back what was painful, unbearable, or unrecognizable to us as Jews.

Most challenging of all, the Christian participants would be a broader group than the usual participants in such conversations. Christian theologians, largely from Europe and North America, who live among Jewish communities, had been working on Christian relations to Jews and Judaism in penetrating, self-critical ways for decades, particularly in response to the challenges posed to Christian theology by the Holocaust. But this meeting would include not only "the usual suspects" but also Christian theologians from South America, Malaysia, Israel, Palestine, and Lebanon. Knowing that Arab Christians would surely think differently about Jews and Judaism than those with whom I was usually in dialogue, I sensed that this would be a difficult few days. As Shanta later commented, this was not to be a dialogue aimed at tea and sympathy, but an honest and painful encounter more like hot sauce and vinegar.

A Jew in Turkey

The World Council of Churches meeting was to be followed by the annual conference of the International Council of Christians and Jews. There had been great excitement about the organization's holding its annual meeting in a predominantly Muslim country for the first time, and the theme of the conference was to be "That You May Know One Another," a reference to a beautiful passage about intergroup understanding from the Koran.

But in the immediate aftermath of the flotilla incident, Israel's relations with Turkey had reached a new low. Diplomatic tensions were high, and it was reported that 10,000 Turks carrying signs, including some calling for the death of Jews, had gathered on a public square to protest Israel's attack. The Israeli government had advised its citizens to reconsider travel to Turkey. Although some conference participants would be coming from Israel, the conference coordinators decided not to cancel the meeting but to use the gathering as a way to bring a positive message of interreligious understanding precisely at this time of tension. In their message to conference participants, they quoted the words of the rabbinic sage Hillel, "If not now, when?" Nonetheless, they suggested that no religious garb (e.g., my *kippah*) be worn on the streets.

Only slightly apprehensive about my own physical safety, I heard my husband's reassuring, sensible voice in my mind, from the days when our children had spent extended periods of time in Israel during the second Intifada. What would be the statistical likelihood, I remembered him saying, of our child being hurt by a random act of violence? Although I was coming to Istanbul during a major diplomatic crisis between Israel and Turkey, this was not likely to translate into anti-Jewish violence on the street. Still, I had to admit that I felt frightened. Should I, in fact, not wear my *kippah* on the street? Would people be looking at me, recognizing that I was a Jew, hating me?

I was aware of my eighty-eight-year-old Jewish mother's fear. I had made the mistake of answering candidly when my mother had casually asked me whether I had any travel coming up. I probably should have told her about my trip only after getting home safely. "Isn't Louis worried?" she asked. No, my husband was not at all worried about my going, sensing, as I did, what a remarkable opportunity this was. "Is Penina worried about your going?" she asked, with greater emphasis. No, in fact, Penina had fully grasped how wonderful it was that I had the chance to go to Istanbul precisely at this time of tension, to build relationships and to serve the cause of peace. Penina had enthusiastically cheered me on, "Way to go, *Ima*!"

When my plane landed in Istanbul, I removed my *kippah*. It felt strange and wrong to be bareheaded, after many years of covering my head in a time-honored Jewish ritual of God-awareness. I tried to be discreet as I peered into the faces I saw at the airport. Would some of these people hate me if they knew I was a Jew?

I napped and showered, then followed my instinct to visit my favorite mosque from a previous visit to Istanbul, the magnificent Blue Mosque. I covered my head with a scarf, in Muslim style, out of respect for the place, and sat in the mosque in silent meditation for a long time. I went where my legs carried me, wandering the picturesque streets whose charm I remembered from my previous visit. After a day in Istanbul, I knew that there was no reason for me not to wear my *kippah*, no reason, in fact, for fear.

Despite the diplomatic crisis, I could relax on the streets of Istanbul. There was no need to fear that I would be assaulted by one of the city's 15 million people. It was not only a matter of low statistical likelihood, but of having pressed beyond instinctive fear of the enemy, to be able to bring myself fully to this place and open to the experiences that awaited me.

Working with Outrage

It did not take long for the interreligious meeting to confirm my expectations of a difficult dialogue. As I had expected, the Palestinian and Lebanese Christian theologians had complex feelings about Jews and

Judaism. Personally committed to reaching out to me, as I was to them, the very mention of the word "Israel" ("people of Israel" and "children of Israel," terms ubiquitous in the Bible that we share) was highly charged. One Christian Arab scholar of the Hebrew Bible summarized a recent meeting of Middle Eastern colleagues, concluding that the word "*Yisrael/*Israel" in the Bible has no connection to any ethnic or national group. It had nothing whatever to do with Jews. My heart translated his words, "My people does not exist." I was outraged. His tone of certainty made his proclamation all the more difficult to hear.

Trying to draw on years of practice staying present in the midst of such encounters, I watched my heart beating urgently and the cascade of angry thoughts pulsating through my mind. I could hardly hear the content of his words any longer, as if the volume had been turned down on the soundtrack, and I could only absorb the energy of rhetorical attack. I tried to observe my breathing, trying to remain engaged even as I began to prepare a response.

At last, his tirade had run its course, and I asked to be recognized. Seeking to reach beneath my anger to a place of grounded authenticity, I addressed him across the table. "I need for you to know," I began, trying to stay in touch with my breath, "that I found your words deeply offensive. If you want to tell me about your life experience, about how your family has been hurt in the conflict with Israel, and about how these experiences have affected how you read the Bible, I want to listen to you. It would be hard, but I would want to know what this has been like for you. But to tell me that the people of which I am a part does not exist—this is not acceptable. I believe that there are certain lines that must never be crossed in inter-religious conversation. Among them is to respect the way in which others construct their own reality. I believe that you have violated this norm."

I had spoken long enough and allowed more anger to come through than I had wanted. Stepping back to yield the space to others, I looked around the table, wondering if I had overstepped my rights as a conversation partner. Would Shanta, a world-class dialogue professional, be sorry that he had chosen me for a seat at this table? Had I brought the group to the brink of conflict that might derail our partnership?

But I sensed support from my colleagues at the table. Not only my Jewish colleagues, who had surely been as offended as I had, and who had each had her own moments of anger as the dialogue had unfolded, but from my Christian colleagues. Silently they communicated support, even respect for my honesty.

As often happens to me at moments of high emotion, I cannot remember what happened next. Shanta had said some encouraging words, urging us to see what had happened as precisely the kind of creative tension of which deep dialogue is made. The next thing I remember is that we left the room for a break in the day's intense deliberations.

Outside the meeting room, several colleagues offered kind words of affirmation for what they considered my honesty, my courage, and my willingness to speak my truth. Female participants huddled supportively with me in the women's room, including Debbie Weissman, an internationally known Israeli interfaith leader[12] and progressive Zionist educator, and Katja Kreiner, a German Lutheran pastor who had spent her career fighting anti-Semitism. I was grateful for their sisterly presence and for their words of assurance that I had done what I had hoped—to speak my truth without blame or recrimination. Later, Susannah Heschel, the other Jewish participant, gave me an exquisite compliment, graciously telling me that I had modeled for her a way of transforming anger into empathy.

I wish I could say that I reconciled with the man whose words had so offended me. I did not find a way to continue our conversation later in the meeting, to go deeper into the pain that lay beneath the words that both of us had spoken. I did, however, share meals with him, and saw that he had a warm smile. While I was never able to tell him so, I saw his heart, and I hope that he saw mine.

Reuniting with a Friend

The World Council of Churches meeting gave way to the much larger annual gathering of the International Council on Christians and Jews. Here I was delighted to find my friend and colleague, Adil Ozdemir, a Turkish Muslim scholar of Islam who teaches at a university near my home. He and his beautiful daughters have graced my family with their presence at

---

[12] Described more fully in chapter 2.

our Passover Seders for many years, always bringing their characteristic blend of humility, piety, and love. I had looked forward to the delight of seeing him, for the first time, in his home country rather than my own. Yet I was keenly aware that we had not yet talked about the flotilla incident, which had occurred after he had already returned home to Turkey for the summer. In a brief e-mail exchange, I felt that his language was a bit harsh, very different from his usual gentle demeanor.

We greeted each other lovingly, as dear friends, and settled into dinner together. We checked in about our children's lives and family events, and I told him about my experiences of the previous meeting. I was anxious to move to the topic I dreaded: How had he understood the flotilla incident and Turkish reactions to it?

A man of deep piety, he began with heartfelt words about the need for faith in the wake of such events. With deep sincerity, he offered the conviction that only God knows what may unfold from tragedies such as this one. I exhaled, and realized that I had been holding my breath, needing to hear him speak these words of faith and reconciliation. While he had clearly disapproved of Israel's actions, and had a different understanding of the events on the *Mavi Marmara* than I did, he was sure that the tension between Turkey and Israel would soon pass. We laughed together at my fearful anticipation of visiting Turkey, recognizing how misplaced had been my worry about encountering hostility or even violence directed at me as a Jew. The incident had most certainly not interfered with our connection with each other. Having reconnected with my Turkish friend, I could relax even more fully into my time in Istanbul, yet another weight of fear lifted from my heart.

Fear arose again as a topic of conversation between Adil and me in a different context later in the conference. We all attended a fine presentation by a scholar of Islam who urged Muslim leaders to develop a more robust culture of self-criticism and epistemological humility. A questioner, deeply engaged in interreligious dialogue work in Europe, asked for the speaker's reactions to his painful experiences of defensiveness in his Muslim dialogue partners, insisting on the perfection of their tradition and their community. The questioner said that he found that defensive stance disturbing and counterproductive in their shared efforts to educate their communities about Islam.

I was struck by the question, as I have had similar experiences in the course of my own work in interreligious dialogue. I have heard Islamic leaders declare that there are no significant differences between different schools of Islam. I have heard some deny that there are any texts of violence in the Koran or significantly violent events in the history of Islam. I have at times experienced resistance to acknowledging the violence committed in the name of Islam in today's world.

Sensing the opportunity to explore the issue more fully, I continued the conversation with Adil at lunch. Being careful not to offend him, I tentatively revealed that I had some feelings similar to those expressed by the questioner. Why, I asked, were so many Muslim leaders afraid to speak openly about the human flaws of the post-Koranic Islamic tradition and the destructive acts of those claiming Islam as their inspiration? I knew he would understand my sense that such defensiveness was harmful to dialogue. Could he help me understand why it was so hard for some Muslim leaders to speak self-critical truths?

Adil looked at me thoughtfully and recalled our earlier conversation about how Jewish leaders had reacted to the flotilla incident. With impressive insight and empathy, Adil asked me to reflect on American Jewish leaders' frequent inability to express their doubts about questionable acts on the part of the Israeli government. He correctly anticipated my answer, that the more American Jewish leaders sense Israel to be under attack (militarily, diplomatically, or rhetorically), the less able they are to speak critically of Israel's policies. He compared this to the chronic situation of American Muslim leaders, knowing that their community is constantly under suspicion, if not downright attack, in the post-9/11 environment.

The idea that Muslim leaders feel defensive in the midst of a climate of cultural assault on Islam and Muslims was not new to me. I have listened to such perspectives many times from my Muslim dialogue partners over the years. But I was struck by the analogy Adil was suggesting between the lived reality of American Muslims, whose religion and communities are subject to scrutiny and vilification, and American Jews, who often see it as their role to defend Israel from diplomatic and rhetorical attack.

Defensiveness is distasteful to look at. It smacks of dishonesty and serves to impede the growth of trust in dialogue. In the presence of defensiveness, I feel pushed away from the possibility of deeper relationship and increased understanding. Whether in another community or in my own, it takes focused intention to look compassionately beneath the barbs of defensive communication to the pain, fear, and need that underlie it.

It took Adil's observation, halfway around the world in a setting filling with possibilities of new understanding, to open me to recognizing that his people and mine are afflicted with a similar malady. The circumstances are so different that the similarity is hard to discern, but there is an important parallel between the defensive posture of Muslim leaders about Islam and Jewish defensiveness about Israel's actions today. When we feel that those precious to us are under attack, we respond defensively. We are afraid to open to the mysterious possibilities of truth-telling, even among presumed enemies.

I was moved by the parallel between the pain of American Jews and of American Muslims. In a moment of openhearted understanding, I could see that people—or peoples—cannot be expected to be at their best when they feel vulnerable to attack, suffering from recent traumas and expecting new ones.

Ultimately, I hope for both of our peoples to have the strength and clarity to override the inbred instinct to close down in self-protection in times of fear and trauma. Although counterintuitive, what is truly needed in such times is not to shut down, as our primal instincts propel us to, but to open the heart and reach out to others. Only in the sharing of our common pain and vulnerability can the dangers we face be transcended. I pray that both Jews and Muslims will be able to support one another in making this shift, moving away from primordial instincts to a more evolved stance of engagement with others. In this shift lies the potential for peace.

The Enemy: One Whose Story You Have Not Heard

As Gene Knudsen Hoffman said, an enemy is one whose story we haven't heard.[13] Later in the conference, I attended a presentation on the Kairos Palestine document. I was familiar with the document, knowing it to be a recent creation of a group of Palestinian Christian leaders, calling

---

[13] Gene Knudsen Hoffman, article, "An Enemy Is One Whose Story We Have Not Heard," *Fellowship: Journal of the Fellowship of Reconciliation*, May/June 1997, on New Conversations Initiative, http://www.newconversations.net.

on the international Christian community to support their desperate call for an end to Israel's occupation of the West Bank. American Jewish communal and rabbinic associations had strongly condemned the document as a one-sided Palestinian polemic, placing full blame for the ongoing conflict on Israel, while failing to recognize the impact of Palestinian violence and belligerent Arab rhetoric on the Israeli people.

On first reading I had written it off as a self-justifying, one-sided account of the complex conflict. For years, I have labored to dissuade Jewish leaders from reciting the Jewish narrative on the conflict without acknowledging Palestinian concerns and perspectives. So too, I expect Palestinians who work for peace to similarly stretch to respect Israeli understandings and fears.

At this meeting, I had the opportunity to learn about the document directly from one of its primary authors. When I had read it online, the document's powerful rhetoric had made me feel that the authors were shouting at me, screaming that they were right and my people horribly wrong. As a real person sitting across the table, my colleague Jamal Khader surely believed strongly in the document. But he spoke without any of the hostility I had expected but with powerful, spiritually grounded conviction. Jamal, a Roman Catholic priest, articulated the goals and message of the document strongly, but it was clear that this was for him a message of faith. Read on the flat computer screen, the document's cry for Christian support of Palestinians in the context of the Christian values of faith, hope, and love seemed like the harnessing of religious rhetoric to strengthen an ideological attack. But the man sitting across the table from me was erudite, dignified, and palpably a person of faith. His religious claims were deeply genuine, and I began to hear his plea.

The conversation continued at a later panel discussion, during which Jamal presented the document more fully. His appeal to the beloved verse in Jeremiah 6:14, "Peace, peace, but there is no peace," was a true religious lament that touched a place of pain in my own soul. His cry of protest was grounded in deep faithfulness and a sense of hope clearly rooted in his own religiosity, despite worsening frustration among Palestinians about the ongoing occupation of the West Bank. Jamal articulated in no uncertain terms what had been ambiguous in the written document—an unwavering commitment to a two-state solution to the conflict, providing for the State of Palestine to live in freedom and self-determination alongside a fully recognized State of Israel, secure and free from fear and insecurity.

Whereas on the page it had seemed just words, in person I knew that his categorical rejection of violence was real. His belief that the occupation distorts the image of God in both Palestinians and Israelis was born of palpable religious conviction. Importantly, there was no doubt but that by "occupation," he meant the lands acquired by Israel in the 1967 war, not the very state of Israel. In the context of the powerful human encounter in the room, I heard him fully affirm Israel's right to exist, and sincerely and honestly call for the end of the occupation not only for its crippling impact on Palestinians but also for its harmful impact on Israel.

Again and again, he spoke the words that soothed my fear, "We care about Israel's security." "We want Israelis to be freed from living in fear." "We want for Israel to be able finally to live in peace." He said repeatedly that we must stop accusing and blaming one another, stop rehearsing historical resentments, and move toward engaged human relationships among the two societies.

I took feverish notes, imagining how I might tell Jewish leaders back home about our encounter. I wondered how I could convey to them the depth and sincerity of this man. I doubted I could get them to believe me that Jamal was unquestionably genuine in his desire for a real peace between his people and ours. But I knew that I had moved from suspicion and fear to open-hearted understanding. I had watched my own heart and mind open during the days of the conference, moving from vigilance about what this Palestinian leader represented to gratitude that I had had the opportunity to know him. I felt that by-now familiar sensation, as if God were prying my heart open.

Years later, subsequent publications from "Kairos Palestine"[14] questioned Israel's very legitimacy, suggesting that Jamal's commitment to Israel's well-being must have been a minority view among the co-authors. Still, knowing him had put a human face to the document for me, so that the Kairos group could no longer be a faceless enemy, as it was for so many in my community.

---

[14] http://www.kairospalestine.ps.

Fear and Trust

I had expected the trip to Turkey to be a journey of conflict and dialogue. It was surely that, offering me more of the kind of difficult dialogue that I have sought out throughout my training as an aspiring peacebuilder. I was given opportunities to practice what I have learned in challenging situations and relationships, and memorable moments to deepen my practice and share it with others engaged in similar journeys.

More than that, my trip to Istanbul deepened my understanding of the dynamics of fear and trust, about the stories and experiences that constrict the heart and mind and the graced moments when tightness opens into possibility and even blessing. In times of fear and distrust, the "other" is seen as the enemy. This is not delusional; we have good reasons for our suspicions. But when we are able to examine our fears, breathe calm energy into them, question them, and pray for their healing, we sometimes find the heart opening into hitherto unimagined possibilities of relationship. This kind of opening makes peace and transformation possible.

Do Not Hate Your Enemy

No Ammonite or Moabite shall be admitted into the congregation of God; none of their descendants, even in the tenth generation, forever . . . because they did not meet you with food and water on your journey after you left Egypt and because they hired Bilaam son of Be'or . . . to curse you. . . .

Do not hate an Edomite, for he is your brother. Do not hate an Egyptian, for you were strangers in his land. Children born to them may be admitted into the congregation of God in the third generation. (Deut. 23:4–9)

Asked to deliver the *d'var Torah* (sermon) at a friend's son's bar mitzvah, I was delighted to see that the portion of the week would be *Ki Teitzei*, which begins with the powerful and tantalizing phrase, "When you go out to war on your enemies" (Deut. 21:10). This phrase has always touched a deep chord in me, promising Torah wisdom on the ethics of war, relationships with our enemies, and how we are to carry ourselves in the midst of conflict—even, dare I imagine, in Israeli-Palestinian relations.

The passage does not give the explicit guidance we might wish for about the wars raging in our world today. But it does teach a great deal about who we are to be as a people, and how we are to be in relationship with those thought to be "the enemy" in today's world.

Chapter 23 of the book of Deuteronomy contains laws governing the Israelites' collective relationship with four peoples who have been their enemies. Two nations, Ammon and Mo'av, are declared to be forever outside the community of Israel: Ammon, who refused to give the Israelites food and water on the way out of Egypt, and Mo'av, who sent the prophet Bil'am to curse the Israelite camp. Because these two peoples intended to do us harm at one point in history, they are to be kept out of our community forever.

But in verse 8, we find the surprising pair of commands: "Do not hate an Edomite—for he is your brother" and the truly stunning verse, "Do not hate an Egyptian, for you were a stranger in his land. Children born to them may enter the community of God in the third generation" (Deut. 23:8). The people of Edom are to be excluded from the community only until the third generation, despite the fact that they committed the same act of aggression against the Israelites as did the Ammonites (Num. 20:14–21). Why the difference? More surprising still is the commandment not to hate the Egyptians, who enslaved and oppressed the Israelites for four hundred years.

Rashi, penetrating the text to its depths, asks the same question. About verse 8, which tells us not to hate Edom, Rashi says, "Do not hate Edom *completely*, even though you have reason to hate them, for they came toward you with the sword."[15] When the text tells us not to hate Egypt, Rashi emphasizes, "Do not hate the Egyptians the slightest bit, though they threw your sons into the river. Why? Because they gave you shelter at a time of need."[16]

Rashi essentially asks our question: "How could we *not* hate peoples that caused us grievous harm, even sought to destroy us?" He accepts the reality that hatred will naturally arise in us when our physical survival has been threatened. Nonetheless, the Torah commands us, after some healing

---

[15] Rashi on Deut. 23:8, s.v. "Do not hate the Edomite."

[16] Ibid., s.v. "Do not hate the Egyptian."

time has passed, to wipe that hatred out of our hearts. Why should we not continue to hate the Edomites? Torah says, because they are our family, related to Esau, the brother of our forefather Isaac (Gen. 36:43). Our hatred for the span of two generations is understandable, even inevitable, but we must work at welcoming them back into our communities and into our hearts again.

Why on earth should we not hate the Egyptians, the paradigmatic, murderous oppressors in our history? "Because they gave you shelter at time of need," welcoming our ancestors into their borders at a time of famine. Rashi understands that we will howl in protest, "But they threw our children into the river!" He recognizes the humanness of this response. But he stands with the Torah's remarkable teaching here, that ultimately we are to remember Egypt not as the despotic regime that sought our destruction, but as the nation that gave us shelter in a time of need.

Some readers may be thinking, "That is not the Jewish way. We are entitled to hate those who have harmed us." But here is Rashi, the greatest Torah commentator of all time, asserting that the Torah teaches otherwise.

We have good reason to hate these two nations, yet we are told to accept them back into our lives after just two generations. But then, we may ask, why are we told to rehearse our grievances against Ammon and Mo'av forever, though their crimes against us were much less serious?

Rashi answers that Ammon and Mo'av sinned against us by tempting us, by strengthening the impulse within us to be unfaithful to God. They sinned against our souls—and that, he says, is a more heinous sin than that of Egypt, who merely tried to kill us! Although this may seem completely counterintuitive, Rashi is saying that what happens to our hearts and souls is more important even than our physical survival.

This insight develops further later in the passage. The end of the same Torah portion exhorts,

> Remember what Amalek did to you on your way out of Egypt, when they came upon you on the road and attacked the weak at your rear, when you were famished and weary, not fearing God. . . . Therefore, . . . blot out the memory of Amalek from under heaven. Do not forget. (Deut. 25:17–19)

Remember Amalek, the nation that attacked you, seeking to cause you great harm. Cultivate that memory—do not forget.

This commandment resonated more and more with the Jewish people as our history unfolded. The commandment not to forget Amalek has become the paradigm for the wicked despot who has sought to destroy us throughout the generations. For many contemporary Jews, the commandment not to forget ("Never Again") is among the most compelling of all Jewish communal imperatives.

But if we return once again to Rashi's commentary, we find that he reads this mitzvah in a very different way. Surprisingly, he says that Amalek attacked the Israelites at the rear of the camp at a time when the Israelites themselves were dishonest in their use of weights and measures. He continues that the Israelites at the rear became separated from the rest of the camp by the cloud, and that without the support of the community, they became lost in sin, leaving them vulnerable to attack from behind.[17]

Rashi goes so far as to suggest that the phrase, "did not fear God"[18] refers not to the Amalekite attackers but to the Israelites themselves. His core understanding of the commandment to remember Amalek is *not* to rehearse the angry memory, not to hate or blame or demonize Amalek, for they were only successful, in his view, because of our own moral and spiritual weakness!

According to this reading, the Torah is suggesting that our primary work is not to fight or hate those who may seek to harm us. Rather, the primary mitzvah is to be vigilant about the state of our own souls, constantly seeking to purify our own inner lives, cleansing our hearts of needless hate, small-mindedness, and self-importance, or anything that may obstruct our connection to God.

One Hasidic commentator, Rebbe Levi Yitzhak of Berditchev, makes this line of reasoning even clearer when he writes:

Not only are Jews commanded to wipe out Amalek, who is the descendant of Esau, but each Jew has to wipe out *that negative part that is called Amalek hidden in his or her heart.* So long as the descendants

---

[17] Rashi on Deut. 25:17, s.v. "remember what Amalek did," and 25:18, s.v. "the weak in the rear."

[18] Rashi on Deut. 25:18, s.v. "did not fear."

of Amalek are in the world—and each of us is also a small world, so when the power of evil in each of us arises (that which leads us to sin) Amalek is still in the world—then the reminder (to wipe out Amalek) calls out from the Torah.[19]

When we become aware that there is Amalek in the world—that is, in the world of our own hearts—then we must hear the call to remember, to struggle against it, to return to goodness and to godliness. The eternal struggle against Amalek, according to Levi Yitzhak, is an inside job, a matter of our own ongoing work on ourselves.

The mitzvah to remember Amalek is a piece of Torah that is often cited as textual evidence that we Jews are to devote ourselves—as to a primary commandment—to defeating those who may ever endanger us again. Surely, this is a strain well represented in our tradition. Our history has amply proven the wisdom and necessity of this command. The challenge is to recognize and deeply consider the other voice within the tradition, a voice that cautions us against allowing our painful history to justify hardening our hearts to our enemies, forgetting their humanity and their own capacity for change.

This voice in no way contradicts the obvious imperative to defend ourselves against real threats. But we are exhorted, whenever possible, to open ourselves to the healing power of time, praying and working to allow the wounds, fears, and angers of the past to recede. This strain of the tradition insists that God's ultimate commandment for the Jewish people is not only to survive, though we must surely do that, but to serve God in the world. The real enemy (and this is so very hard to remember) is not the external despot but our own *yetser hara* (the "evil inclination"), the negative instincts within us, to make choices devoid of wisdom and compassion, to imagine that we can live our lives without divine guidance. The ultimate force of the command to remember, then, is not to rehearse thoughts that reinforce anger or blame, but to rededicate ourselves to the ongoing work of cleansing our own hearts of all that is less than godly.

---

[19] Rabbi Levi Yitzhak of Berditchev, *Kedushat Levi, Drash L'Purim*, s.v. "*zachor et asher* etc. *v'atah ayef v'yageah v'lo yarei elohim*," trans. Rabbi Jonathan Slater.

What has all this to do with the ethics of war? The Torah is telling us that if are going to wage war—against other nations, other communities, or individuals in our lives, we must be certain that we have done our own inner work first, struggling against the inner Amalek, the impulse to hostility, vengefulness, or self-absorption within us. Only when we have met this prior condition—and how often can we honestly say that we have fully explored and purified our own motivations?—only then may we enter into conflict and consider ourselves blameless.

These surprising Torah texts suggest a counter-tendency to the one presumed to predominate in Jewish sources, that fighting for our own survival and waiting for the other side to do justice is our primary national imperative. Rather, in this stream of thought, our primary obligation—both as a people and as individuals—is to live lives as righteous and godly as we can, even in the presence of real adversaries in the world. In the midst of conflict, this means reaching higher than the feelings of bitterness, trauma, and victimization that naturally arise in response to wounding. We are to cultivate healing so that we may return to the primary purpose of life: pursuing justice and kindness for all people (not only for ourselves). Our tradition, in its wisdom, knows that this transformation does not come easily. Rather, it is a matter of lifelong practice of the sacred values at the core of our lives.

Peacebuilder Portraits

As soon as I began meeting with peacebuilders in Israel and Palestine, I knew that I needed to share their stories with others back at home. As is well known, the news media spend far more time covering the work of warmakers than that of peacemakers. I wanted to amplify the voices of the many thousands of grassroots peacebuilders who work quietly every day laying the groundwork for coexistence and respectful engagement between people with long histories of terrible grievances against one another. Their work is remarkable, edifying, and worthy of celebration and support.

I also want to disseminate their inspiring stories because their work generates hope. Hope can be hard to come by in contemplating a long-entrenched conflict, and despair, in turn, convinces many that reconciliation efforts are futile. Thus, supporting hope by publicizing evidence of peace work unfolding every day on the ground serves the cause of peace. The stories of these peace workers could fill volumes. I offer here accounts of just a small handful of peace heroes whom I have the privilege to know.

The Parents' Circle: Bereaved Families Supporting Peace, Reconciliation, and Tolerance

I have had many opportunities to encounter the inspired work of the Bereaved Parents' Circle, from private conversations to public meetings to the documentary film *Encounter Point.* In the presence of these unique peace activists, I always feel deep pain for their losses, awe and admiration for their courage, vision, and wisdom, and a great sense of hope. This meeting was no exception.

As always, the Bereaved Parents' Circle had sent two bereaved persons—one Israeli and one Palestinian—to speak with our group in Jerusalem. The two men, obviously close friends, exchanged friendly banter, then agreed that Rami Elkhanan, the Israeli, would speak first, beginning with his own story of loss. His fourteen-year-old daughter Smadar had been killed in a terrorist attack while shopping for school supplies in downtown Jerusalem. With remarkable vividness and honesty, he narrated how he had become filled with rage and "an urge for revenge that is stronger than death." The anger did not abate when Yitzhak Frankenthal, the founder of the Bereaved Parents' Circle, came to him and invited him to come and speak with Palestinians who had also lost children to the violence in the region. Why would he want to speak with such people? In any case, he needed to get on with his life.

But he could not go on with his former life, he said, because he had become a different person. "Such a loss changes you," he said. And, as he gradually came to discern, it presents you with a choice.

You can hold on to the anger which is the natural first response to such an excruciating loss, or you can channel your feelings into working to prevent more such losses to other families. "The pain of loss," he said, "is like nuclear power: it can be used to bring light and energy or to create great destruction." "We are the only club I know," he said wryly, "whose deepest wish is to have no new members."

Mazen then told his story of loss. In April 2002, during the height of the Second Intifada, his father was killed by Israeli soldiers on his way home from Jerusalem. He did not carry a gun or stones or any other weapon. Mazen said powerfully, "He was killed for no reason." The family received a phone call that the hospital had a sixty-two-year-old man with more than sixty bullet wounds in his body. The ID found on his person identified him as Mazen's father.

The audience, with great sadness and tenderness, sat in sacred silence as he told his story. It becomes clear that although each of the narratives of the five hundred families in the Bereaved Parents' Circle is unique, they blend together into a single story: one anguished lament over the death of innocents and the endless, futile cycle of violence.

Rami and Mazen, having spoken to many different groups around the region and around the world, told us some remarkable reactions they have encountered in speaking of their losses and their work for peace. After a presentation together, Mazen told us, a sixteen-year-old Palestinian girl approached the two with her father, telling them that she had turned to her father and asked, "Dad, if I were killed in the violence, would you do like Rami and Mazen and work for peace?"

They told us that again and again people on both sides ask the same desperate question: "If we make peace, can you assure us that we can trust the other side, that we will be safe?" Mazen and Rami said that this is like a patient who is told that his leg must be amputated to prevent deadly toxins from pouring into his system. When the patient asks the doctor, "Can you guarantee that if you remove my limb then everything will be OK?" the doctor cannot honestly offer such a guarantee. But the doctor can assure the patient with certainty that if the limb is not amputated, an already dire situation will grow worse.

Rather, Rami and Mazen love to rehearse stories and images of hope. They recall the terrible attack on a Gaza apartment building, intended to kill a terrorist leader, in which many children died in their sleep. They want us to remember that, following the attack, Jews donated blood to help wounded Palestinians, and Palestinians have done the same. If asked, "How can you give blood to 'the enemy'?" such people would respond, "It is better to give blood than to spill it." Later, the forum sponsored a project titled "Blood Relations," in which Israelis and Palestinians donated blood to be shared by both Israelis and Palestinians wounded in violence across the region. The core inspiration of the project was the question, "Could you hurt someone who has your blood running through their veins?"[20]

Most of all, Mazen and Rami and their colleagues intentionally offer themselves, their own stories, and their own friendship as an image of hope. Knowing that they make a striking picture, sitting at the head of the table, calling each other "brother," and treating each other with obvious affection, they told us, "Take this picture with you, the picture of the two of us together. Tell people that it is possible for Palestinians and Israelis to work together for peace. And if it is possible for us, who have paid the highest price, it is possible for anyone. Tell people that there are things about which we disagree, things about the past and about strategy. But tell them that we agree about tomorrow, about what we want for our children." Sitting around the seminar table, many of us in tears, we left knowing that we would tell their story to whoever would listen.

Sheikh Ghassan Manasra, Anwar Il Salaam/ Lights of Peace Center, Nazareth, Israel

I first met Ghassan Manasra at a funky restaurant in Minneapolis, where he and his colleague Eliyahu McLean, partners in a visionary project called Jerusalem Peacemakers, were having a quick dinner before their fifth speaking engagement of the day on a high-energy fund-raising tour. I had met Eliyahu, but I looked forward to my first-ever meeting with a sheikh. I imagined a bearded older man in traditional garb, remote and otherworldly. Instead, Ghassan, dressed in casual Western clothing, greeted me with eyes that sparkled with love for the world. He immediately opened his arms in a gracious gesture of pleasant anticipation. I was being invited into relationship with a man with an enormous heart.

I peppered Ghassan with questions about his work: teaching Sufism to Israeli Jews and Muslims, teaching Hebrew to Israeli Arabs and Arabic to Jewish Israelis, and conducting intrafaith dialogue across the broad spectrum of the Muslim community in Israel. The work was inspired and revolutionary, yet what impressed me most was the light in his eyes and the

---

[20] The Parents' Circle Families Forum, http://www.theparentscircle.org.

spirit of generosity, genuineness, and love that he embodied. After dinner, he spoke with gentle dignity to a synagogue filled with two hundred Jews, Christians, and Muslims. He closed his words with a haunting Islamic chant. I was enchanted.

Months later, I accepted Ghassan's invitation to his home for dinner. His home on the Mount of Olives, in his family for generations, looks out on a breathtaking view of Jerusalem. A majestic Jerusalem panorama lay before us; one could practically reach out and touch the Dome of the Rock. Ghassan delightedly introduced me, the woman rabbi from Minnesota, to each of his children. The children smiled obediently and shook my hand, and then withdrew. His wife, Laila, wearing the *hijab*, listened with intent interest as her husband and I conversed in fluent Hebrew. We spoke of our shared prayer for peace in the land we both love, of the critical importance of interreligious reconciliation, of commonalities between our two faiths, and of dreams to work together to bring American Jews, Christians, and Muslims to visit Israel.

On a subsequent visit, I brought my husband back to the Manasra home. I again heard the story and personal meaning of Ghassan's lineage as the son of a renowned Sufi sheikh, heir to a family that proudly traces its line back to the Prophet Muhammad. We looked respectfully at the prominent portrait of Laila's father, also a preeminent Sufi sheikh. Laila was less shy this time, willing to use her Hebrew, not only a gracious hostess but a woman seeking relationship. I sensed her pride in her own family line, a dignity born of generations of family prominence and piety. Yet she smiled broadly as her husband told the story of blessing their fifteen-year-old daughter's decision not to wear the head covering, delighting in the blossoming of their daughter's self-knowledge and confidence. She looked lovingly at her husband as he choked up when telling the story of how their teenage son had been seriously wounded in an attack intended to deter Ghassan from his pioneering work, and the way in which their son had awakened from his coma with the words, "Father, we must continue our work."

Speaking elegant Hebrew, Ghassan radiated pleasure in our presence, from the Hebrew and Arabic prayers with which we began our meal together, to the strictly vegetarian meal Laila had prepared on dairy-only dishes reserved for religious Jewish guests, to his warm and attuned responses to our every question and observation. Ghassan told marvelous tales of his encounters with conservative Muslims. It was obvious that his rare combination of traditional learning, personal warmth, piety, and humility won people over, as when confronted by a conservative colleague over his mission to bring Islam fully into conversation with the modern world. His gentle invitation, "If I am wrong, please help me understand," began the dialogue. Many conversations later, the conservative leader began to absorb his understanding of an Islam grounded in deep respect for and unity with other religions, an Islam profoundly committed to peace and reverence for all of God's creation.

We roared with glee as Ghassan, aware of our connection to Judaism's Conservative Movement,[21] dubbed himself a "Conservative Muslim." We listened with wonder and deep respect as he engaged in a penetrating critique of the gap between the teachings of Islam and the lives of some contemporary Muslims. He decried the evils of Wahhabism and the fool-hardiness of the Muslim world's failure to modernize, unite, and learn from the West. With prayerful humility, he described his work to create bridges between Muslims, Jews, and Christians, between Jewish Israelis and Palestinians, and between Islam and the West.

As the evening drew to a close, Ghassan and Laila, with classical Middle Eastern hospitality, gave us samples of our favorite dish to take home, and walked us out to our car, stopping to marvel at the magnificence of Jerusalem shimmering below. Members of the extended family living in adjacent homes appeared and greeted us warmly. We exchanged loving greetings, looking forward to future meals at our home in Minnesota or, more likely, here in Jerusalem. Our hearts were bright as the lights of Jerusalem, as we prayed for his success and reveled in the blessing of our friendship.

On another occasion, I was again a guest in Ghassan's home, this time during Hanukah. As a house gift, I brought him a *hanukiyyah*, Hanukah candelabra. I offered it to him lovingly, explaining that it was a token of my appreciation for his work in bringing light into the world. I need not

---

[21] "Conservative Judaism" refers to the movement in Jewish life, created in the late nineteenth century, whose mission is to balance deep faithfulness to Jewish law and tradition with awareness of how the tradition has changed and must continue to evolve in response to changing historical developments.

have explained; he understood perfectly. The previous evening, he had led an interfaith celebration of Hanukah, in which the candles were lit and reflections on light shared by Jewish, Christian, and Muslim leaders. He was delighted by my gift.

Despite the lights of Hanukah all around Jerusalem that week, it had been a dark time. I had come to Israel hoping for good news, yearning to discover more openness to a political resolution of the conflict than was evident from the media. My two weeks of conversations had confirmed that things were, if anything, more stuck than ever. I was in need of precisely the sort of teaching that comes so readily to Ghassan as a Sufi teacher, the image of the light of God warming us from within, and the practice of cultivating love in the heart. I wanted someone to tell me that there was a way to make things go faster than the excruciatingly slow work of relationship building. He could not, for, like me, he believes there is no way to real peace but the gradual process of opening hearts.

But somehow, in Ghassan's presence, I was reminded that the work of peacebuilding is God's work, and I must be more patient. I had visited a holy man, and I left feeling inspired and more peaceful than I had felt in some time.

Amnon Sadovsky, Teacher, Hand in Hand School, Jerusalem

The title of the evening session was "Can/Should There Be a Joint Narrative?" "A joint narrative?" I thought, with some skepticism. Having spent years learning about the profound differences between Israeli and Palestinian perspectives on the past hundred years in our troubled land, I felt skeptical. I had been to peace camps where ethnically homogenous groups from the region were asked to create timelines of the conflict; the timelines they drew up were radically different, both in terms of which events were considered of importance, how these events were referred to, and, of course, how they were interpreted. I knew of books and curricular materials that attempted to juxtapose the two narratives—even this, I knew, was a radical effort. An integrated narrative?

Amnon is a Jewish Israeli history teacher at *Yad B'Yad*—Hand in Hand—one of five such bilingual, bicultural schools (Jewish and Arab) in all of Israel. He is a sweetheart of a man, teddy-bearish in build, soft-spoken and thoughtful, yet passionate about the potential for turning history from a weapon in the conflict into a vehicle for understanding and reconciliation.

Idealistic but far from naïve, Amnon teaches history to Jewish and Palestinian Arab kids at *Yad B'Yad* and leads dialogue groups for Jewish and Arab Israeli teachers. Amnon did not mince words about how difficult the dialogues could be. At times it was hard to get enough participants to come; at others, sessions exploded into loud argument and despair.

Visiting the school the next day, we saw Jewish and Arab children playing together in the schoolyard, easily shifting between Hebrew and Arabic depending on whom they spoke to, and talked with children who told us that in their classrooms they saw a room full of friends, not children defined by nationality, religion, or ethnicity. Yet the school faces a host of thorny issues: How to apportion the class time allotted to the teaching of Judaism, Christianity, and Islam? How to honor Friday, Sabbath for the Muslim children but not for the Jews and Christians? How to teach events on the Israeli calendar such as Holocaust Day and, most difficult of all, the day that Jews call "Israeli Independence Day" and Arabs call "*Naqba* Day," marking the day of the announcement of Israeli independence as a "catastrophe" for their people?

Amnon spoke with educational sophistication as he described efforts to create an integrated narrative. The vision was to de-emphasize issues about which Jewish and Arab Israelis cannot yet agree (e.g., Was Zionism a return to a homeland or a colonialist project of Western powers? Were local Arabs evicted from their homes in 1948 or did they flee?), and focus on topics that can be shared by all who love the land. It takes great creativity to identify meaningful subjects about which all students and teachers can agree in connection with this land, and that is precisely what is being pioneered at *Yad B'Yad*. Children are taught the history of the land itself (rather than of its separate national groups), cultural and religious rather than political and national history, and stories of times and places in history when tolerance and coexistence have reigned. At times, aspects of local history are taught through an examination of multiple family narratives, shedding light on different facets of the historical story.

My skepticism melted in the presence of this ground-breaking effort and this visionary educator. He teaches and models the practice of empathy and respect in the hardest possible context. His work, educating children in a laboratory of coexistence, exemplifies the values of mutual acceptance and respect for all.

Souliman Al-Khatib, Peace Activist, Ramallah

I first met Souliman Al-Khatib at the makeshift office of the Abu Sukkar Center for Peace and Dialogue in a tiny town in East Jerusalem. A sweet and warm young man with sparkling eyes, an endearing combination of humor, humility, and obvious charisma, he told a remarkable story of transformation.

Souli (as I later came to know him) had grown up in Hizme, a tiny Palestinian town in northeast Jerusalem that had long been involved in what he called "political activism." His family had suffered from the Israeli occupation of the West Bank and believed that the only solution was military, leading several family members to engage in what they called "violent resistance." (He smiled ironically as he said this, well aware that from the Israeli perspective this would be called "terrorism.") At the age of twelve, Souli joined the Fatah movement (illegal at the time under Israeli law) and engaged in acts such as throwing stones and Molotov cocktails at Israeli soldiers. At the age of fourteen, in 1986, prior to the first Intifada, he and a friend stabbed two Israeli soldiers (wounding them, he interjected apologetically, not killing them). Sentenced to fifteen years in Israeli prison, he eventually served ten and a half years, with time off for good behavior.

Souli told us that the Palestinian political prisoners were placed in an area of the prison different from that of nonpolitical criminals, and that the political prisoners self-organized a kind of "university" within the prison, including daily study groups, in which many received the equivalent of high school and college education. Souli learned Hebrew (which he at first thought of as the "language of the enemy") and English, read classic works of Western literature, philosophy, and political theory, and studied Jewish history. Gradually, he recalls, his mind began to open, and he began to understand that the Israeli-Palestinian conflict was more complex than he had previously understood. Over time, he concluded that there was no military solution to the conflict. By the time of his release from prison,

Souli was determined to turn his natural talents for leadership toward the work of peace activism.

By the time the Second Intifada broke out in September of 2000, he was among those Fatah activists who opposed violence, believing that the conflict needed to be addressed by building relationship between Israelis and Palestinians. In January 2004, Souli joined Breaking the Ice, a small expedition of Israeli Jews and Palestinians traveling together to Antarctica, seeking to demonstrate the power of Israeli-Palestinian collaboration. The participants climbed a mountain and renamed it "The Mountain of Israeli-Palestinian Friendship."

Soon thereafter, Souli partnered with other Palestinians who had rejected violence, creating a relationship with Israeli Jews who had come to refuse to serve their required time in the Israeli army because of Israel's occupation of the West Bank and, at the time, Gaza. The resulting organization, Combatants for Peace, began with a painful series of private dialogues between twenty-five Israelis and twenty-five Palestinians. Gradually, the group coalesced into an educational program, teaching young people in both communities to reject violence and to pursue understanding and reconciliation between Israelis and Palestinians.

Later I reconnected with Souli at an Israeli-Palestinian peace camp in Northern California. I learned that he was in the United States for some time, available to speak to groups to spread his message of hope and nonviolent engagement. My husband and I eagerly brought Souli to Minneapolis/St. Paul, where we hosted a parlor meeting in our home and arranged for Souli to speak to several college classes and to a Conservative synagogue. For two days, Souli was a guest in our home, the first time we had had the opportunity to host a Palestinian. As it turned out, we were the first Jewish family that Souli had known in this way. Our daughter struck up a long-standing friendship with Souli, and one of our sons was so moved by what he heard that he wrote a college application essay about the profound and wonderful confusion caused in him by coming to know Souli as a lovable and admirable human being. Souli still occupies a special place in the heart of our family.

Souli later partnered with Gadi Kenny, an entrepreneur turned peace activist, in creating Wounded Without Borders. This group draws together Israelis and Palestinians who were wounded in the conflict, including the

Jewish warden of one of the Israeli prisons in which Souli had served. Unlike most collaborative peace projects in the region, whose members are largely leftists within their own societies, this group comprises people with more hawkish views on the conflict. The dialogue process has been difficult and rich. Even during the war in Gaza in 2008–9, the group continued to meet and build relationships with one another. Souli and Gadi have also worked to build "People's Peace Houses"—centers built expressly to house extended Israeli-Palestinian encounter programs.

Souli is now one of the people I see every time I go to Israel. For years, Souli, like other peace and dialogue activists, had a long-term permit to cross from his home in Ramallah into Israel, so he always came to Jerusalem to visit me when I was in the country. On a recent visit, due to what he said was an administrative change, Souli was without the required permit, and he asked me to come to Ramallah to see him. Having been to the West Bank many times but never alone, I noticed how frightened I was boarding a Palestinian bus to travel the short distance from East Jerusalem to Ramallah. The Palestinians at the bus station and on the bus were strangers to me, and so my images of them as "the enemy" were intact. I had to pray my way through my fear during the thirty-minute bus ride.

But Souli, as always, greeted me like an old friend, and we spent a completely delightful day hanging out in coffee shops, where Souli was a magnet for Palestinians and internationals interested in peace and dialogue efforts. When it was time for me to go, Souli produced a gift bag with two beautiful scarves, one for me and one for my daughter. Souli and I laughed at my fear in coming. This man was a friend of our family, in no way an adversary.

Alick Isaacs, Jewish Scholar, Philosopher, Peace Activist

A friend in New York City, a wonderful Israeli rabbi and justice activist, had lovingly told me that I must meet Alick Isaacs next time I was in Israel. "He does remarkable peace work! You must meet him!" Thus, our encounter was graced from the start. Alick's initial e-mails reflected the affection one feels on meeting the friend of a special friend, and we eagerly arranged to meet at a café in southern Jerusalem often frequented by peace and justice activists. Our one-hour appointment went on for well over two hours.

It was thrilling for me to encounter this soft-spoken, brilliant Orthodox scholar who shared my fervent desire to use Jewish text to teach and cultivate peace. More precious still, we seemed to share a common language in talking about the spiritual experiences that had led each of us into this work.

Alick told me a bit about his journey, revolving around two defining moments of violence.[22] Born and raised in Great Britain in a religious Zionist family, Alick had a lifelong connection to the State of Israel. As a fourteen-year-old, he was badly beaten in an anti-Semitic attack by a group of boys. On the ground, suffering their blows, Alick knew that he would make *aliyah*, or "ascent," to make his life in Israel. He did just that, moving to Israel and entering the army immediately after graduating from high school.

Years later, serving as a solder when the First Intifada broke out in 1987, Alick was given orders to beat Palestinians and destroy their property. He understood the profound significance of his having moved from being beaten to the one committing violence against others in the name of his beloved state. From that moment, he knew he would study the problem of peace and violence in Jewish text. A peacebuilder's journey had begun.

Alick studied sacred Jewish text in yeshiva, then earned an interdisciplinary PhD in history, philosophy, and education at the Hebrew University. A man in his early forties, Alick has already written several books. One describes his experience of the Second Lebanon War. Another constructs a theory of Jewish peacemaking that encompasses the complex and often contradictory tendencies within Jewish tradition on the subject. His approach seeks to uncover a complex understanding of peace and violence within the underlying structure of Jewish sacred text.

But Alick is an activist as well as a philosopher. He has created a pilot project that has, improbably, brought together renowned settler rabbis and arch-leftist leaders of the secular peace camp (many considered "extremist" ideologues by one side or the other). Alick's goal is nothing less than to

---

[22] This story is now told in his book, *A Prophetic Peace: Judaism, Religion, and Politics* (Bloomington: Indiana University Press, 2011).

create a new kind of peace camp in Israel that would unite "doves" and "hawks" in commitment to peace as a Jewish and Israeli guiding principle. The goal is not to discuss borders, refugees, settlements, or other specific matters of policy. It is about creating a broad alliance of Jewish Israeli leaders—unheard of in this fragmented society—to articulate the profound value of peace for Judaism and for Israel. The core question for discussion is not "What shall we do?" but "What does peace mean to you?" Alick envisions the creation of a peace campaign that would unite left and right, secular and religious, pragmatic and ideological people, providing to this meaning-hungry society a nourishing and inspiring vision of peace as a way of finding purpose in their lives.

Alick spoke with the sophistication of an experienced dialogue activist as he recalled meeting with individual participants before convening the group, spending hours listening to them in order to win their trust and respect. He related things he had heard the rabbis tell the leftists that would have been unbelievable had I not heard them from someone so utterly trustworthy. One rabbi, he said, told a secular leader, "The problem is not the Palestinians. We could accept a solution with them. Perhaps our settlement would move back within the borders of Israel. Or perhaps we would stay where we are, living in the new state of Palestine. The real problem is between you (secular Israeli Jews) and us (Jewish settlers). If only you could acknowledge us and hear our truth about the threat of secularism to the soul of Israel, then we could make peace together."

Alick's work is grounded in the writing of Abraham Isaac Kook, the first Ashkenazi chief rabbi of the State of Israel, who embodied a rare combination of universalist mysticism and passionate devotion to the particular way of the Jewish people, made real in the teachings of *halacha* (Jewish law). For Rabbi Kook, the Jewish people's particularity is essential to its purpose of serving the world. Likewise, the world would be diminished if any of the other unique strands of the human family were to disappear. Thus, Israel's crisis in the world today and the challenges faced by Zionism are to be seen as an opportunity sent by God to help bring Judaism to a new stage in its collective evolution. Alick continues in Kook's footsteps, modeling a rich and respectful way of living with difference in our broken world.

Zoughbi Zoughbi, Wi'am Palestinian
Conflict Resolution Center, Bethlehem

We arrived at Wi'am on a punishingly hot summer day in Bethlehem. A staff member of the center immediately served cold water and Turkish coffee to our group in a Middle Eastern gesture of hospitality. Moments later, Zoughbi appeared, a large man with a large presence. He began to tell us about Wi'am, the grassroots conflict resolution center that he directs. The name "Wi'am," he told us, is a feminine word in Arabic, meaning "*agape*" or "cordial relationship." As he described the work of the center, I kept changing my mental framework for understanding what this place was. A mediation center that helps individuals and families resolve interpersonal conflicts. An educational center that teaches methods of nonviolent conflict resolution to children and adults. A training center for mediators and human rights activists. A community center that finds jobs for needy people, sells handcrafts created by community members, and organizes its constituents to creatively address the challenges that their communities face.

Zoughbi, educated in the United States, spoke fine English and exhibited mastery of both Western modes of conflict resolution and the traditional Palestinian reconciliation practice known as *sulha* (from the Arabic and Hebrew root meaning "forgiveness"). Sensing the perspective of his audience, he spoke inspiringly of the need to teach peace and reconciliation, from the individual to the national level, yet he knows when it is wiser to use the more cautious language of "culture of acceptance," when speaking with people who are discouraged and bitterly skeptical of the language of peace in this war-torn land. He lamented the collapse of civil society in the Palestinian community and bemoaned the impact of the occupation on local infrastructure. Yet he yearned for healing in the "dysfunctional family of Abraham."

I was deeply moved by Zoughi's obvious leadership ability and by his vision of working for peace and reconciliation on every level—personal, communal, and international. I was delighted to learn that Zoughbi was serving on the City Council of Bethlehem at the time, bringing his blend of psychological insight, conceptual sophistication, and big vision to this depressed city. Irrationally exuberant about this man's power to bring positive change to his people and to our shared land, I rushed up to him after the formal session and asked whether he was active with the Palestinian Authority. I wanted him to run for Prime Minister of Palestine, keenly aware that both societies are in deep need of gifted leaders who can inspire the confidence of their people and move with integrity toward peace and justice. He smiled, taking in the compliment, replying (with a politician's savvy?) that his work is with the people of Bethlehem. I thanked him, and gladly bought a beautiful piece of traditional Palestinian embroidery for my daughter, supporting the work of the center.

Center for Humanistic Education, Kibbutz Lohamei Hageta'ot (Ghetto Fighters Museum), Northern Israel

The museum at Kibbutz Lohamei Hageta'ot (Ghetto Fighters) is now a very different place than the one created in 1949 by the survivors of the Warsaw ghetto. The difference was clear immediately when Tania Ronen, our tour guide/educator, intentionally introduced herself not by the usual designation, "child of survivors" (which she was), but as a "second-generation Israeli." As her story unfolded, it became clear that this formulation symbolized a significant shift in identity, reflecting a radically new perspective on how to teach the Holocaust.

Tania spoke, as one would expect, with exquisite sensitivity to the Holocaust memories exhibited and transmitted at this museum. "We all have our memories," she said eloquently. "They have a right to be there; we must honor all of them and make a dedicated space for them." She narrated the symbolism in various architectural features of the remodeled museum, such as a skylight, intended to let light in to expose dark times in history, but also to create an open space, she said, where spirit could rise. She emphasized that on longer tours she guides people on a walk on the roof itself, inviting them to contemplate the danger of falling into the darkness, of being consumed by memory.

Her central questions as an educator and tour guide are, "What do I want visitors to do with the information the museum conveys?" "What do we want our young people to learn from the horrors exhibited here?" "How do we take this story into the future, to create a new life for our people?" The answer: the founders of the museum and their children are now using their story as a powerful means of teaching humanistic values such as human dignity, tolerance, and embrace of difference. These people, who have every right to hold fast to their particular story of victimization, are now loosening their grip on the uniqueness of their story. In the twenty-first century, they no longer want to insist that this story of genocide is sui generis and incomparable. Rather, they are insisting that this story be shared with the world as a spur to creating a better tomorrow for all people.

I was stunned and thrilled. I have been one of a number of teachers and Jewish leaders urging a reconsideration of the place the Holocaust plays in Jewish identity. Devoted as I am to honoring our people's history of persecution and genocide, I have been concerned about the ways in which Holocaust education can be used as a negative motivator for Jewish identity or, worse, how the Holocaust narrative can be used to elevate Jewish survival above other values equally central to Judaism. When I have spoken and written about these things in the Jewish community, I have always felt that I was breaking a taboo, pushing against deep wounds and anger at the very suggestion of holding our traumatic memory differently.

Yet here was Beit Lohamei Hageta'ot, the first holocaust museum in the world, founded in 1949, advocating just this sort of change in perspective. But there was more.

The museum's department of education has within it a Center for Humanistic Education that was directed by Raya Kalisman and David Netzer at the time I was there. In a presentation titled "Bridge Over Troubled Waters: Painful Past in the Service of Humanistic Dialogue," they introduced us to a remarkable Holocaust education program, in which homogenous groups of Jewish and Arab Israeli teenagers undergo an intensive process of studying the Holocaust as a bridge to democratic values, civic responsibility, moral judgment, and commitment to human rights. Working closely with the renowned Facing History and Ourselves program,[23] the educators deftly guide the students to consider the many different uses to which memory—especially charged traumatic memory—can be put. Implications for contemporary Israeli politics were unspoken but clear.

---

[23] http://www.facing.org.

Graduates of this thirty-hour program are eligible to join in a "multi-cultural bi-national seminar," in which teenagers engage in Jewish-Arab dialogue, applying the humanistic values they had explored in their Holocaust study. The encounter is no simple thing. In contemporary Israel and Palestine, the story of the Holocaust is charged with profound national, political, and religious passions. For Jews the Holocaust represents the culmination of two thousand years of exile and persecution suffered by our people and therefore the final demonstration of the need for a Jewish state as an existential necessity. For many Palestinians, by contrast, the Holocaust is a bludgeon used against their people, the excuse employed by colonial powers to rob them of their land. In Israel itself, many (perhaps the majority) still hold fast to the Holocaust as a unique and incomparable Jewish story; the notion of teaching the Holocaust as a vehicle for universal moral education is still controversial at best.

Yet some two hundred teens each year engage in these profoundly difficult dialogues, sitting together, wrestling with the multiple personal and national narratives that define their lives. Some sixty of the graduates of this program have gone on to conduct civic awareness projects within their own communities, coming back together—Jews and Arabs—once a month, to share their triumphs and challenges. These student activists consciously work at reconstructing their own deeply held narratives, laboring together to create a more moral, humane, and democratic society, not despite each group's traumatic memories, but because of them.

The museum and its educational programs serve as a remarkable model of altruistic and courageous self-reflection. In the face of the most tragic stories of trauma, these educators teach the art of examining the construction of one's own national identity. In so doing, people discover that interpretations of collective memory are not immutable. With a measure of humility and a strong desire to serve the cause of peace, these people release some of the hold of the traumatic past in order to create a better future for all.

Hanan Abu-Dalu, Kids for Peace

Attending an international interfaith dialogue conference, we sat in a beautiful retreat center in the southern part of sprawling West Jerusalem, minutes from the Green Line and from Bethlehem. The morning's plenary session promised to be intense, even explosive. Three women—one Jewish Israeli, one Christian, and one Muslim Palestinian—were listed on the conference program to address the essential issue, "My Community and the Land."

The Christian Palestinian woman never came, and we never learned why. The Jewish moderator let us know with deep remorse that, despite the conference planners' intensive efforts to be sure that no Palestinian participant would be detained at a checkpoint on the way to the conference, Hanan, a Muslim activist with the program Kids for Peace,[24] had, in fact, been delayed. Yet when she rose to speak, we saw not a hint of anger or frustration. The graceful, eloquent woman before us, dressed in Islamic garb, was infused with the humility and God-consciousness that I have come to know as Islam at its best.

Still, I braced myself, wondering whether a talk on a Palestinian's claim to the land would be hard for me to hear. To my surprise, Hanan began, in a gentle and heartfelt style, to define the term "my community" in the session's title. "Of which community shall I speak?" she asked, and proceeded to articulate, in descending order, the identities that most define her: her identity as a human being, as a Muslim, as a Palestinian, and as a woman. Without any question, she asserted with quiet power, her primary identity was as a human being, grateful to God for life. Instantly I began to breathe more deeply. This beautiful woman, covered from head to toe, was telling me that she could speak of her attachment to the land only after she had acknowledged that at heart, she was at one with all of us, with all people. I was in the presence of a holy woman.

She continued describing the components of her identity. As a Muslim, she said, she knows herself to be a creature of God, endowed with qualities of the divine, meant to worship God and to serve others. Her Muslim identity, she said, teaches her that the way to be a better human being is not to be a better Muslim but to revere God by honoring all of God's creatures and expressing commitment to the well-being of all people. "Drawing closer to God," she said, "is why I'm here." When life circumstances (such as this morning's encounter at the checkpoint? I wondered) lead her away from God, she must choose that which will bring her nearer.

---

[24] Kids for Peace: Uplifting Our World through Love and Action, http: www. kidsforpeaceglobal.org.

Her identity as a Palestinian, she said, was not nearly as important to her as her identity as a Muslim or as a human being. (What if more people in this war-torn land thought of their lives in this way, I thought, leaning forward to absorb her every word.) She acknowledged the suffering of her people but insisted that as a Muslim her task was not to assign blame or to act the victim, but to make change from within oneself, as Allah commanded. "There is no monster out there," she said. "It is only your inner weakness that makes you see the other as a monster."

When she spoke of her identity as a woman, she again expressed gratitude, thanking God for being created a woman. (I thought of the Jewish blessing that I recite every morning that expresses the very same spiritual impulse.) If you give women power and education, she said, they will create better men and a better society. Again, she was presenting herself as at one with us, with all mothers around the world who change the world by the impact we make on our sons and daughters.

After the panel, I embraced her and offered words of blessing. I wanted to take the image of this righteous, humble, and powerful Muslim woman home with me. She categorically disproved the stereotypical story about Muslims I so often encounter, and she serves in my memory as a living example of how religiosity at its best leads to humility, mutual respect, and hope.

Al-Aqabe: Building a Peace House

On a recent trip to Israel, our family friend, Palestinian peace activist Souliman Al-Khatib, offered me an adventure I could not miss. The purpose of the journey: to explore the possibilities of creating a Peace House, a much-needed retreat center for use by Israeli-Palestinian dialogue and reconciliation programs. A small group of Israeli, Palestinian, and international peace activists traveled together for the day, along with a peace-minded Israeli architect.

Heading into the north-central West Bank, the terrain was starkly beautiful. The time passed quickly, as we took turns telling each other how we had been drawn into peace work. We were even good-natured enough to weather the frustrating one-hour stop at one of the many checkpoints that dot the West Bank. The issue: the soldiers who staffed the checkpoint could not get confirmation of the written documents the Israelis in our car had presented to indicate that they were permitted to travel into the area of the West Bank we were visiting.

Finally we reached our destination, a primitive but beautifully maintained tiny Palestinian village called Al-Aqabe. Our host, the beloved head of the village, Hajj Sami Saddiq, a warm and dignified man in his early sixties, sat in a wheelchair, because of a crippling injury he suffered from a stray Israeli bullet in 1972, as he worked his fields near an Israeli army training camp. Hajj Sami had suffered greatly, but in surprisingly quiet tones, he told us that fifty of his villagers had been similarly injured over the years. He wanted us to know that 95 percent of the buildings in his village have standing demolition orders issued by the Israeli government. Remarkably, he spoke without anger. Over and over again, he told us that theirs is a peace-loving village, wanting only to live quietly with their neighbors in peace. They had renamed the entry road to their village, "The Gandhi Peace Road." When I asked what had led him to care so deeply for peace, he said simply, "We all live here. Sixty years from now, we will all be dead. Why not live together in peace?"

The place was magical, both the terrain and the peace-loving culture of the village inspiring hope and tranquility. We were treated to an elaborate lunch and several rounds of coffee and tea in different homes. A "Peace House" in this exquisite place would be a beautiful thing.

I would have floated home to Jerusalem on the wings of that prayerful vision. But as we drove toward the Jerusalem neighborhood where I was staying, we encountered snarled traffic, police barricades, and shouting. Very near my apartment, some ten thousand religious Jews from around the country and the West Bank had gathered near the Prime Minister's official residence to protest Prime Minister Netanyahu's 2009 order to freeze some settlement construction for ten months. Harsh slogans shouted from the dais rippled through the crowd.

Broken-hearted, I edged through the passionate crowds to make my way back to my apartment. These were Jews like me, but shouting with what appeared to me to be hard-hearted insistence on their desires to the exclusion of the rights of others. What of the vision of a house of peace? My heart was heavy, but I took refuge in the memories of the day's journey and in the Jewish prayers for peace I recite every night.

Building Bridges for Peace

Outside, war raged in Israel and in Lebanon. Hezbollah rockets terrorized more than one-third of Israel's civilian population, causing extensive property damage and personal injury. In response, Israeli rockets flew north, devastating areas of Lebanon. We frantically tuned in each hour for the headlines; each news report brought images of destruction and hate; hopelessness reigned. Yet on a small college campus in Colorado, I was privileged to witness a group of young women building a very different reality.

During the summer of 2006, seventy-five young women from Israel, the West Bank, and around the United States attended a two-week intensive program in dialogue and relationship-building sponsored by the visionary program, Building Bridges for Peace. It was the program's thirteenth year, but this year the staff feared that conditions on the ground might deter participants from coming, or that the trauma of war might overwhelm the program's capacity to transform stereotypes into deep understanding, changing suspicion, fear, and hatred into love. In fact, not a single participant stayed away. The young women came, full of emotion, youthful vitality, and girlish energy, with their capacity for hope and transformation, incredibly, intact.

The young women, sixteen to twenty years of age, and their counselors, ages twenty to twenty-five, plunged quickly and deeply into the essential issues that divided them, exploring the dynamics of the conflict that have kept the people of the Middle East at war since long before they were born. One day paper bags were hung from the walls of the meeting room, marked with evocative words like "soldier," "martyr," "Hezbollah," and "occupation." The girls wrote their thoughts and feelings about these trigger words and placed them anonymously into the paper bags. By the next day, the staff had written all the anonymous responses on large sheets of paper. The participants walked around the room in complete silence, horrified by the stereotypes, hatred, and pain that so many of us carry, and struck by the starkly contrasting meanings these realities have for the different communities.

The next day, homogenous groups (Israeli, Palestinian, and American) created and presented timelines of their peoples' histories. We were all confronted with a visual image of the different realities inhabited by the Israelis and Palestinians. The two groups were worlds apart even in their description of the most basic "facts" of the conflict that defines all of their lives. Girls began to struggle with the program and their counselors; hopelessness began to take hold. Every few days news filtered in that loved ones had been killed back home. They held one another and took turns wiping one another's tears.

Not all their time was spent in difficult conversation. The girls played and made art together, did volunteer work in the community, and did all the things that girls do to create relationship. And at each meal time, they erupted into song. They sang serious, meaningful songs expressing yearnings for a better world ("If I Had a Hammer," "Lean on Me" and "Imagine"), and they sang silly, joyful songs, dancing around the dining hall with youthful exuberance. They sang songs of peace in English, in Hebrew, and in Arabic. At such moments, it seemed that nothing divided them. Enemies were becoming friends.

At late-night staff meetings, counselors released the emotion accumulated during the day, when they labored to respond to participants' unanswerable questions and worked to maintain the safe, sacred, and hope-filled container of the program. One particularly painful night, two young women who looked remarkably alike—one a beautiful, eloquent Palestinian college student and one a beautiful, eloquent Israeli who had just completed her army service—fell into a deep sense of hopelessness. What if the kids' anguished doubts were right? Was change really possible in their troubled, beloved land? How could they imagine going home, now a place full of violence, hatred, and fear?

The two young women began to cry, each in her own place in the circle, until they stepped into the center of the circle and embraced each other. They held one another for a long time, two beautiful dark-haired, dark-skinned girls, comforting one another, easing the pain and fear by carrying it together.

When we thought the campers were ready, we challenged them to a demanding empathy exercise. Having placed the girls in heterogeneous dyads (an Israeli with a Palestinian from the West Bank, an American with an Israeli Arab, etc.), we asked them a series of questions: for example, "How do you feel about being an American/Israeli/Palestinian?" "How do you feel about the checkpoints?" "What comes to your mind when you hear that a bus was blown up?" "What do you think of Hezbollah?"

But this time, instead of speaking their own opinion, the girls were asked to answer as they thought their partner would (a religious Israeli answering for her militant Palestinian partner, and an African American girl answering for her partner, an Israeli Arab). And then each girl listened as her partner, taking in the experience of being deeply heard, elaborated on her own answer, helping the speaker understand "the other side" even more accurately and fully.

Afterwards, we asked the girls what they had gained from this exercise. Their answers were profoundly moving. "It's good for me to know what the other side is feeling." "I realized that the other side also has pain." "Wow! I didn't know that in some ways they feel the same way I do." "I felt so supported and understood." "I grew more hopeful because I felt I'd been heard. I felt she understood me and felt my pain."

As the end of camp drew near, a palpable sadness descended. Loving friends clung to each other with a sense of urgency, yearning to spend every last moment together. In a closing circle, many of the young women talked about the pain of going home to a place full of violence and hatred, where no one would understand their experience of having an enemy become a beloved friend. Others offered blessings, exhorting one another to believe in the world they had fashioned together and to claim their role as leaders in creating a more peaceful, loving future.

At the closing lunch, shared with an appreciative community of supporters in Denver, an Israeli girl and a Palestinian girl spoke to the crowd about their experience, and they embraced. And one last time, the girls sang in Hebrew and Arabic: *Od yavo shalom aleinu . . . Salaam. Leyahela alayna isalaam . . . Shalom.* May peace come to us and to all the world—*Salaam, Shalom.*

What are we to learn from these peacemaker portraits? Surely, these are heroic and visionary individuals, in some cases capable of almost superhuman acts of empathy and hope. But these are real people, all of whom embody the primary characteristics of peacebuilders. They are people of humility and vision. They exemplify passion for peace, respect for others and curiosity about others' lives. They are willing to challenge their own certainties and able to engage in critical self-reflection. They are remarkably gifted individuals. But, as we will summarize in the next chapter, they are living examples of traits that can be taught and learned, qualities that exemplify the practice of peace.

Hearing the Cry of Our Enemy

In a Rosh Hashana sermon, my colleague Rabbi Ed Feld asked, "What are we supposed to hear when we listen to the Shofar?"[25] Based on a Talmudic discussion, he teaches that we are to hear our enemy's cry of pain.

> Abaye said: The disagreement[26] regarding how to sound the *teru'ah* (one of the notes in the Shofar service) must revolve around the following: The Biblical text says, "It should be for you a day of sounding the *teru'ah*" [Num. 29:1]. . . . And it is written of the mother of Sisera [a Canaanite general in the time of the prophet Deborah, Judg. 4:7], that [when she understood that her son had died], "the mother of Sisera looked out the window and she lamented" [Judg. 5:28]. One opinion is that this means that she groaned [and therefore the *teru'ah* should sound like a gasping sound], and one opinion is that she wailed [and therefore the *teru'ah* should sound like staccato wails].[27]

In this remarkable passage, the Talmudic sage Abaye explains a debate of the earlier authorities about how the *teru'ah* blast, the third of the three notes in the shofar service, should be sounded. Abaye argues that the argument turns on whether the *teru'ah* should sound like deep sighing or like uncontrollable weeping. In either case, the rabbis agreed that the model for these sounds of distress was the mother of Sisera.

We recall that Sisera was a Canaanite general in the time of the prophet Deborah. God had promised to bring the Israelites victory over Sisera, so

---

[25] Rabbi Ed Feld, "Call of the Shofar, 5768," website of Rabbis for Human Rights–North America, http://www.rhr-na.org.

[26] Between Mishnah *Rosh Hashana* 4:9 and the *baraita* (extra-Mishnaic source of the same period) quoted at BT *Rosh Hashana* 33b.

[27] BT *Rosh Hashana* 33b.

Deborah called the people to battle. His army routed in war, Sisera fled and hid in the home of Yael, who gave him milk to lull him to sleep, then killed him by striking a tent pin into his head (Judg. 4:21). In Deborah's triumphant song of victory, she describes Sisera's mother (unnamed in the text) looking out the window, weeping, as she realizes that her son will not return home from battle.

Deborah's biblical song unambiguously rejoices over the death of the Israelites' enemies. This text is one of many in the Bible that regard victory in war as an expression of divine blessing, comparable in this respect to the Israelites' Song at the Sea (Exod. 15:1–19).[28] It is an eminently understandable human instinct: when the enemy who endangered us is defeated, we are moved to celebration.

But the Talmudic sage Abaye grasped the poignancy of the image of Sisera's mother desperately gazing out the window and weeping, a model of every mother who has ever waited in vain for her son to come home safely from war. Living over a millennium later, Abaye no longer regards Sisera and his family only as an enemy to be vanquished and reviled. Abaye can sense the human suffering in the scene, recognizing an archetype of the mother desperately weeping for her son lost in battle. The nameless mother of Sisera is no longer a foe; she is a human being, a bereaved mother, for whom all people are stirred to compassion.

Rabbi Feld's penetrating reading of this text implies that what we are to hear when the shofar is sounded is the cry of human suffering, not only of our own people but of all people, even of our "enemy."[29] Some may say, "Impossible!" "Only angels could be that compassionate!" "Why should we not rejoice at the death of our enemies?" But the Rabbinic tradition builds into the shofar service, a central highlight of High Holy Day practice, a requirement that we open ourselves to the universal cry of human suffering.

This is a moment when Judaism, like all great religions, calls us to rise above our baser human instincts. In this case, the call to a life of *teshuvah*

---

[28] Deborah's Song in Judges 5 was chosen by the Rabbis to be the *haftarah* (parallel prophetic reading) for *Parashat Beshallach*, when Exodus 15 is read.

[29] This suggestion also appears in *Maḥzor Lev Shalem,* ed. Ed Feld (New York: Rabbinical Assembly, 2010), 115.

(repentance), virtue, and integrity, involves reaching beyond our initial human aversion to our "enemy," to recognize the humanity in all people. At the climax of the liturgical year, we are taught to open to the pain of the "other," thus allowing us to envision for a moment a world at peace.

5

The Ways of Peace

We began in chapter 1 by examining the nature of conflict, exploring similarities among different kinds of conflict, investigating the differences between constructive and destructive conflict, and learning about the human brain's response to threat and discord. In chapter 2 we explored interreligious engagement, in which the fundamental fear of difference can present an impediment to the embrace of the religious other or even tolerance of the other. In chapter 3 we studied a deeply felt ideological conflict within the Jewish community, in which historic fears and passionate identity issues produce the classic dynamics of polarized communication. In chapter 4 we surveyed grassroots relationship building efforts in the context of the Israeli–Palestinian conflict, in which both communities carry profound histories of wounding and grievance and live with chronic fears of annihilation.

Throughout this exploration, I have investigated various dimensions of conflict as they are discussed in sacred Jewish texts and exemplified in a set of illustrative experiences and portraits. Many of these examples have highlighted identified peacebuilders—persons with special expertise in the insights and techniques of conflict transformation, whose work is to facilitate encounter between estranged people or groups. Such people have special skill and certainly remarkable experience. At the same time, I have used their stories to highlight the process of heart-opening, relationship building, and peacemaking as a practice to which all thoughtful people are called. My deepest purpose in this book has been to persuade you, the reader, to serve as a peacebuilder in the midst of your own unique life.

Peacebuilding, as I understand it, is not the exclusive purview of diplomats, elected officials, or conflict specialists. It is not only for people who live in international conflict zones or violent neighborhoods or work in mediation centers. It is for all people who take seriously the biblical call to "seek peace and pursue it." It is a way of being in the world, a way of bringing peace, of being peace[1] in everyday encounters, in personal and professional relationships, in the communities of which we are a part, and in our life as a nation. In this expansive sense, we implicitly choose in every human interaction whether to act with nonviolence and respect or with animosity and judgment. Living out a commitment to peace is a full-time job, something we may do everywhere we interact with people in our lives. It is for all of us, and it is a life's work.

From this broad perspective, peacebuilding practice is an expression of spiritual virtues valued in most religious traditions, such as kindness, compassion, gentleness, generosity, patience, and respect for all people. In this final chapter of the book, I explore the way of the peacebuilder—the cultivation of the traits that prepare and enable us to live as a source of peace and blessing in the world, to contribute to relationships of mutual respect, kindness, curiosity, and human connection, wherever we live.

I do this by drawing on the ancient Jewish tradition of *Mussar*. The Hebrew word *mussar* means both "correction" and "instruction," and "*Mussar* literature" hence refers to "a genre of spiritual-ethical exhortation"[2] that began in the tenth century and has continued to develop in the present. This literature spawned a movement,

> developed primarily in Lithuania in the second half of the nineteenth century. Founded by Rabbi Israel Lipkin of Salant, it sought to explore the composition of the human soul and provide a series of techniques to help minimize the "disconnect" so often experienced between our actions and our ideals.[3]

---

[1] I borrow this phrase from Thich Nhat Hanh, *Being Peace* (Berkeley, CA: Parallax Press, 1987).

[2] Ira F. Stone, *A Responsible Life: The Spiritual Path of Mussar* (New York: Aviv Press, 2006), xvi.

[3] Ibid.

All serious students of Judaism know that Jewish tradition has a decidedly behavioral bias. By far, most Jewish sacred imperatives relate to action, and that which is prized most highly is not attitude or inner faith but behavioral expression of these beliefs. The Mussar tradition, while completely committed to the traditional Jewish legal system of religious and ethical practice, systematizes Jewish values for the inner life. One finds in works of Mussar an articulation of the central *middot*, or soul traits, that the traditional Jew is to cultivate throughout a lifetime. What is more, the Mussar system offers ways of developing and reinforcing these traits, in what I have long thought of as a spiritual version of cognitive-behavioral therapy. These are not characteristics that can be acquired once and for all but must be assiduously practiced throughout our lives if we are to root them deeply in our minds, hearts, and actions.

This chapter, then, will explore seven of the qualities of being I consider central for the practice of peacebuilding and, more broadly, for the development of the heart and soul of the peacebuilder. In each case, I discuss the trait as it appears in Jewish text and in everyday life, explain why this quality of mind and heart is essential for peacebuilding, and offer suggestions for its cultivation.

> "To walk in all God's ways. . ." [Deut. 12:22]. These are the ways of the Holy One: "gracious and compassionate, patient, abounding in kindness and truth, extending kindness to thousands, forgiving iniquity, transgression and sin, and granting pardon . . ." [Exod. 34:6–7]. Just as God is gracious and compassionate, you too must be gracious and compassionate, and give freely to all. "Adonai is righteous in all God's ways and loving in all God's deeds" [Ps 145:17]. As the Holy One is righteous, you too must be righteous. As the Holy One is loving, you too must be loving.[4]

I read this text in the light of another Rabbinic passage. Pondering the verse, "Follow Adonai your God" (Deut. 13.5), the Rabbis ask, "What does this mean? Is it possible for a mortal to follow God's Presence? . . . Rather, the verse means to teach us that we should follow the attributes of the Holy One, Blessed be God."[5]

---

[4] *Sifre Deuteronomy, Ekev 13.*
[5] BT *Sotah* 14a.

As we have seen many times, the Rabbis, understanding the Torah to be divine, take every letter, word, and turn of phrase as nothing less than a precious message from God, inviting our deep understanding and faithful response. The Rabbis are generally comfortable with anthropomorphism, but on this occasion the Rabbis rightly interrogate such biblical expressions: "Follow God? Walk in God's ways? What could it possibly mean to follow a God who has no physical being? And how would we dare to do so?"

The question is penetrating, and the answer is clear. Expressions such as "follow God" or "walk in God's ways" are to be understood not literally but metaphorically. We cannot physically follow a God who has no body. Rather, we are commanded to emulate the characteristics of God. Of course, created in the divine image, we are ourselves endowed with the same characteristics, but since they are most fully manifest in God's own Being, to imitate God's ways is our highest calling.

Now comes the tricky part. If we honestly consider what attributes God embodies in the Torah, we would have to list quite a range of traits. Anyone with cursory knowledge of the Torah knows that there are passages in which God is pictured as angry, jealous, vengeful, and even violent, as well as countless passages in which God is portrayed as the infinite source of justice, compassion, and goodness. Interestingly, our text quotes the verse from the Golden Calf narrative in Exodus that we have discussed earlier, from which the Rabbis excise a description of God as rigorously pursuing justice against the guilty, highlighting only God's compassionate, kind, patient, and forgiving nature.

In this text, the Rabbis state that the God we are to emulate, in whose image we are to shape our lives, is the God of the first half of the verse in Exodus: "gracious and compassionate, patient, abounding in kindness and truth, forgiving to thousands, forgiving iniquity, transgression and sin, and granting pardon." This is the God in whose image we are created. In a variety of Rabbinic and *Mussar* texts, these traits become the basic curriculum[6] for spiritual formation and for the fashioning of a righteous, reverent life. They are also central to the soul of the peacebuilder. As God

---

[6] In using the metaphor of a "curriculum" for spiritual formation, I draw on Alan Morinis's use of the term in *Everyday Holiness: The Jewish Spiritual Path of Mussar* (Boston: Trumpeter Books, 2007), 3, though I use it somewhat differently here.

is kind and compassionate, you must be kind and compassionate. As God is patient and forgiving, you too must be patient and forgiving. As God's name and essence are peace, so too must you be a force for peace in your life.

Kindness

Once Rabban Yohanan ben Zakkai was walking with his disciple, Rabbi Joshua, near Jerusalem after the destruction of the Temple. Rabbi Joshua looked at the Temple ruins and said: "Alas for us! The place that atoned for the sins of the people Israel—through the ritual of animal sacrifice—lies in ruins!" Then Rabbi Yohanan ben Zakkai spoke to him these words of comfort: "Be not grieved, my son. There is another equally effective way of gaining atonement even though the Temple is destroyed. We can still gain atonement through deeds of lovingkindness." For it is written: "Lovingkindness I desire, not sacrifice" [Hosea 6:6].[7]

Rabbi Simlai taught: "The Torah begins with deeds of lovingkindness and ends with deeds of lovingkindness."[8]

These two beloved texts offer a glimpse of the importance of "deeds of lovingkindness" in Jewish tradition. In other texts, this category includes such mitzvot (imperatives) as honoring parents, hospitality, visiting the sick, accompanying the dead to their final resting place, and providing for a poor bride's wedding needs.[9]

The first poignant text provides a window into the Rabbis' grief and disorientation at the destruction of the Temple, the center of Israelite and early Rabbinic religion. The text strikingly suggests that deeds of loving-kindness can substitute for animal sacrifice, previously the core of the Israelite atonement process, as well as the central expression of devotion to God. Other Rabbinic texts would include prayer and study among these central substitutes for Temple worship; in any case, there is no more elevated status than this. The author of this text is thus expressing

---

[7] *Avot d'Rabbi Natan* 4:5, translation from *Siddur Sim Shalom*, 68.
[8] BT *Sotah* 14a.
[9] BT *Shabbat* 127a.

something akin to the Dalai Lama's oft-quoted response to the question, "What is the nature of your religion?" He is said to reply, "My religion is kindness."

To say that the Torah is a book of loving-kindness from start to finish, as in the second text, is similarly to assert the centrality of deeds of loving-kindness in Jewish religion.[10] To describe the Torah as suffused with kindness from start to finish is to assert that acts of kindness are (or should be) what religious life is all about. But the all-encompassing quality of this description of the Torah suggests that loving-kindness is more than a matter of particular deeds. It is an inner state of being as well, a spirit of loving intention toward all beings that is described as the most essential quality of the divine and the one that we are to emulate in our own lives.

One recent Shabbat morning, on entering the synagogue, I was immediately greeted with a particularly exuberant hug from the three-year-old daughter of a good friend. My spirits immediately soared as I responded to this precious child's affection, lavishly offering her hugs, kisses, and delighted attention. Then she moved on, and making her way around the sanctuary, she readily found similarly loving arms throughout the congregation. I felt so happy for this little girl, whose mothers have created for her such a warm and embracing circle of loving community. But my attention was drawn to the grownups, who were readily drawn out of their own Shabbat reflections to offer love to this child—and many other children—of the congregation. A wave of love moved around the room, evident in the delighted smiles, hugs, and playful games offered by each adult. The happiness was contagious. Or perhaps, more accurately, there was a stream of love moving through the room, waiting to be evoked and expressed.

I remember once hearing the renowned and beloved singer-songwriter Debbie Friedman (may her memory be for blessing) observe that it tends to be easy for us human beings to be loving with babies and old people. The challenge, Debbie suggested, is to offer that kind of easy affection toward everyone.

---

[10] One might well challenge the author's characterizing the Torah in this way. What of all the violence in the Torah, much of it instigated by God? The author of this text knew these passages at least as well as we do, and is once again engaging in selective exegesis to elevate and emphasize the loving qualities of God.

Similarly, I have heard that the root meaning of *metta*—the Pali word for kindness—is related to the word for rain. The image is one of caring and warm regard—a central dynamic in the world—falling on all people, like the rain, without direction or exception.

I have been deeply affected by the Buddhist practice of *metta,* or loving-kindness meditation. On several occasions I have spent a full week in silence at a Buddhist retreat center, one of a large community of people, each of us spending all of our waking hours reciting traditionally inspired phrases of well-wishing toward oneself and others. "May you be safe and protected from harm." "May you be healthy and strong." "May you be happy." "May you be at peace." The practice proceeds from offering these wishes for well-being toward oneself, then toward different categories of loved ones, then to "familiar strangers,"[11] then to "difficult persons,"[12] then to "all beings."

I always find this practice profound. It evokes very powerful sensations in my body (perhaps a rush of the "tend and befriend" hormone, oxytocin), inspires strong feelings of care and connection toward all people, and leaves me feeling remarkably joyful and full of love. Although it is a bit less powerful to do this in my own personal prayer at home, I know that my days are different and my life more loving when I spend time with this practice each morning before offering my traditional Jewish morning prayers.

Human kindness lies at the core of peacemaking practice. Kindheartedness flows naturally and effortlessly toward those people we consider to be close to us, toward those we know wish us well, such as members of our own family (when these relationships are working!). When human connection is ruptured, conflict emerges, and the natural good-heartedness between people freezes or erupts into animosity. To the degree that we—either as parties to the dispute or as third parties—can bring more kindhearted intention into the situation, the possibility of reestablishing human connection is naturally enhanced. Peacemakers thus embody the

---

[11] This is my teacher Sylvia Boorstein's suggestion for translating the category of "neutral persons" in Buddhist texts, since our minds jump to judgment about people so readily that it is rare that we have neither positive nor negative views of anyone.

[12] Sylvia's adaptation of the traditional category of "enemy."

theological truth that all of us are family, therefore all in a necessary web of caring for one another. When the web is torn by painful alienation, much less violence, all of us suffer and long for repair.

Kindness Practice

Consider dedicating five or ten or twenty minutes each morning for this practice. (When your mind protests, "I don't have time for this!" consider responding, "You don't have time *not* to do this!") In a quiet place where you will not be interrupted, sit comfortably on a chair or on a cushion on the floor, in a physical posture that evokes both alertness and calm. Spend a couple of moments noticing physical sensations: places where part of your body touches the floor or the chair, where your arm touches your lap, or where there is a bit of discomfort. No need to do anything complicated or struggle to get anything right. Just notice. Then bring your attention for a couple of moments to the sounds in the room. Even in a very quiet indoor place, you may hear sounds of nature outside, the hum of the fan, or even the sound of your own breath.

Then bring your attention to your breath itself. Again, nothing complicated. There is no right or wrong way to do this. Do not be the slightest bit surprised if you find all sorts of thoughts springing into your mind, including whole lines of narrative thought that draw you far away from the breath. This is precisely what minds are supposed to do. But very gently, without force or judgment of any kind, coax your attention—just for these few moments of dedicated practice—back to the breath moving in and out of your body, filling you and emptying, moving through you without any need for your control.

Then begin to recite these phrases, first toward yourself, in a Jewish adaptation of the Buddhist *metta* practice.[13] "May you be blessed and protected from harm." "May your life be filled with light and grace." "May you be loved and blessed with peace." Try saying each blessing on the in-breath, then feel it resonate in your body on the out-breath before moving on to the next phrase. If that pacing leaves your mind too open to distraction, try saying the first phrase on the in-breath, then

---

[13] These phrases are adaptations of the priestly blessing, found in Numbers 6:24–26.

the second on the out-breath, the third on the in-breath, then release on the out-breath.

When you notice your mind carrying you away into judgment ("this is a stupid waste of time"), self-doubt ("I'm sure I'm not doing this right"), or just plain thinking (the to-do list or the task of planning this or that encounter you might have later in the day), gently invite your attention back to the phrases. Start by offering them toward yourself, then experiment with offering them to someone who evokes gratitude or love in you, then to someone with whom you have a casual relationship. If you find yourself loving the practice, ask yourself how many times a day you might be able to wish these phrases of well-being to people who randomly cross your path.

The practice of offering kindness to others and to oneself lies at the very heart of the practice of peacebuilding (as well as being a central aspect of a virtuous life, by any definition). Particularly in the midst of conflict—when we encounter frightening difference or strong disagreement, when we are wounded or pained by the actions of others in our lives or in the world—fear, pain, and anger naturally crowd out the natural flow of kindness that arises when the heart is at rest. The spontaneous stream of positive regard we may have for a child or in response to the unexpected kindness of strangers emerges from a heart that is broad and expansive, feeling safe and appreciated. When we work every day to train the heart for kindness, as in the practice I have described or by some other method, we make it much more likely that we will be able to call on our own natural goodness even in the midst of a difficult conversation or challenging situation.

Compassion

I have a vivid memory of the sensation of entering the front door of the hospital each morning when I served as a hospital chaplain. Whatever thoughts had occupied me or feelings had possessed me on my way to work, a wave of compassion moved through me when I walked through the door. Entering the hospital's central corridor, I was surrounded by the sights and sounds of the hospital: busy medical personnel rushing to their next task, patients in wheelchairs or wearing protective masks or using various tools to help them walk or breathe, family members with many strong emotions unabashedly displayed on their faces.

Some days I thought of the words of the chief executive of the first hospital where I worked, a physician who regularly called our hospital "a temple of healing." Virtually every day, whether in words or as an unspoken intuition, the thought arose: there are people in pain here. Walking into the territory of suffering each day exposed me to pain. Entering this territory on a daily basis exercised what my friend and colleague Rabbi Alan Lew called "the compassion muscle."

Make no mistake. There are many moments of my life when I am mean-spirited, nasty, and self-centered. That very morning I might have been irritated by a driver or by a member of my own family. But crossing the threshold of the hospital evoked an automatic compassion response in me. I immediately wanted to help—to let a slow-moving person go ahead of me, to ease their way, to discern which of the distressed people I encountered might appreciate a kind word. Stepping into a place where the truth of human suffering cannot be avoided, my own desire to help was automatically evoked.

The Hebrew (and Arabic) word for compassion, "*raḥamim*," derives from the word "*reḥem*," meaning "womb." Compassion is like the infinite and ever-flowing love of a mother for her child. The root of the word challenges us to find that most powerful capacity for love within ourselves, not only toward our own children, but toward all children and all beings. Especially, compassion is to suffer along with people in pain, be it large or small—neither to push the pain away, deny it, nor distract ourselves from it. Compassion is to be with pain, trusting that, just as a mother's arms comfort her crying child, love soothes the heart of suffering. Compassion is that deep love for people in need and in pain, drawn on our deepest instincts for caring for others. This no doubt explains why images of compassion appear so prominently in Jewish prayers for healing, as we hope for God, who is called "*Haraḥaman*," "Compassionate One," to soothe our pain.

The words "*Ḥen vaḥesed v'raḥamim*," "grace, kindness, and compassion," frequently appear together in classical Jewish sources, in a single multifaceted description of divine or human love. If we must identify the particular connotations of the different words, compassion is perhaps deeper, more focused on situations of pain, whereas kindness is broader, applied to all beings, without exception.

Compassion is deeply connected to empathy, the ability to feel a measure of another's feelings or imagine another's perspective. Empathy is very different from sympathy, with which it is often confused. In sympathy, we feel sorry for the painful circumstances that afflict another, and we are glad that we are not similarly afflicted. In empathy, we know that we are not immune to the other's troubles. As human beings, we know that "but for the grace of God go I." We are only temporarily spared their sorrow; our turn will come.

Compassion, empathy, and kindness are perhaps the skills most essential for peacebuilding. To meet conflict positively and productively requires genuine caring for both self and other—or, if we are a third party, for both sides, and to all those affected by the rupture in relationship. It does not require agreement with the other's position or denying one's own convictions. It does not require desire for long-term relationship or even a sense of "liking" the other. It does require an ability to see all parties (including ourselves) as fully human, vulnerable to pain, hurt, and fear. It also depends fundamentally on our willingness and capacity to imagine how the dispute looks from another's perspective. Without these capacities, conflict and estrangement rarely heal.

"Love your neighbor as yourself; I am God" (Lev. 19:18). This most central verse in the Torah has spawned a rich library of Jewish commentary throughout the ages, with exegetes seeking to penetrate the internal logic of the seemingly impossible command. Some find in it a reminder that the other is a person much like we are—imperfect and prone to mistakes, vulnerable to sufferings large and small, a finite creature doing the best we can moment by moment. Just as most of us naturally forgive ourselves for our errors, citing contextual factors to understand why we fell short (I was tired, stressed, off-kilter that day), we ought to similarly seek to understand the life challenge that may have led the other to hurt us.

Some commentators ponder the intriguing juxtaposition of the command to love one's neighbor with the enigmatic statement, "I am God." Surely, this phrase appears in other places in the Torah as well, but why here? For example, Bechor Shor[14] comments laconically, "And your love for Me should cause you to forget your hatred of your fellow."[15] That is, he poses the question, Why does the statement, "I am God," appear immediately after our commandment? This juxtaposition, he suggests, exhorts us to bring awareness of God—that which is Ultimate for us—to mind when we find ourselves hating another. If you love God, if you revere the wonders of creation, if you are grateful for the gift of life, if you are committed to living righteously and reflectively, then you cannot possibly hate another person who is, just like you, a creature of this same marvelous universe. When we can remember this, as the tradition exhorts us to do, conflicts look very different and are much more amenable to resolution.

Compassion Practice

The nature of human life is such that we need not look far to find opportunities to practice compassion. As I said earlier, entering a medical facility where human frailty cannot be denied or visiting a frail or bereaved person is perhaps the best training ground for exercising the compassion muscle. But everywhere we turn, we can choose to pay compassionate attention to what we see, starting with the sometimes tortured contents of our own mind. Throughout our day, there are countless moments to practice compassion: toward the morning news, the obvious distress of someone ahead of us in line at the airport ticket counter, a frustrated toddler and fatigued parent in the grocery store, or the couple arguing at the table near us in the café. All of these are places where human pain is all too evident. In every one of these situations, we have the choice to turn away—to put in our ear buds, close our hearts by blaming one party, respond with anger, deny what is happening, or distract ourselves. We have another choice: to lean forward toward the suffering, welcoming it as an opportunity to breathe more compassion into the world and into our own hearts.

Throughout your day, when you see someone in pain, directly or even via the news media, practice mentally moving toward the pain rather than recoiling from it, as our first instinct often leads us to do. Bring your heart

---

[14] Joseph Ben Isaac Bechor Shor, twelfth-century biblical commentator.
[15] On Leviticus 19:18, "I am God."

closer, seeking to understand and empathize with the person's distress. If you are physically present, try breathing for a moment in rhythm with their breath, sharing their experience for a moment. You might even wish them well in your mind, breathing in with the wish that their pain be relieved by your presence and breathing out with a hope for comfort.[16]

So, too, anger is an expression of pain. The next time you find yourself irritated or quarreling with someone, take a moment to try to imagine their perspective on the situation. No matter if their viewpoint makes no sense to you. Just for a moment, without rejecting your own view of the situation, envision how this person might tell the story of the conflictual moment to her partner or journal at the end of the day. If you can't even guess how it might seem from their point of view, make up a hypothesis. Try to see this moment of life experience from a very different perspective.

What might have made a person behave this way or think or speak this way? A bad driver cut you off on the road? Maybe he is driving a loved one to the hospital in an emergency. The voice at the call center is nasty? Perhaps she was just abused by another customer or fired from her low-paying job. A politician expresses a view that is anathema to you? Make up a story that might explain how a person's life experience could possibly lead them to hold this view so fiercely. Developing such a habit of caring response trains us to meet the experiences of our lives, moment by moment, with compassion.

Generosity

I walked into the evening prayer service that I have led this year, since my mother's death, in order to have the prayer quorum required for the daily recitation of the *Kaddish*, the Mourners' Prayer. I was happy to see Elaine's kind face. Her presence is always warm and comforting, especially so now, since she served as a hospice volunteer during the last days of my mother's life. After hugs and greetings, Elaine went to her bag and pulled out a small plastic food storage container, handing it to me with a sheepish grin. I immediately recognized it as one that my husband and

---

[16] This thought lies at the heart of the Buddhist *tonglen* practice. See, for example, Pema Chodron's explanation of *tonglen* at the Shambhala website: http://www.shambhala.org.

I had given her to take home leftovers from Thanksgiving dinner at our home, several months back. She apologized for the delay and joked that she really had not wanted to return it because it was such a perfectly useful size. Of course, without hesitation, I told her to keep it. (It was worth about $2.99.)

As we chatted before the service, my eyes were drawn to the lovely pair of earrings she was wearing. Just like my mother, I am wont to stop in the middle of a sentence to admire someone's earrings before playfully returning my attention to the conversation. Elaine told me where she had bought the earrings, and immediately said, "Do you want them?" I laughed and protested that I had only meant to admire her earrings, not to take them from her. She pressed her point, but I resisted. The conversation ended when the prayer service began. But after the service, Elaine reached out to me, taking both my hands in hers, and pressed the earrings into my hands.

It was a simple exchange, yet it warmed my heart. In a small, everyday sort of way, a spirit of generosity moved naturally between Elaine and me. She really liked my little kitchen implement, and I knew it would give me far more pleasure to give it to her than to put it back in its place in my cabinet. Clearly, she felt the same about her earrings. The exchange of caring energy between us made me happy.

It is a truism that giving can bring as much pleasure to the giver as to the recipient. (This is undoubtedly the spiritual essence that underlies the materialist excess of Christmas gift-giving in America.) Giving feels good—whether simple gift-giving, a gesture of thoughtfulness on a loved one's birthday, or volunteering one's time to help a person in need. It is such a bedrock, visceral experience that I suspect it derives from an ancient evolutionary source.

But in troubled relationships, the natural flow of generosity is blocked. Reconciliation becomes possible when both sides gradually come to feel that mutual goodwill is more satisfying than holding onto feelings of hurt and anger, woundedness and betrayal. I daresay that every act of peacebuilding—whether in individual relationships or around the globe—requires this kind of leap, in which the benefit of moving beyond past hurts is experienced as more nourishing than the paradoxical pleasure of living within the victim story.

It is one of the enduring puzzles of entrenched identity conflict that the pain over harms committed by the other side comes to feel somehow gratifying, reinforcing self or group identity, and conviction of how right we are. In the midst of the conflict, anger at the other and holding fast to the list of legitimate grievances make us feel strong and clear, when really we are imprisoned by traumatic memories. It is only the impulse to generosity—whether individual or collective—that can reveal how much more whole we are when our relationships are based on amity and collaboration rather than on suffering and woundedness.

Is there really any connection between the powerful work of transcending histories of wounding and the kind of simple, daily experience of exchanging small gifts reflected in my evening with Elaine? Do such small, everyday acts of generosity make any difference?

All of the soul traits we explore in this chapter can be expressed in large and small ways, but they draw on similar instincts within us regardless of scope. When we take advantage of small, effortless opportunities to practice a particular trait, we train a muscle, making it more likely that we will have the capacity we need when a more challenging occasion arises. Like any skill-building process, practice begins with the easy and proceeds to the difficult. It is not surprising that we often feel unable to draw on inner resources of compassion or generosity when the situation requires it, given that contemporary life trains us moment-by-moment in the very opposite of such virtues. Much spiritual practice consists of bringing attention to daily opportunities to strengthen a particular ability. When we do so, our capacity increases at a glacial, incremental pace, until one day we surprise ourselves and are able to leap into spiritual or moral proficiency we did not know we had.

The classical Jewish text on generosity is Exodus 25, when Moses calls on the people to come forward with donations from their own meager possessions to build a sanctuary, a focal point for the divine presence, in their journey through the wilderness. Remember, this was a people only recently liberated from slavery, who left Egypt in a rush of urgency and terror. Even taking account of the jewels given to them by the Egyptians (Exod. 11:2–3), how could they have had the items needed to adorn a dwelling place for the divine? Yet the text tells us that people came forward with precious metals, fabrics, and stones, as well as building materials, oils, and spices. The overflow of donation is described alternately as a gift of the heart and a gift of heart-wisdom.

But the Torah's description of the giving campaign begins with a strange statement from God. The words are usually translated as "Speak to the children of Israel, that they bring (or give) Me an offering; from every person whose heart is moved to give, take My offering" (Exod. 25:2). But the Hebrew word translated as "bring" or "give" actually means "to take." God literally says, "Speak to the children of Israel, that they may *take* for me an offering." The giving is described as an act of taking.

This may simply mean "taking" up a collection for the sake of God.[17] But the linguistic peculiarity of the verse leads the Hasidic commentary *Birkat Avraham*[18] to a penetrating description of the nature of giving and receiving.

> We would have expected Scripture to say, "They shall *give* to Me" [but it actually says, "They shall take to me"]. What this means is that you are to *take Me*: any time we are in need of anything, we are not to turn to any means [other than God], but understand that it is only when we "*take Me*" that we will be able to receive what we need.[19]

The rebbe uses the text's ambiguous word choice to make a bold statement about the nature of spiritual life. The "taking" described in the verse is far more than a historical reference to a building campaign in the wilderness. Rather, it teaches that we must take God/the Ultimate/ Truth/Oneness deeply into ourselves. Only when we ground ourselves in what is ultimately meaningful to us can we receive the help we need at difficult moments in our lives. That is, in order to give, we must take, and in order to receive, we must make a gift of the heart.

This lyrical piece of commentary has strayed far from the literal meaning of the text to teach about the reciprocity of giving. God/Life/the Universe

---

[17] See, for example, Rashi on Exodus 25:2.

[18] Rabbi Avraham Weinberg, of the Slonim dynasty of Hasidism, twentieth-century Poland.

[19] *Birkat Avraham, Terumah*, #1, p. 203, adapted from translation by Rabbi Jonathan Slater for Institute for Jewish Spirituality, www.ijs-online.org.

wants to give to us, the rebbe teaches, to satisfy us when we are in need, but this only works if we have first opened our hearts to the beauty and wonders of life. The same is true, of course, in human relationship. It is extremely difficult for us to give—even when doing so would benefit us—unless there is at least potential for goodwill in the relationship (think of the inability of members of Congress to compromise with those on the opposite side of an issue). Conversely, the most objectively valuable gift is unwelcome if we have not taken the other into our lives (e.g., a beautiful engagement ring after a breakup). Giving requires receiving, and taking in goodness requires a gift of self. Giving is reciprocal.

Generosity (or the lack thereof) operates just as well in human relations even when no material object changes hands. Joshua ben Perachya taught, "Judge every person on the scale of merit."[20] The statement uses a courtroom metaphor, inviting us to imagine our responses to people and situations on invisible scales of justice. Our internal scales, unfortunately (probably also for evolutionary reasons), seem to be weighted naturally toward blame, negative judgment, and skepticism. When we hear a piece of gossip, witness an unexpected interaction, or read a disturbing piece of political news, the mind so often leaps to the worst possible explanation. Only later, when we learn more, are we sometimes confronted with the fact that our negative assumptions were inaccurate.

It is particularly difficult in our contemporary society, dominated by cynicism, sarcasm, and a brutal critique of "the other," to try to reverse this bias in judgment of self and other. We may be completely unaware that we have the option to choose a positive interpretation—giving the other the benefit of the doubt, looking for a generous interpretation of another's behavior, actively looking for the good in another or in ourselves. Those of us who are blessed with loving relationships in our lives know the immense power of a loved one's affirmation, when someone assures us that they know we did the best we could, that we meant well, or that we will surely do better next time. The truth is, we can be that loving voice for ourselves and for the people in our lives any time we choose to.

---

[20] Mishnah *Avot* 1:6.

Generosity Practice

There are opportunities every day to choose generosity both of the material kind and of mind and spirit. Try making an intention in the morning to actively look for opportunities to be openhanded with your time and possessions. (The trick is to do this in a way that is not ungenerous to yourself, such as working more hours than is good for you because a co-worker looks tense.) Plan for one day to give some change when encountering a homeless person or to spend extra moments greeting people you generally pass by in your workplace. There is much to be learned from observing the variety of reactions we may have to such a practice.

Even more frequently, moment by moment throughout the day, we can try just noticing how often the scales of our minds shift toward judgment. It can be an interesting experiment to count how many times a judgmental opinion comes to mind in a single day or even a single hour. This is not for the purpose of condemning our own negativity or blaming ourselves for malevolence. Rather, with compassion, curiosity, and wholesome intention, if we notice that tens or scores or even hundreds of fault-finding thoughts take up residence in our minds each hour, we can have compassion for ourselves about how truly challenging it is to cultivate a more gracious attitude toward ourselves and toward others in our lives.

Self-Awareness

I had a terribly hard time with Purim this year. The strange and delightful Jewish festival is based on the biblical book of Esther, considered by many to be a literary parody, yet one that resonates deeply with the Jewish soul. Esther, a Jewish orphan, wins a national beauty contest and becomes queen of an ancient Persian empire without revealing her identity, just as the king's viceroy decides to kill all the Jews. Through a mixture of court intrigue, serendipity, courage, and faith, Queen Esther is able to claim her power, reveal herself, and prevent the annihilation of her people. Hence the mardi gras nature of the festival, in which congregants young and old dress up in the most outlandish and paradoxical costumes possible, celebrating the reality that, against all odds, sometimes things turn out very differently than we feared.

So far so good. As the murderous monarch came to be a well-known phenomenon in Jewish history, it is easy to understand why the Book of Esther's story of persecution resonated with reality, and its happy ending was a soothing antidote to lived reality. The problem is that the book's account continues by describing a genocidal rampage conducted by the Jews of the empire, in which over seventy-five thousand Persians were supposedly killed, though the book repeatedly insists that the Israelites took no spoils from the vanquished (proof, some would say, that the whole account is tongue-in-cheek). The Jew on the street, echoing traditional Jewish commentators, believes as a matter of course that no such genocide happened. "Jews would never do such a thing. This is just a Purim joke."

I love costuming and have always delighted in the sight of the sanctuary filled with young children dressed as ancient Persian characters and adults dressed as their least favorite political and religious characters, in joyful parody. (Personally, I have a long tradition of dressing up as a submissive woman, and my husband does a mean Rhett Butler imitation.)

But this year I simply could not laugh at the violence—*our* violence—in the story. I love the carnival atmosphere that takes over the synagogue, and I can continue to wrestle respectfully with the difficult text in the study hall. But I cannot recite the book in its topsy-turvy, comic chant, knowing that in the end, whether in jest or not, our people are said to wipe out another.

On the Shabbat prior to Purim, we read the biblical story of Amalek, the wicked descendant of Esau, who attacked the weak and weary stragglers of the Israelite camp on their way out of Egypt (Deut. 25:17–19). As we have seen, the Israelites are commanded to blot out the memory of Amalek and never to forget. Throughout Jewish history, Amalek has come to serve as the paradigm of the murderous enemy, identified with characters as diverse as Haman (the villain of the Purim story), the Roman empire, Hitler, Stalin, and Yasser Arafat. For many Jews, these are among the most challenging texts and images in the Torah.

As noted above, I have long been drawn to the Kabbalistic interpretation,[21] carried forward in Hasidic literature, that understands Amalek not as an external enemy at all, but as the *yester hara* ("evil inclination"), the impulse

---

[21] Zohar 3:160a.

to evil that lies within each of us. This exegetical move to interiorize Amalek is profound. First, this means that there is no commandment to hate and surely no license to do violence to anyone. By this logic, everything that we might label "enemy," "other," heinous or horrific, lives within every human being. There is no sanction to blame the other, for he or she is us. We can only recognize that we are all made of the same stuff, including both the loving and the hateful, both the compassionate and the violent.

This teaching stunningly dissolves the pattern of demonizing and dehumanizing those seen to be foreign or threatening. It short-circuits the victim narrative, cutting off the telling of the story of suffering as if another was entirely to blame. There is nothing to blame but the human condition itself. Evil is within us all, and all human beings are engaged in the same sacred internal struggle to empower the righteous parts of ourselves and disempower the negative. This means that evil is still a formidable opponent, but we can exercise significant power over it, moment by moment, throughout our lives. The "other" is a human being just as we are, laboring to cultivate the internal good and suppress the wicked.

Clearly, the authors of this interpretation were extremely well acquainted with the existence of evil in the world. Those who named the battle with Amalek as intrapsychic in no way denied that there are truly evil, murderous people in the world. The same literature that produced this interpretation also produced extended reflections on the reality of evil. They knew this feature of life at least as well as we do.

I believe that the rabbis who developed these understandings were making a boldly empowering statement about spiritual life. Is evil a reality in the world? Certainly. Are thoughtful people to struggle to understand the presence of evil in a world of God's creation? Without a doubt. But these are theological questions that have relatively little direct impact on our daily lives. In naming Amalek as our own evil inclination, the rabbis teach that we are to spend our best energies not reflecting on philosophical imponderables and not on reminding ourselves of the sins of our enemies but on living the very best lives we can. The rabbis are teaching that the most important battle of our lives is the herculean effort to choose kindness, compassion, generosity, and justice, even when our baser instincts direct us toward selfishness, greed, and hate. Through a rigorous and lifelong practice of self-awareness and self-examination, we can make a real difference in the quality of our lives and of those around us. On this battlefield, we can exert real power.

Such self-awareness is essential throughout our lives, and most especially in situations of conflict. Regardless of the specific content, in entrenched disputes we become focused on our own rightness and the other's wrongness. The more severe the hurt or fear, the more protracted the conflict, and the more directly the clash touches on core identity issues, the louder the voices of "I am right" and "They are wrong" become. When the strongest voices—both external and within our own minds and hearts—are screaming these polarized certainties, it is all but impossible to listen for something new, gain new understanding into the other's motivation, or to recognize our own doubts. Thus the "inner Amalek" idea exhorts us to stop shouting the enemy's name and stop pointing blaming fingers. Instead, we are to look deeply inside ourselves to see how we ourselves might contribute to the conflict and how we might instead work for its resolution.

Another piece of Rabbinic guidance helped me make a measure of peace with Purim. It is well known that, along with the other absurd frivolities of the day, the Talmud declares it an affirmative religious obligation to become so drunk on Purim as to be unable to distinguish between "cursed be Haman" (the evil) and "blessed be Mordechai" (the good).[22] This is striking, because this same literature often inveighs against drunkenness. But here, on Purim, when reversals of fate are the order of the day, we are to become so inebriated that we cannot tell right from wrong.

The Rabbis trust that we will recognize that the commandment to drunkenness on Purim is the exception that proves the rule. Three hundred and sixty four days a year, clear awareness is a virtue. Seeing clearly what is before us and within us is essential to righteous living. We cannot live a moral life without making clear and thoughtful distinctions between right and wrong, helpful and hurtful behavior—both in others and in ourselves.

Once again, from the topsy-turvy world of Purim emerges a key principle of spiritual life: in faithful living, we must cultivate the capacity for keen and clear awareness of self and other. In the midst of conflict, it is at best insufficient (and usually destructive) to see only the other's flaws. We must be well practiced in looking inward and asking with sober rigor,

---

[22] BT *Megillah* 7b.

"What part do I have in this? In what ways have I harmed or confused the other? What mistakes have I made that have contributed to the spiral of conflict?" Only by asking such courageous introspective questions do we work to eradicate "Amalek" from the world, and contribute to the cause of peace among people.

Self-Awareness Practice

I once heard of a Buddhist teacher who posted little notes around her home and office with the deceptively simple words, "Are you sure?" written on them. I have often found this penetrating question to be a potent invitation to self-reflection. When my mind is filled with stories, narratives and counternarratives, even attacks and counterattacks, this question is an external voice of wisdom interrupting the silent cycle of hostile thoughts—questioning my certainties and inviting me to take a quiet look inward.

Try designating an occasional day for the following practice. Counter-intuitively, pledge to pay close attention to whatever or whoever irritates you today. Whenever you sense annoyance or anger in yourself, use that uncomfortable sensation as an internal reminder to ask yourself what about that person or subject bothers you. Ask yourself such courageously honest questions as, "What is it about this person that bothers me so much? What pain in me does his or her behavior touch? What part of this is more about me than about her?" Such rigorous introspection is uncomfortable, but when the full truth is recognized, there is generally much to explore within, even in response to "objectively" annoying behavior.

This practice is at times obvious and familiar: for example, a person may irritate me, through no fault of his own, because he resembles someone who once hurt me grievously. When the mind and heart are at rest, it takes little effort to recognize this. But in the midst of conflict—when another challenges us on an issue that arouses passion, strong anger, or deep fear—our every instinct bids us to maintain our vigilant surveillance of "the other." In this practice, we are pressing against those ancient impulses. This is not a lion racing to annihilate my family sleeping in their tent. This is a person, just like me, living his life, holding her beliefs as I hold mine. She is not really the enemy. The enemy is the impulse to hostility that lives within both of us. Together, in the service of peace, we can vanquish this harmful inner adversary.

Humility

A remarkable set of Rabbinic commentaries asks why, of all the beautiful places along the Israelites' route from Egypt to the Land of Israel, Mount Sinai was chosen for the revelation of the Torah. One Rabbinic midrash imagines various mountains vying to be chosen as the place of revelation. One mountain said, "Let the Presence of God rest on me," and the other mountain replied, "Let the Presence of God rest on me." Mount Tabor explained why it should have the honor. Mount Hermon countered, asserting why it deserved the honor more. The midrash seems to describe a clamoring of arrogant, competing voices, decibel levels rising.

> Then a voice out of the high heavens rang out and said: "The Shechinah (Divine Presence) shall not rest upon these high mountains that are so proud, for it is not God's will that the Shechinah should rest upon high mountains that quarrel among themselves and look upon one another with disdain. God prefers the low mountains, and Sinai most among these, because it is the smallest and most insignificant of all. Upon it will God let the Divine Presence rest."[23]

I love the imagery of the mountains engaged in a loud, derisive chorus of self-promotion. "I'm the better mountain, most worthy of honor!" "No! I'm far more impressive than you!" This mythic portrait affirms that arrogance and mutual disdain occur among God's creations, but that God prizes humility. God is not impressed by one mountain's noteworthy history or another's natural beauty, and certainly not by their willingness to deride the other. God is most impressed by the humble attitude of Mount Sinai. It is neither the most physically imposing of the mountains in the region, nor does it yet have an inspiring story associated with it. The most pleasing of them, and the most worthy of praise, is the lovely

---

[23] Adapted from Louis Ginzberg, *Legends of the Jews* (Philadelphia: Jewish Publication Society, 1968), 3:82–83.

Mount Sinai, simply doing what mountains do, its very existence giving praise to its Creator.

The midrash may seem quaint and foreign. After all, in contemporary American society, it is assumed that the most impressive and self-promotional candidate will win the prize. In our cultural context, humility may be the hardest of the soul traits to understand and embrace. It is regularly confused with humiliation, and its close cousins, shame, low self-esteem, self-denial, and self-loathing. Who would want a spiritual practice that would deepen rather than heal a core pain that afflicts so many of us? Many women, in particular, have been taught to downplay our gifts and accomplishments, a dynamic that in turn reinforces male dominance in a supposedly gender-blind society. In this cultural moment, self-aggrandizement is seen as a necessity for success. Humility, by contrast, means to be a loser and a failure.

A quick look at the Torah challenges this understanding, teaching that Moses was "the most humble person on the face of the earth" (Num. 12:3). Moses was the leader who endangered his own life to protest injustice, challenged the most powerful monarch in the world, spoke to God face to face, and became the leader of a great people. What kind of humility is this?

My colleague Alan Morinis writes insightfully, "Humility sounds so much like humiliation that it's easy to get a very wrong impression of this soul-trait."[24] The two English words do in fact share a common root. However, both words share another etymological ancestor: *humus,* from the Latin for soil or earth (not to be confused with the beloved Middle Eastern food *hummus*), defined as a "mass of partially decomposed organic matter in the soil. It improves the fertility and water retention of the soil and is therefore important for plant growth."[25] This is lowly stuff indeed, yet the definition hints at its fruitfulness.

The Hebrew word for humility, *anavah,* is related to roots that refer to oppression and poverty. Surely, these circumstances may engender feelings of humiliation. But this etymology also suggests that humility

---

[24] Alan Morinis, *Everyday Holiness: The Jewish Spiritual Path of Mussar* (Boston: Trumpeter, 2007), 46.

[25] *Collins English Dictionary—Complete and Unabridged* (HarperCollins 1991), http://www.thefreedictionary.com.

refers to core realities of the human condition. To be a human being is to be an advanced and reflective creature, but also to live in a finite and vulnerable body, dependent on others who are equally fragile. And yes, the word "human" also derives from "humus," as in "a creature of earth."[26]

This etymological journey opens a new vista for understanding the virtue of humility. To be humble is to carry ourselves in the world in a way that is cognizant of our humanness. We are of the divine and of the earth, the apex of creation and the creatures most capable of harming others. We are magnificent creatures and also supremely fragile. We are no more and no less than fully human beings. Perhaps most important, we are neither more nor less than our fellow humans.

This leads us to Maimonides'[27] classic teaching that "humility is not the opposite of conceit, for that would be self-effacement, but rather stands between conceit and self-effacement. Humility is not an extreme quality, but rather a balanced, moderate, accurate understanding of yourself that you act on in your life. That's why humility and self-esteem go hand in hand."[28] Morinis graphically illustrates a continuum of feelings, ranging from self-debasement to humility to pride and then to arrogance,[29] with both humility and pride near the healthy center of the spectrum. Humility, he teaches, is "occupying your rightful place in life, neither too much nor too little."[30] Living with humility means living with awareness of both the fullness and the limits of our power and place in the world.

This also helps explain why Bahya ibn Pakuda[31] wrote, "All virtues and duties are dependent on humility."[32] This would be a puzzling teaching but for the understanding of humility as a life fashioned in awareness of

---

[26] Walter W. Skeat, *Concise Dictionary of English Etymology* (Hertfordshire, Eng.: Wordsworth Editions, 1998).

[27] Maimonides, or Moses ben Maimon, commonly known as "the Rambam," was a preeminent Jewish philosopher and codifier of Jewish law in the twelfth century. He was born in Spain and died in Egypt.

[28] Morinis, *Everyday Holiness,* 50, based on Maimonides, *Eight Chapters*, chap. 4, 67.

[29] Ibid.

[30] Ibid., 45.

[31] Bahya ibn Pakuda was a Jewish moral philosopher in eleventh-century Spain.

[32] Morinis, *Everyday Holiness,* 46.

our full and paradoxical identity as human beings—both our gifts and our vulnerabilities. We cannot practice ethical virtues or create a righteous life *either* if we regularly forget how remarkable and powerful we are *or* if we masquerade as invincible, superior beings. Both of these images are distortions of reality and therefore harmful to others, to ourselves, and to God's world.

Once during a silent day of prayer in the midst of a spiritual directors' training program, I wandered through the fields behind the retreat center. I don't remember what in particular was occupying my mind and heart prior to this walk, but I know that I have spent much energy in my life navigating the turbulent waters of low self-esteem. I looked out at two cows in the pasture, and I suddenly realized that neither of these cows would ever compare itself to the other, thinking either, "I am a much more beautiful cow than she is," or "My milk is nowhere near as tasty as hers." Shifting my gaze to the trees, I knew that no tree would ever compare itself to another, suffering from self-disparaging thoughts or haughty separation from her fellow. I burst out laughing, a deep, healing laugh of recognition about the absurdity of the thought-prison in which I had been captive for so long.

Unlike cows or trees, we humans are capable of developing false images of self and other, leading to endless suffering and strife. Fortunately, we also have the reflective capacity to recognize how our thoughts can distort reality and cause us needless pain. This kind of clear-eyed reflection enables us to see how we can do good and avoid doing harm in the world, as Bahya's emphasis on humility suggests. Only in this way can we use our roots in the soil of the earth to produce growth and fruitfulness for ourselves and for those around us.

Humility and its corollary, respect for others, are essential capacities for contributing to peace and wholeness in our world. Much conflict derives from outright greed or fear-driven hoarding of resources so that some are privileged at the expense of others. Remember that in Morinis's conceptualization, humility is to occupy as much space as is my natural right in the world, neither to diminish my own place nor to rob others of theirs. So, too, when disputes arise from competition for scarce nonmaterial resources such as love or honor, parties may try to acquire all the love and recognition available, denying others that which is justly theirs.

When controversies stem from identity-based clashes of ideology, participants in the conflict essentially claim all existing space for themselves, as when Democrats and Republicans wish the other would go away. (I have a bad habit of occasionally challenging ideologically inflamed people at my dinner table, asking whether they actually think there is no room for "the other side" in our nation or in our world. The challenge rarely accomplishes its desired goal.) When we live out of humility, we can lay claim to that which is rightfully ours, including speaking up for our views, but we are careful not to deny the other's right to his or hers. With such attitudes, many conflicts would quickly dissolve, or at least transform into respectful exploration of difference.

That is to say, conflict is intertwined with disrespect for the other. This works in two directions. When one side fails to respect another's rights, needs, or perspectives, destructive conflict will invariably ensue. However, when disputes have become entrenched, both sides tend to lose all respect for each other, coming to see the other side purely as an enemy—as evil, insane, or stupid. Thus, conversational contexts that promote mutual respect—based on the other's humanity, if not respect for the other's point of view—can help prepare the ground for conflict transformation. Respectful communication automatically moves the embattled parties toward greater possibility for disagreement that is constructive, even generative, for relationships and communities.

Humility Practice

Alan Morinis invites us to call attention to how we share space with others. When you are sitting on a bench, do you tend to spread your stuff all over, leaving little room for others? In a public seating area, do you place your things on an empty chair and fail to remove them when someone else needs the space? Or is it your tendency to diminish your own needs, squeezing or twisting yourself into a pretzel to make room for another, acting as if you have no right to be comfortable?

We can track the implications of these same traits in nonspatial contexts as well. When you are sitting in a meeting or classroom in which people are sharing finite airtime, how often do you insist on sharing your thoughts at length, oblivious to the resultant lack of available time for others to share? Or conversely, how often do you defer to others, assuming that you have little to contribute?

Any time during the day when we share resources with others—be it space, time, recognition, or love—we can engage in the practice of humility. Again, the point is not to find ever more reasons for self-disparagement but to compassionately investigate how we live in relationship and in community with others. Do you often claim all the space or time available, as if others will or should defer to you? If so, you can experiment with stepping back and inviting others to take their rightful places. Do you tend to express your perspective as the only view possible? If so, you might stop for a moment and ask yourself, "Is it possible someone else at the table knows something I don't? Might I have something to learn from another's perspective?" Or, if your pattern is to avoid claiming what is yours, consider taking a step forward, asserting the legitimacy of your own needs and perspectives, really, your own personhood. When you do speak, if it helps, think of the cow in the field and let my story make you smile.

Curiosity

We have seen the midrashic image of God choosing Mount Sinai to be the place of revelation because of its humility. Another one of my favorite answers to the question of how the place of revelation was chosen is that the Torah needed to be given in the wilderness, in a place of spacious openness, rather than in the city. In the city, there is so much stimulation (if the Rabbis only knew!), so much information, so many things to attend to. Minds are filled to overflowing and there is no mental space for new truth to enter. In the wilderness, there is open space in the physical landscape. So, too, some commentators imagine that in the midst of such a journey, the mind and heart are uniquely open to new knowledge and inspiration.

Rabbi Menachem Mendel Morgensztern of Kotzk of nineteenth-century Poland carries the metaphor further.

> Only a person who is like the wilderness is worthy of having the Divine Presence rest upon him, and is worthy of the light of Torah. The words "like the wilderness" mean that even if he is learned

and has worked hard to learn Torah, he must know in his soul that he has not yet touched the [fullness of] Torah.[33]

According to this image, a faithful human being, even after decades of dedicated study of sacred teachings, must cultivate open space in the mind and heart. The teachings, whose source is divine, are infinite, and so no human being can ever know it all. We must always leave space in our minds for more learning and new understanding.

A similar story is told of a university professor who came to the Japanese master Nan-in (1868–1912) to inquire about Zen. With an arrogant air, the professor challenged the teacher to elucidate the essence of the dharma. The master reached to a small table beside his chair and began pouring himself a glass of water. The glass filled to overflowing and he continued to pour, as water spilled over onto the floor. The professor watched for a time and then asked in an exasperated tone, "It is overfull! No more will go in!" Nan-in responded, "Like this cup, you are full of your opinions and speculations. How can I show you Zen unless you first empty your cup?"[34] There is no learning without humility and curiosity.

I had helped create a large community event with the rather ambitious goal of getting two hundred Jews in a room together to talk openly and respectfully about the Israeli-Palestinian conflict without the session erupting into explosive rhetoric and minds more closed than before. The program began with a panel discussion among four community leaders, representing the spectrum of views in the Jewish community. The panelists, all extremely articulate and knowledgeable people, were asked to answer specific questions, including queries about their personal relationship to the conflict, to evoke authentic communication rather than recitation of rote talking points.

After brief responses to the initial questions, the panelists were each asked to pose a question of their own to another panelist, to help clarify or deepen their understanding of the other's view. Our instructions had

---

[33] Menachem Mendel of Kotzk, cited in *Itturei Torah,* ed. Aharon Yaakov Greenberg (Tel Aviv: Yavneh Publishing House, 1986), 5:9.

[34] *Zen Flesh, Zen Bones*, compiled by Paul Reps (Garden City, NY: Doubleday, Anchor Books, 1961), 5.

been very clear: these were to be questions of curiosity, genuine attempts to comprehend another's view better. These were not to be rhetorical attacks or continued efforts at persuasion masquerading as questions. (I often say that a question that begins with, "But don't you think . . . ?" is rarely a question of genuine curiosity.)

A fascinating thing happened when we reached this part of the panel discussion. Of the four panelists, three completely ignored the request to pose a question of curiosity, simply using the time to continue their own speeches about their own positions. One panelist—a local academic with a fine intellect and keen understanding of the nature of dialogue—shared with everyone present just how hard it was for her to think of something she was genuinely curious about in another's position. (She did come up with an appropriate question, to which her colleague responded with an extended speech that he had obviously delivered many times.)

Later, this woman (a good friend) told me how much she had appreciated the program. Two hundred Jews had, in fact, sat in a room and listened to one another in facilitated small group conversations about Israel without shouting or mutual recrimination. It was a significant achievement for those present and for the community. The most striking part for her, though, was the moment when, sitting on the panel, she realized how difficult it was for her to formulate a question of curiosity about the others' views. This woman is an acclaimed scholar and renowned teacher and writer. On this occasion, she was astute and honest enough to observe how her own natural curiosity had been almost completely blocked.

My friend's experience was not unique. All of us were naturally inquisitive as children. Although children's wide-ranging (and sometimes embarrassing) curiosity mellows into socially acceptable parameters as they grow, most thoughtful people continue to eagerly welcome new knowledge and understanding about the world around them. It feels good to learn new information and perspectives, to meet people with backgrounds different from our own, to travel to places unfamiliar to us.

But in the midst of polarized conflict, locked in an intellectual version of combat, with the limbic brain on high alert, we can only repeat our own version of things as loudly and powerfully as possible. The opposing view is regarded as incomprehensible, foolish, ignorant, or unconscionable. It is a straw person to be demolished if possible or at least strenuously defended against. Just as we cannot show physical weakness when a wild animal is attacking us, in rhetorical battle we instinctively present the most powerful, aggressive form of our own belief and see only the flaws in the other's view. I certainly know the feeling.

I have long seen listening as the single most important skill for dialogue across conflict, whether interpersonal, intergroup, or international. I have come to recognize that the restoration of curiosity about one's opponent is an equally important capacity. Like the other traits we explore in this chapter, it is part of a way of being in the world. To the extent that we consider ourselves superior to or unconnected to others, our natural desire for knowledge about them will be shut down. The result is that we live in worlds of our own construction, listening only to the people we deem worthy, reading only the commentators whose views match our own. The irony is that this attitude of self-satisfied superiority makes us ignorant, without access to sources of possible wisdom beyond our chosen circle of acceptable people and opinions. In the process, we impoverish ourselves, denying ourselves the possibility of learning new ways of seeing the world.

By contrast, an attitude of curiosity means that opportunities for learning and expansion of our horizons are everywhere. Every moment of our lives can be a laboratory, an occasion for growth both interpersonally and intellectually.

Most people are not nearly as astute as my friend, who was able to notice and admit that she was honestly not interested in her rhetorical opponent's views. The deceptively simple act of stopping to observe that our natural capacity for curiosity is locked down can be a moment of awakening in the midst of conflict. In such a precious moment, when we notice that we actually don't have any interest in what a Democratic or Republican voter in the United States or a Likud or Meretz voter in Israel thinks, we might feel a pang of regret for the lost opportunity to learn something more about God's world. This might lead to a brief moment of humility and honesty, in which we admit to ourselves that we actually do not know everything about the other side or even about the issue we are discussing.

Can you think of a moment when someone unexpectedly inquired about an important aspect of your life? Generally this is an experience of respect, an affirmation that you are important enough for the other to want to know more about you. It is an experience that fosters connection, as you share something you value and see that the other person wants to hear and understand your perspective.

When even one side in a dispute interrupts the continuous flow of aggressive communication to ask a question of genuine curiosity, a crack may appear in the previously impenetrable wall of animosity. The very expression of interest and inquiry creates a thaw in frozen rhetorical combat, inviting the two parties to step beyond their well-worn embattled positions and experience one another as whole human beings, not only straw figures representing an objectionable point of view.

During a life-changing week in Israel, during which my call to work for peace was ignited, a sacred text was revealed to me in an unusual context. My husband and I had been in Jerusalem, visiting our son who was in Israel for the year. My head was spinning with images of my visits with dialogue centers and meetings with peace activists. We stopped for coffee to debrief at a fashionable café in downtown Jerusalem. As we prepared to leave the café, I excused myself and headed to the restroom. On the graffiti-filled inside wall of the ladies' room in that café I saw the following words. I later learned that they were written by Israel's renowned poet, Yehuda Amichai (1924–2000). Coming to me at that important moment in my life, I heard these words as the voice of God.

> From the place where we are right
> flowers will never grow
> in the spring.
> The place where we are right
> is hard and trampled
> like a yard.
> But doubts and loves dig up the world
> like a mole, a plough.
> And a whisper will be heard in the place
> where the ruined
> house once stood.[35]

---

[35] *The Selected Poetry of Yehuda Amichai,* ed. and trans. Chana Block and Stephen Mitchell (Berkeley: University of California Press, 1996).

In this exquisite poem, which has become sacred for me, Amichai evokes the image of certainty as hard, parched earth from which nothing can ever grow. Amichai knew all too well that we humans love to feel certain. It makes us feel powerful, important, and safe. But really, it makes us ignorant and impotent, blocking the change and growth on which vibrant life depends. What allows new things to grow and helps new ideas and relationships to flourish is the ability to admit what we cannot know and to open ourselves to what others may have to teach us..

Curiosity Practice

Warning: these thought experiments may seem exceedingly simple. But, unless you are quite an advanced being, you may well find out that they are not as simple as they appear.

1. Set an intention for a day to watch for moments when you are not curious. Notice those times when you have no desire to know anything about a person you are sitting with or a person you read about. Stop and ask yourself: Why do I have no interest in this person, whom I know must be a multifaceted and complex human being, like myself? This may correspond with moments when you feel very sure of yourself or certain of your opinion about something. (For some of us, such occasions may be surprisingly common.)

2. When you have practiced for a period of time observing when the healthy, generative impulse of curiosity is blocked in you, you are ready to work on stretching your capacity. You might want to practice by eavesdropping on conversations you hear in a café or elevator or on the street. Remember: this is not for the purpose of gathering fodder for gossip or judgment, but to appreciate the human beings who happen to be near you. What would you need to know about these people to understand the conversation they are having? Watch your assumptions that you already know. Yes, your intuition may be correct, but do you really know what makes them say the things they are saying?

3. More difficult: practice listening to a radio talk show, particularly one that represents a different political persuasion than your own. Again, bring a spirit of inquiry to what is happening inside you. Would you like to know what would lead a person to think what the host or caller seems

to think? What don't you know about this person's life? What would you have to learn to really know why they see the world the way they do? Watch for false certainty, then ask yourself what you might ask this person if he or she were in your living room. What might you learn if you did?

4. Now you might want to challenge yourself to think of questions of curiosity to ask of people in your life whose views are very different from your own. How could you formulate a question that would help you understand your sibling's political perspective, the polar opposite of your own? What words and tone of voice might you use to invite a co-worker of a different religion to help you understand something you have long found puzzling or offensive about their religion? How could you ask an estranged friend to explain what was true for them when they did or said something that hurt you?

Caution: this is not as easy as it sounds. Think about how the person you have in mind might respond to the words you are using. Remember: if they respond defensively (rightly or not), you will not achieve your goal of evoking honest communication that will contribute to your understanding. Unless you are very gifted or very practiced at this, you might need to adjust the words and formulation of the question many times before you have a question that will do more good than harm when you actually pose it.

Equanimity

For ten years (which are, thankfully, behind us), my husband and I commuted between two homes, two thousand miles apart. I was an unlikely frequent flyer, for, although I like to travel, I am quite frightened by turbulence in flight. One terrifying night, the plane began to pitch and rock in high winds. Other passengers continued to eat their dinners. I began to pray the last line of *Adon Olam,* half the line on my in-breath (*Beyad'cha afkid ruchi*—In Your hand I place my soul), and half the line on my out-breath (*be'eit ishan ve'a'ira*—when I wake and when I sleep).[36]

The plane continued to lurch for what seemed like a long time. Occasionally, I wondered at what point I should switch over to saying

---

[36] Last line of *Adon Olam* prayer, traditional Jewish prayer book, adapted from Psalm 31:6.

the *Shema,* to be recited just before the moment of death. I then brought my attention back to the calming rhythm of prayer and breath. My fear did not leave me, but my breathing slowed, and I was able to drop into a place of deep prayer. For a moment, I considered what would happen if I died that night. I mentally checked on my loved ones, knowing that they were all safe and happy. I touched a place of deep calm about where I was in my own life. For a moment, it was OK.

Using this prayer in the midst of airplane turbulence has become a practiced habit for me, so that I reach for the verse automatically when I feel the plane begin to reel and bounce. I wish I were as consistent in using this verse in the midst of the large and small storms of doubt, fear, sadness, and anger that blow through my mind on a regular basis.

Many Jews think that equanimity is not a Jewish value. It is true that Jewish practice is dynamic, encouraging us to struggle, working every day to purify ourselves and better the world, learning and growing until the day of our death. But equanimity, referred to in Jewish sources as "*menuhat hanefesh*" (soul-rest),[37] does not mean a flat line of serenity or apathy, impervious to the natural joys and sorrows of life. Soul-rest means a capacity to ride the turbulent waters of life, as often as possible, without completely losing our balance, perspective, or sense of who we are.

Buddhists express this beautifully: "Praise and blame, gain and loss, pleasure and sorrow come and go like the wind. To be happy, rest like a giant tree in the midst of them all."[38] A bit like the Psalmist's "tree planted by streams of water,"[39] this statement addresses a truth about human existence that transcends religious difference. Life brings us all kinds of experiences. Some make us happy; others make us sad. The mind and heart respond, just as they should, and then create elaborate interpretations of events, which in turn cause us even more pain. When every word of praise gives us that "died and gone to heaven" feeling and every slight expression of criticism sends us crashing, our well-being is as unstable as the stock market. This is not the path to wholeness or to peace.

---

[37] Rabbi Menachem Mendel of Satanov, *Cheshbon Hanefesh*, ed. Dovid Landesman (Jerusalem: Feldheim Publishers, 1995).

[38] Attributed to the Buddha, Beliefnet website, http://www.beliefnet.com.

[39] Psalm 1:3. The image here appears to be only one of fruitfulness, but its opposite is described in the next verse, "like the chaff driven away by the wind."

There is an alternative. When we cultivate the sense of being in God's hands—in traditional, anthropomorphic language, or regularly reach for a place of wholeness within us that is present regardless of external circumstances, we pitch and rock somewhat less in response to life's "slings and arrows of outrageous fortune." We can say, "This, too, shall pass," both to a moment's adulation and to a time of great suffering. We still rejoice over good news and grieve over tragedy, but with a more developed capacity for balance or tranquility, we are less likely to forget who we are and who we want to be in the world. We are more likely to remember that this is one moment's experience, and that tomorrow will bring another. Quoting the Psalmist again, "Weeping may tarry for the night, but joy comes in the morning" (Ps. 30:6).

If you find yourself protesting that this is a state virtually impossible to achieve, you are right, for biological reasons alone. Our bodies are bathed with comfort chemicals in response to love and pleasure and flooded with stress hormones in times of threat. What is more, as we have seen, in response to perceived danger, a different part of our brain is in charge, at least initially. No wonder we so often feel thrown off course in our lives, uttering words and committing acts large or small that later mystify us and cause us remorse.

This is why it is so essential for conflict interveners and peace-seekers to cultivate groundedness, particularly in the midst of the high reactivity of conflict. Precisely because the brain so often responds to difference and disagreement as to mortal threat, parties to conflict are, to a greater or lesser extent, in the grips of their limbic brains. The reactivity of that self-protective part of the brain that can alert and energize us to fight or flee danger makes us unhelpfully reactive to every word, gesture, and nuance of our opponent's communication. One side's prepare-for-battle stance instinctively alerts the other that there really is danger here, usually without either one's conscious knowledge that these neurological mechanisms are at work. One side's biological fear mechanisms frighten the other, and the rhetorical battle escalates. Under these circumstances, it is exceedingly difficult for the parties to be calm enough to recognize what is happening and wise enough to reach for a reflective part of the brain to take charge of the interaction.

Those of us who desire to serve the cause of peace must practice tools for self-awareness and centering, so that we can more quickly identify the signs that we are in the grip of the limbic brain's habitual supersensitivity to possible danger. Only by repeatedly practicing the skill of noticing how our body feels in this state (for me—heart pounding, chest constricted, thoughts racing, palms damp, and fists clenched) will help us return more quickly to the best of ourselves. Only then will it be possible for us to respond to the conflict situation with calm, clarity, and compassion. I say "possible," because my own experience is that, having thought about these issues for many years, I regularly forget to practice what I preach.

Equanimity Practice

Countless books have been written about ways to center ourselves in the presence of stress. Since conflict activates the same neurological and biological mechanisms as stress, these same practices are precisely what we need. If you have a long-standing practice of conscious breathing, breath prayer, body scanning, or biofeedback in response to stress, you have already been developing capacities that are essential for peace-seeking work. If you are new to this kind of practice, consider the following:

1. Next time you find yourself arguing with someone—either in person or in your mind—stop just as soon as you can and bring your full attention inward. What is happening in your body? What physical sensations do you notice? Do you notice patterns of thought that are different from when your mind is at rest? Is your breathing different than usual (are you breathing at all)? If you can, jot down a few notes on a scrap of paper or an online notepad so you can return and do this exercise again and again.

As you do this exercise repeatedly, you will gradually gain familiarity with your own particular experience of conflict. This, of course, depends on your ability to notice these sensations and patterns with compassionate, nonjudgmental curiosity. Whatever you find is just perfect, since the goal is to learn as much as you can about how your own body, heart, and mind respond to discord. The more you know, the better chance you will have to engage self-awareness next time.

2. The next step is to explore what helps you calm down in the midst of a fight. If you know that what works best for you is to take a "time-out"—to leave the room or take a short walk to clear your head, this is a wonderful practice. It is also very useful to have ways to calm yourself

right in the midst of the conflict space when physically taking a break is not an option.

If you have a meditation practice, this is a priceless resource. For example, close your eyes (or look down at the floor just ahead of your feet) and bring all of your attention to the task of watching three full breaths from start to finish. Observe the in-breath from the very bottom, where it begins. Watch it fill you, until it reaches the very top. Then watch the out-breath till you have completely released the breath. Do this for three breaths, then five or ten, if you can. Notice if you feel any calmer before returning to the situation at hand.

For people with a more body-based practice, try consciously moving your attention away from whatever thoughts are moving through your mind. Concentrate instead on the sensations in your body by placing your hand on your chest or your belly. If you have a bit more time, gently guide your awareness to explore the parts of your body in turn, starting with the soles of your feet, very slowly and gradually working your way up to your thighs, midsection, chest, shoulders, neck, face, and head. This can powerfully shift your attention from the stormy scene in your mind, grounding you in the here and now.

If a verbal prompt is helpful for you, pick a phrase to repeat over and over again, synchronized with your breath. Pick something simple like "Right here; right now." Or something lyrical like Thich Nhat Hanh's, "Breathing in, I see myself as a mountain; breathing out, I feel solid."[40] Or choose a sacred phrase from your tradition, like my use of "In Your hand I place my soul, when I wake and when I sleep," or "Hear O Israel, Adonai our God, Adonai is One." Do this five times or ten, or for as many moments as you can, until you feel that the turmoil in your mind has settled down.

If what will be most potent for you is a visual image, close your eyes, get settled in your body and watch a couple of breaths move in and out. Then bring to mind a place where you feel completely safe and nourished. Let the inner portrait fill with visual detail. See the many beautiful details of the place and the people who are there, and allow yourself to feel the

---

[40] Thich Nhat Hanh, *The Blooming of a Lotus: Guided Meditation Exercises for Healing and Transformation* (Boston: Beacon Press, 1999), 10.

sensations that that place conjures for you. Stay there for as long as you can. Then bring yourself gently back into the room where you are, and see whether a measure of calm has returned.

It is good to have a wide repertoire of such tools that are particularly potent for you, so that you can settle into the one that feels right in a particular moment. Remember, there is no right answer to the question of how to center yourself back into a place of calm and clarity. Whatever works for you is a gift that you should treasure and practice, practice, practice, so that these tools will be readily available for you at the moment you need them. Remember that whatever happens next in the tense situation, your calm presence will make a positive difference.

Strength

All of the *middot* I have explored so far, and much of the content of the book, have emphasized what some may call "soft" characteristics. I have written a great deal about kindness and compassion, about generosity and curiosity, and about softening and opening the heart. In so doing, I fear that I may have reinforced a common misconception, that the work of peacebuilding is fluffy or "touchy-feely," for the soft-hearted but not for strong and clear-headed realists. Some readers will readily recognize a gender dynamic in my emphasizing traits like empathy, caring, and respect for others.

It is certainly true that conflict transformation demands highly developed capacities for empathy, humility, and kindness. But this work also requires qualities normally thought of as "strong," such as courage, clarity, determination, and boldness.

I once heard an interview with Congressman John Lewis, a veteran leader of the civil rights movement and a close colleague of Dr. Martin Luther King Jr.[41] Congressman Lewis spoke eloquently about the quality of love at the heart of the movement—love for one another within the movement's "band of brothers and sisters," and even love for those who violently opposed their work. This is hardly soft and fuzzy love. The movement's mission—to respond to violence, racism, and hatred with dignity,

---

[41] "John Lewis on the Art and Discipline of Nonviolence," at *On Being with Krista Tippett*, http://www.onbeing.org, March 28, 2013.

compassion, faith, and even love—required almost unimaginably fierce commitment and strength of spirit.

Dr. King urged his followers to study the work of the consummate nonviolent peacemaker, Mahatma Gandhi, who placed the concept of *satyagraha* ("soul force," based on the Hindi, "zeal for truth") at the center of his philosophy and method,

> to designate a determined but nonviolent resistance to evil. . . . According to this philosophy, . . . practitioners of *satyagraha* achieve correct insight into the real nature of an evil situation by observing a nonviolence of the mind, by seeking truth in a spirit of peace and love, and by undergoing a rigorous process of self-scrutiny.[42]

It is hard enough to imagine facing an armed and vehement opponent. Ask yourself: Had you joined civil rights activists in one of their demonstrations, would you have had the determined clarity of mind and strength of conviction to respond with dignity and grace to vicious words and physical force?

Judaism is not a pacifist tradition. A clear preponderance of Jewish sources defends—even requires—responding with violence when necessary to protect life, so it is not my purpose to advocate for Gandhian notions of nonviolence. But Gandhi's and King's teachings vividly illustrate the kind of spiritual strength, powerful will and faith, and resolute commitment that peacebuilding work often requires. At times what is required is the boldness and courage to speak truth and to act. At least as frequently, the peacebuilder's might is expressed in restraining oneself from speaking or acting in harmful ways, or in refusing to rush human processes that inevitably take time.

What we do find in Jewish sources are texts like the one that serves as the title of this book. Let us examine this text more closely.

> Who is the greatest of heroes [or, "the most mighty"]? One who conquers one's own impulse (to evil), as it is said, "Better to be forbearing than mighty, better to master one's own self than to

---

[42] "*Satyagraha*," in *Encyclopaedia Britannica*.

conquer a city."[43] . . . And others say, [Who is the greatest of heroes?] One who makes an enemy into a friend.[44]

The author of this and similar sources calls attention to a paradox of human nature: holding back, refraining from speaking or acting until the time is right, is not passivity. On the contrary, it takes tremendous strength to resist the impulse to do harm when we are frightened and angry, to stop and think before we respond in kind to a verbal attack. It can take all the spiritual force we can muster to scour the contents of our own soul when we would much rather rehearse the outrages committed by the other. The hero's might is apparent; these acts of powerful self-awareness and self-discipline are invisible yet they frequently demand more rigor than we can muster.

Engaging mindfully with conflict, or helping others to do so, is hardly for the faint of heart. Working skillfully with discord requires courage to stay in the fire of conflict—that many would rather flee, to tolerate strong emotion in oneself and others without betraying our own values, and to powerfully oppose parties that are acting in unjust or dangerous ways. Responding wisely and fruitfully in the midst of conflict requires speaking one's truth clearly and compellingly, but without violating the dignity of the other. Walking Buber's "narrow ridge" of human encounter, we must rigorously honor both our own truth and the other's dignity. In the midst of impassioned debate, when it is most difficult, we must strive to recognize both our own weaknesses and the other's strengths.

Insisting on defending the dignity of all parties to the conflict, especially those whom we find threatening and those with whom we profoundly disagree, represents a bold commitment to core values, just when the rubber meets the road. Surely, it is relatively easy to love those who love us back. It is in the presence of an opponent that our moral mettle is most truly tested. When ancient instincts impel us to strike back at our adversary—verbally if not physically—it takes passionate commitment to basic moral principles to refrain. So, too, in intergroup or international contexts, determination to engage the other side without causing additional

[43] Proverbs 16:32, translation adapted from *The Writings Kethubim: A New Translation of the Holy Scriptures according to the Traditional Hebrew Text* (Philadelphia: Jewish Publication Society, 1982).

[44] *Avot d'Rabbi Natan* 23.

harm demands a courageous willingness to defy social and international convention that violence is the normal and expected mode of response.

Working for peace is about kindness, love, and humility, but it is also about boldness, courage, and fierce determination to work for the highest good rather than merely for immediate relief of our momentary fear, anger, or frustration. It can be some of the most challenging work we ever do, and the only kind of heroism to which we can aspire on a daily basis.

Strength Practice

The training ground for moral strength and courage is the terrain of our everyday lives. Just as the physical therapist wants the client's injured joint to work optimally in both directions, in this practice we must train both in self-restraint when we are overwrought and in boldness when we are frightened or timid.

Set an intention for today to notice when you get angry—so angry that you are moved to do or say something you'd be embarrassed to admit to a partner or friend. It could be your reaction to a driver on the road, to the billing office at your internet provider, to a Facebook entry, or to a loved one. Or it can be just as fruitful to watch for a vehement internal reaction to a commentator or political figure on the news or online.

The first step is to notice those moments at which you want to make an obscene gesture, scream, curse, or threaten. If you tend to be quick to anger, you may have multiple experiences to work with on a particular day. (Give yourself credit for at least noticing an outburst after the fact, for such moments of awareness can lead you to learn a different way of responding in the future.) Take a breath and ask yourself: What will I accomplish if I respond in this instinctive way? Will I feel better for more than a moment? Will I do harm to myself or to another? Does responding in this way match my sense of who I want to be in the world? All of this in a fraction of a second, of course, before the fuse bursts into flame.

Keep a small tablet or electronic device near you so you can keep a record of these occurrences. Just noticing how often this happens to you each day or each week is itself a powerful learning tool. Better still, choose a trusted partner who will engage in this practice with you, checking in at the end of each day or once a week to report: How often were you able to restrain yourself from doing or saying something you would later regret? If awareness kicked in only after you exploded, how did you feel afterwards? (Was the momentary sensation of relief and self-righteousness followed by a moment of regret or embarrassment?)

If you find this valuable, challenge yourself to notice such moments a little sooner in the process. That way the occasional flashes of anger become opportunities for learning, for strengthening the muscle of self-discipline, for expressing not your momentary rage but your deeper values. Remember, it can take much more strength and agility to walk down a hill than to climb upwards; preventing ourselves from tumbling into danger is a very active, rigorous practice.

If your work is to develop more boldness in relationship, watch for occasions when you feel hesitant to speak. For example, at a meeting at which you share airtime with more assertive speakers, notice the inner monologue that may keep you from claiming time for your contribution. ("How can I get a word in here without stepping on someone's toes? Do my words really need to be said? The others are smarter/wiser/more experienced than I am.") Then push yourself to jump in and speak.

Likewise, notice moments when you find yourself at odds with another. If you are a person who generally avoids conflict or doubts her own perspectives, see how many times in the coming week you can speak up for what you believe, bringing your full self into the disagreement, even as you recognize the other's humanity. Remember, if you do not express your own view, the encounter is not dialogue but monologue, since your opponent's view is the only one being heard.

During a recent week-long retreat at a Buddhist retreat center, I found myself in a state of quiet joy unlike anything I had experienced before. In complete silence except for occasional talks by the teachers in the serene meditation hall, two hundred retreatants had come to devote themselves to the Buddhist practice of loving-kindness meditation.

Pray for Peace

Each of us received the same instructions—to silently offer wishes of well-being to a variety of people, using classical Buddhist phrases or words of our own. "May you be safe. May you be well. May you be happy. May you be at peace." On the first day we were to offer well wishes to ourselves, since cultivating our own reservoir of loving-kindness is what best enables us to develop kindness toward others. On the second day we were to offer the same hopes toward someone so beloved to us that the very thought of that person immediately makes us smile. As we developed increasingly powerful sensations of the power of loving-kindness in us, we moved toward wishing for the well-being of people that we hardly know and even to people who had hurt us, if and when we felt ready to do so, and ultimately, to all beings in the world.

Having been on such retreats before, I knew that the next step was to experiment with offering blessings to everyone in the room and eventually to everyone in our lives. I had heard a teacher suggest that we wish for the well-being of every person who crossed our path as we walked silently around the retreat center, on the way to or from lunch or the meditation hall. The moment I would see someone coming in the opposite direction on the path, I would silently recite, "May you be safe. May you be well. May you be happy. May you be at peace." I began to do the same for people who crossed the path of my thoughts. As someone in my life spontaneously floated into my awareness (a friend, a community member, an estranged family member, a despised political figure), I offered the phrases to that person as well. "May you be safe. May you be well. May you be happy. May you be at peace."

The practice was flowing through me. In those blessed moments and hours during which my concentration was strong and focused, I genuinely wanted the best—the basic blessings that I know all people desire—for everyone who crossed my path, either physically or imaginatively.

Then I noticed something really interesting. I realized that I felt as if I had gotten very fat, as if my belly and chest had filled up with loving-kindness. Then I realized that I felt happy. Very happy. That overstuffed feeling shifted into feeling full of joy. It was so wonderful, in that moment, to have kindly feelings toward everyone. It was something like the mysterious way in which helping another or giving a gift to another brings us joy. But I wasn't doing anything or giving anything. I was just walking around the retreat center, full of love for everyone.

Of course, the experience did not leave me in a permanent state of total love and kindness. Nor did it leave me with a craving to reproduce the experience on any particular schedule. It was a moment's experience that came and went, as all experiences do.

But I did leave with a powerful and precious memory to reflect on. As I thought about what had happened for me that day, the memory became a kind of prayer. Remembering that sensation of feeling full of love and joy for all the people in my life and for myself, I knew that this was the way I wanted to live, as much and as often as possible. I knew that this was what my work on peacebuilding is about: trying to bring a measure of kindness and blessing to everyone I encounter.

It is as simple and as challenging as this. The desire for the well-being of all people is what moves us to work for peace, and this same desire makes it possible for us to care for all people in any conflict. Though we may be more connected to one "side" or more inclined toward one viewpoint in the dispute, on a deeper level, we sense a bond of common humanity with everyone involved. We want what is best for all of them. Like a parent responding to estrangement among her children, she wants for all of them to be happy, for all of them to thrive, for all of them to be free of the pain of ruptured relationships.

This is what I wish for you and for all people who honor the cause of peace. I want for you to believe that it is a meaningful and attainable goal in our lives to touch the natural desire of our hearts to feel kindness, to embody caring in our relationships, in our communities, and in our world. I hope that this ground of kindheartedness toward all people will move you to bring a healing presence to conflict wherever you encounter it— from arguments in your family and workplace to deeply broken personal relationships in your life to connections of open-hearted curiosity with people of religions and political views different from your own. I want your benevolent sense of caring for all who live on God's earth to move you to help ease pain and restore connection in the human family.

Most of us ordinary mortals cannot live this way all the time, but we can live this way some of the time, and surely that makes a difference. The more of us adopt this goal as an intention for our lives, the more peace and harmony there will be in the world.

Grant peace, goodness and blessing, grace, kindness, and compassion upon us and all Your people Israel. Bless us, our Parent, as one, with the light of Your face, for in Your light You have given us, O God, the Torah of life, love of kindness, justice, blessing, compassion, life, and peace. May it be good in Your sight to bless Your people Israel at all times and at every moment with Your peace. Blessed are You, God, who blesses the people Israel—and all the inhabitants of the earth—with peace.[45]

This beautiful prayer, offered every morning of the Jewish year, and in a slightly different form in evening prayers as well, asks for God's blessings of peace upon us all. Strikingly, the prayer associates peace with a host of other blessings: grace, kindness, compassion, justice, and life itself. Perhaps in this prayer we are asking God for an array of separate blessings. Or perhaps, this text teaches that peace is inextricable from goodness, ease and well-being, justice, good health, and harmony. These are the blessings for which everyone longs.

Prayer for peace has become a central practice in my life. We cannot know how prayer works in the world. But I know that the more we pray for peace, goodness, health, harmony, and grace for all beings, the stronger will be the power of peace and kindness in the world.

This book is an expression of my own prayer for peace. In these pages I have shared my heart's longing to help restore connection between divided families, religions, communities, and national groups. I have journeyed to understand the dynamics of destructive conflict among groups and among individuals, in the hope of becoming a healing presence wherever I encounter harmful dissension and alienation among people.

This book is also an invitation—really an exhortation—to you, to pray and work for peace in your own way in the midst of your own life. I ask you to pray for peace in whatever way is authentic for you. Pray for peace in your words and in your deeds, at home and in your travels. Act out your prayer in relationship to those nearest to you and to those who seem like the enemy. Be this prayer, and take it with you wherever you go, every day. Know that you are part of an enormous circle of peace-seekers all over the world. May our prayers multiply, and may the actions that flow from our prayerful intentions help create a more peaceful world, the kind of world that God desires for all of us.

---

[45] "*Sim Shalom*" prayer, Jewish prayer book, translation mine.

Glossary

Avot d'Rabbi Natan—literally, "Fathers according to Rabbi Nathan," a volume of commentary on Mishnah Tractate *Avot* (Fathers), printed as a separate minor tractate of the Talmud.

Beit Midrash—study hall, academy of Torah learning, especially of the Rabbinic period.

Halacha—Jewish law.

Hillel—great rabbi of the first century before the Common Era.

Kabbalah—(literally, "receiving"), refers to the body of Jewish esoteric teachings and Jewish mysticism, especially from the twelfth century onward.

Maḥzor—traditional Jewish High Holy Day prayer book.

Midrash—literary, legal, or folkloristic commentary on a biblical text; also genre of literature or freestanding homiletical composition.

Mishnah—literally, "Learning." The Mishnah is the sixty-three-volume foundational work of Jewish law, compiled around 200 C.E. by Rabbi Judah the Prince, reflecting the first stage of Rabbinic law, including sources from several centuries of reflection in Rabbinic academies in Palestine.

Mitzvah—Jewish religious commandment or imperative, rooted in the Torah (Five Books of Moses). Plural: *mitzvot*.

Shabbat—Jewish Sabbath.

Shammai—great rabbi of the first century before the Common Era, often in disagreement with Hillel.

Siddur—traditional Jewish prayer book.

Talmud—literally, "Study." The Talmud is the sixty-three-volume corpus of Rabbinic law, lore, and commentary, representing several centuries of Rabbinic legal and literary reflection following the redaction of the Mishnah. The term generally refers to the Babylonian Talmud (BT), edited in the early sixth century, as opposed to the Jerusalem—or Palestinian—Talmud (JT), edited in the early fifth century.

Torah—literally, "Instruction," connotes the Five Books of Moses (first five books of the Bible); more broadly, may refer to the whole corpus of Jewish sacred texts.

Tosefta—literally, "Addition," is a collection of Rabbinic materials (prior to 200 C.E.), parallel to the Mishnah in content and organization, edited in the late fourth century C.E.

Yeshiva—literally, "sitting." This is the institution of sacred Jewish learning, through the ages.

Index

Praise for *From Enemy to Friend*

"This is a beautiful book by a very unique American rabbi. It will be a blessing for Jews, Muslims, and Christians—and members of all world religions—in America and in other parts of the world, who are genuinely interested in understanding how Judaism, and especially Jewish spiritual practice, can help all of us bring the pursuit of peace into our personal, communal, and national lives."

—Rabbi Ron Kronish, Founder and Director,
The Interreligious Coordinating Council in Israel

"Rabbi Amy Eilberg provides beautifully clear, wise, and deep instruction to help each of us fulfill the injunction, "Seek peace and pursue it." She expertly guides us regular folk in becoming pursuers of peace ourselves, rather than relegating the work to politicians or professional peace-workers. Informed by contemporary brain science as well as modern psychology, her program is both practical and spiritually-based. Eilberg shows us how to transform our minds and hearts from fear to faith, training us to interact with "the other" as a moving adventure of learning and discovery instead of as a source of threat. This book absolutely has the power to change our world for the better."

—Rabbi Nancy Flam, Co-Director of Programs,
Institute for Jewish Spirituality

"[Amy Eilberg] brings the deep wisdom of centuries of Jewish teaching together with contemporary research, her own thinking, and the gravitas of her personal experience to focus on re-weaving the fabric of our common life. In addition to being a gifted practitioner and a complex thinker, Rabbi Eilberg is authentically human. In these pages, she walks us through her challenges as well as her triumphs, making it easier for us to imagine contributing to tikkun olam, the healing of the world, by changing the ways we treat our enemies."

—Robert R. Stains, Jr., Public Conversations Project

"This amazingly comprehensive synthesis of contemporary understandings of conflict resolution integrated into the context of the ancient and enduring wisdom of Judaism as reflected in its sacred texts will be accessible to readers across parochial boundaries because Rabbi Eilberg's voice, thoroughly captivating as a narrator, is invitingly honest, courageous, and kind."

—Sylvia Boorstein, co-founding teacher,
Spirit Rock Meditation Center

"In *From Enemy to Friend* Amy Eilberg tells us what true peace means and offers strategies for living a life based on the pursuit of peace. She exhibits a profound understanding of the problems faced when Israelis and Palestinians, as well as Americans—particularly Jewish Americans—discuss their passionate differences regarding the conflict in the Middle East. Eilberg's book provides us with a beginning point and, more importantly, the inspiration to follow our own paths in making our world a far more accepting and rich place in which to live our lives."

—Rabbi Steve Gutow, President & CEO,
Jewish Council for Public Affairs

"In this much anticipated book, Amy Eilberg inspires and defines a new field, inviting Jews to join her on the spiritual adventure of the twenty-first century: encountering the 'other' with curiosity and compassion. Digging deeply into her knowledge of Jewish text and tradition, Rabbi Eilberg gently but firmly shows us what it might mean to become *rodfei shalom*—pursuers of peace. I cannot imagine a more important journey, nor could I hope for a wiser guide."

—Rabbi Nancy Fuchs Kreimer, Director, Multifaith Studies and Initiatives, Reconstructionist Rabbinical College

"Weaving classical Jewish wisdom, spiritual teachings drawn from many traditions, writings on conflict resolution, and highly instructive personal vignettes and testimony into a seamless whole, Amy Eilberg constructs an engaging, provocative, and discomfiting book that calls upon its readers to question deeply held and seemingly intractable positions. Her voice is gentle, wise, and modest. Yet, her moral insistence that peace is attainable shines on every page. In the end, this book is one of hope. It has the rare virtue—if only we, her readers, possess the openness and courage—of changing how we are in the world."

—Rabbi David Ellenson, Chancellor, Hebrew Union College-Jewish Institute of Religion

"With courage, clarity, and humility, Rabbi Amy Eilberg teaches readers to honor their own truth and other's dignity. *From Enemy to Friend* is a compassionate guide to the hard but essential work of peace-building."

—Rabbi Burton L. Visotzky, Jewish Theological Seminary

"From beginning to end, *From Enemy to Friend* is a hospitable book. Grounded in the sacred texts and tradition of Judaism, Rabbi Eilberg presents 'seek peace and pursue it' as the principal commandment in Jewish tradition. Implicitly, she encourages her readers to see similar values in their own spiritual traditions. Through personal narratives of 'peacebuilding' within Judaism, interfaith relations, Israel and Palestine, within families, she calls the reader to consider the pursuit of peace as a way of being for all people, in all of our relationships."

—Marilyn Salmon, United Theological Seminary of the Twin Cities

"Lucidly written, combining theological reflection and analysis with practical handles, *From Enemy to Friend* is an honest telling of the engagement of one rooted in her Jewish tradition in interreligious relationships and cooperative efforts towards peace. Rabbi Eilberg brings learnings from her many years of chaplaincy experience, conflict resolution work, and interfaith dialogue to flower in this book. It's helpful to all who engage in interreligious dialogue and cooperation."

—Rev. Dr. Shanta Premawardhana, President, Seminary Consortium for Urban Pastoral Education (SCUPE)